BAEN BOOKS
BY WM. MARK SIMMONS

❖

Halflife Chronicles

One Foot in the Grave
Dead on My Feet
Habeas Corpses
Dead Easy
A Witch in Time

A Witch in Time

or Something Wiccan This Way Comes

❖

WM. MARK SIMMONS

BAEN

A WITCH IN TIME, OR SOMETHING WICCAN THIS WAY COMES

Copyright © 2019 by Wm. Mark Simmons

A Baen Books Original

Baen Publishing Enterprises
P.O. Box 1403
Riverdale, NY 10471
www.baen.com

ISBN: 978-1-4814-8390-2

Cover art by Alan Pollack

First printing, April 2019

Distributed by Simon & Schuster
1230 Avenue of the Americas
New York, NY 10020

Library of Congress Cataloging-in-Publication Data

Names: Simmons, Wm. Mark, author.
Title: A witch in time / Wm. Mark Simmons.
Description: Riverdale, NY : Baen Books, 2019. | Series: HalfLife chronicles
 ; [5]
Identifiers: LCCN 2018055721 | ISBN 9781481483902 (hardback)
Subjects: | BISAC: FICTION / Fantasy / Paranormal. | FICTION / Fantasy /
 Urban Life. | GSAFD: Horror fiction.
Classification: LCC PS3569.I4774 W58 2019 | DDC 813/.54--dc23
LC record available at https://lccn.loc.gov/2018055721

Printed in the United States of America

10 9 8 7 6 5 4 3 2 1

Dedication

❖

This one is for all of my dedicated readers
Who patiently waited for closure.

Do I dare
Disturb the universe?
In a minute there is time
For decisions and revisions which a minute will reverse.
For I have known them all already, known them all . . .
> —T.S. Eliot,
> "The Love Song of J. Alfred Prufrock"

The time is out of joint. O cursèd spite,
That ever I was born to set it right!
> —William Shakespeare,
> *Hamlet*, Act I, Scene 5

Tempus fugit (time flies)
> —Ovid (Publius Ovidius Naso),
> *Fasti (The Book of Days)*

Time flies like an arrow; fruit flies like a banana.
> —Groucho Marx

Chapter One

Everyone thinks the Great Battle against the Forces of Darkness is all about silver bullets, holy water, and consecrated crossbows. Mystical martial arts passed down through arcane academies. Profane prophecies and secret societies bestowing ancient wisdom, sacred weapons, and kickass tattoos.

Nobody ever talks about picking up the dry cleaning, doing the dishes, or mowing the lawn.

Actually, I'm not going to talk about them, either. Other than to say I hadn't done any of those things for a number of months.

Instead, I'm going to say a few words about meeting with the accountant. As humdrum tasks go, it would seem to belong on the Mundane List. Along with doing the laundry, taking out the trash, the brushing of teeth, and regular showers.

None of which I had done within recent memory either.

Meeting with the accountant was different for three distinct reasons.

One: I was pretty sure that mine wasn't really human . . . not that I had any room to be judgmental about that sort of thing.

Two: It was absolutely required on a monthly basis and I had to drive to the Louisiana–Texas border to do it.

And, three: It got me killed . . . again.

It's a two-hour drive across northern Louisiana from Monroe to just beyond Shreveport and back. Round-trip: just over four hours.

Between sunset and sunrise: little wiggle room around the summer solstice. It's a huge inconvenience, potentially fatal even without complications, and had made me grumpy even before I'd turned into a reclusive misanthrope.

With hygiene issues. To say I was in a "funk" these days went beyond the metaphorical turn of phrase. The requirement to take the trip every thirty days—and, therefore, shower and wear moderately clean clothes—was probably the only thing keeping me from turning into a walking Petri dish.

If I were a normal guy with a normal financial portfolio I could have just used some kind of spreadsheet software like QuickBooks or a TurboTax clone. More importantly, I could avoid the Herculean tasks of standing under a showerhead and figuring out which pile of clothes on the floor were, well, the least repellent. It's amazing what a little Febreze can accomplish with the right permanent-press ensemble. Still, I was fast approaching the point where the only things that distinguished me from vagrants and homeless mental patients were my apparent lack of a rag, a squeegee, and a purloined shopping cart.

See, here's what people who have never been clinically depressed don't understand: They assume it's all about "feeling sad." But "sad" is just the leading boxcar on the Freight Train of Grief: The next ninety-nine are mostly about "boredom." Ennui. Feeling *tired*. With a capital T.

No sadness, no weepies, no "woe is me." No—. . . *thing*. Nothing. Just an intense, profound weariness. It's not long before such things as dressing or undressing—or even eating and sleeping, for that matter—seem terribly unimportant and require huge efforts of will and taxing amounts of energy to accomplish. And to what purpose? Sooner or later, you just have to do them all over again.

Life's a bitch when you're no longer human, everyone you love has been sucked into an alternate dimension, and you're hunted by things that think a bloodbath is the same thing as a food fight.

Trust me: that last sentence is neither allegory nor hyperbole.

But as much as it annoyed me to leave the house—much less drive two hours each way—meeting with the accountant made it possible to keep buying those silver bullets, vials of holy water, and sacred weapons.

Kickass tattoos are worth diddly-squat when the Minions of

Darkness are coming at you and you are fresh out of consecrated ammo.

So, once again, I ran the clippers over my beard until my face emerged with that stubble effect that looks so crappy or pretentious on anyone but an upscale male model. Come to think of it . . . no, don't get me started. . . .

The follow-up with a blade was exceedingly unpleasant until I remembered that shaving cream was part of the equation. I finished with only half of my face resembling Freddy Krueger's. I dutifully used both soap *and* shampoo in the shower—though cream rinse seemed beyond my best efforts to care. Finally: deodorant and some flavor of body spray that was supposed to induce amorous assaults by roving gangs of supermodels.

And I was done. For another month, anyway. By then I would have to decide whether I wanted to do a load of laundry or order more clothes over the internet.

Up until the first time I died I hadn't needed professional accounting services. Now I required a financial *consigliere* capable of keeping me off of the NSA watchlists: not easy when you have a dozen different identities, most of which shot the human actuarial tables all to hell. Being rich is a lot more complicated when your investments are linked to accounts that predate your birth by several centuries. Try explaining funds deeded to you by a Carpathian madman who is still hunted by the Vatican, not to mention certain factions that are barely hinted at in ancient nursery rhymes or the fevered imaginings of Stephen King, Guillermo del Toro and the Brothers Grimm.

So, once again, I executed all of the security protocols, adding an extra thirty minutes and eighteen miles to the drive to ensure I wasn't being tailed. I wondered what I would do if my enemies ever realized that drone technology was now accessible through their local toy stores.

For now I only had to contend with threats that fell toward the other end of the tech spectrum. For example: The light patina of zombie "juice" still splattered across the hood and windshield from last month's trip tinting the glare of oncoming headlights so that they glowed like strands of greenish, radioactive pearls.

One of these nights I would have to take the time to find a twenty-four-hour car wash.

But not tonight. I hated anything that interfered with my carefully timed routine. So you may imagine my ire when I arrived only to discover that my money magician had stood me up.

I was annoyed for all of five minutes.

Our monthly assignations were set in stone: Diggs totally understood my need to make it home before dawn and that any wiggle room couldn't be imparted to the front end of my journey. So she was never late. In fact, Marsha was so unerringly punctual that I was pretty sure the U.S. Naval Observatory clock set itself to her cell phone and tablet.

I killed a half hour waiting in her driveway dialing her numbers: home, office, cellular, sat-phone, ex-husbands, a peculiar little cross-species tavern in the back of a defunct auto repair shop. Nada. I sat in my car mulling the repercussions of her disappearance while Stephen Hawking was on the radio explaining how our attempts to recreate the Higgs boson "God particle" could result in the annihilation of the entire universe.

And maybe seriously damage a couple of adjacent ones . . .

That didn't get me too excited. My last two therapists had claimed that I had a "personal death wish" but I'd learned not to invest too much hope in doomsday scenarios by now.

If anything about the interview gave me pause, it was the impression that they were presenting the conversation as if the renowned physicist were still alive. Hawking had passed away a couple of years ago—at least I was pretty sure that he had. But then, I had started to question my own memory of late, so . . .

I shook my head and turned off the radio: I had matters of greater import to attend to right now.

I spent the second half hour breaking in and creeping Diggs's house: lights off, no one home, everything neat as a pin—no signs of struggle or rapid departure. No notes, either: front door, back door, refrigerator door. Her car was in the carport. If she had a second vehicle, I didn't know about it. The hairs on the back of my neck suddenly stood up like a mob of meerkats on Ritalin: *time to leave.*

Marsha Diggs was only the latest demi-human to go missing from the covert section of my contacts folder. There had been discrete inquiries as to the whereabouts of Stefan Pagelovitch in Seattle and Dennis Smirl in Chicago in recent weeks.

I was honestly—but tactfully—unhelpful in my responses to both demesnes. I really *didn't* know anything. As usual. But, even if I had, I wasn't going to point the way for the kinds of busybodies that might be hunting a master vampire, or a shapeshifting um—well— "Enforcer." And if something had already happened to either of those bad boys, it was likely to be way out of my league. As just about anything from the shadowlands usually turned out to be.

So, I wiped all the surfaces I remembered touching, deleted all of my messages from her antiquated answering machine, and slipped back into my SUV like a bead of mercury navigating the inclines of a gravity tilt switch. Turning the key in the ignition, I felt the necrophagic virus start to stir. Although this was not officially a fight-or-flight situation the *shadow* that now inhabited my limbic system picked up on my rising stressors—my annoyance from the long drive and my growing disquiet over Diggs's disappearance— and defaulted to its preferred response setting: I was suddenly hungry.

Or, rather, more aware of how hungry I *always* was now.

I pulled out of the drive and circled the block twice, then drove a set of random figure eights on my way back to the highway to see if anyone was trying to follow. The fact that no one did was more irritating than if I'd picked up a tail of sinister black sedans with helicopters hovering overhead in stealth mode. I didn't know whether to be angry or frightened that Marsha was AWOL. I split the difference by deciding to stop off for a late-night snack.

That's the other thing about depression: It makes you stupid.

Chapter Two

The woman struggled feebly on the rumpled bed.

Her wrists were trapped between the brass bars of the headboard by a pair of handcuffs. Her eyes were half-closed while she panted through a slack and half-open mouth. If she had started her captive state in wild and frantic mode, she seemed to have exhausted herself before my arrival. Her nude body writhed slowly now, undulating across the bunched sheets like a sleepy reptile seeking a warmer spot on an already sunny rock. The light from some three dozen candles scattered about the room honeyed her pale skin and cast shadows that accentuated the curves and crevices of ripened flesh.

My immediate and autonomic response was a reminder that I had reached the stage where differences between food and sex were beginning to blur out of clear definition. In fact, as I paused just outside the doorway I felt a powerful tingling sensation near my groin.

I ran my tongue across my lips to moisten them, trying not to let it snag on my fangs in the process. This whole drinking-blood-for-sustenance thing was kind of pointless when it was your own veiny goodness filling your mouth. The extended canines, curving down between my lateral incisors and first molars, were sharp enough to slice through all three layers of human skin and a quarter inch of fat and muscle to reach the more interesting veins.

I had learned to be very careful of my tongue.

The tingling sensation near my groin repeated itself, turning out to be something more familiar and less disturbing: My hand plunged deep into a front pocket and extracted my cell phone. Set on "vibrate." Mama Samm D'Arbonne's name blinked in the display.

I stepped back down the hall and into the greater darkness and took the call. "Not a good time, Sammathea," I murmured.

"Am I interrupting somet'ing, *cher*?" Her honeyed alto implied an arch to her eyebrows and her Cajunized endearment came out as "sha."

"I was just getting ready to eat."

"Hmmm . . . midnight snack? Or early breakfast?"

I looked at my watch. I had hoped for a banquet but I was behind schedule and it was starting to look like more of a couple of quick bites and home again, home again, jiggity-jig. "What do you want?"

"I want you to get out more, Christopher. You been spendin' too much time alone. Alone is not good for you."

Not exactly alone right now. "Why do you care? You haven't exactly been chummy the last couple of years."

"I been busy—"

"Admit it: You've been keeping your distance ever since that whole nanite-enhancement thing freaked you out."

"Dat's ancient history!" she snapped.

"Yes," I snapped back, "it *is* history! The EMP wiped out the nanobots in my system over three years ago so you and the rest of the female population of the planet are safe."

She chuckled. "Maybe it more like you the one who outta danger."

"Hardy," I said dryly, "har. So, what's your excuse? Staying away because I'm irresistible even without the weapons-grade pheromones?"

The hesitation in her response was no more than two seconds but felt more like ten. "Like I tol' you, I been busy—unlike some folk I could name. I lost most of a lifetime's worth of mojo wit' that Cthulhu bidness and I been workin' on getting it back. Had to travel some . . ." She stopped herself and I could feel her annoyance through the phone. Well, technically, I could detect the subvocal stressors in her voice starting to build, but, since it was inaudible to the human ear, you might as well call it "feeling."

"I gots a job for you," she said, getting back on track.

"I have a job," I said, feeling my own not-so-subvocal stressors start to rise.

There was nothing subvocal about her snort. "What job? You ain't teaching college Lit, no more. You just living fat and sassy off'n them investments dat your good buddy Vlad set you up wit.'"

It was my turn to snort: She knew how I felt about the guy who had stolen half of my humanity. "You're not the only one who's been busy. Staying alive has kind of turned into a full-time job." *That and holding on to the tattered, fraying freak flag of my sanity.*

"Yeah, well just staying hunkered down in that big ole empty house only give you the illusion of security seein' as how everyone dat matter knows where you live now!"

Yeah.

You'd think that saving the world and sending a Great Old One back to its own dread dimension would earn me a break. Maybe even put some second thoughts in the pinched skulls of all of the lesser monsters out there still looking to "make their bones."

Yeah, not so much . . .

"So, how's that mojo recharge coming?" I grumped back at her. "You must be filling up and filling out if that awful minstrel-show dialect is any indication. Is the medium becoming an extra-large?"

This time the pause was noticeably longer. "You might do well to remember to whom you are speaking," she said, sounding uncannily like a Bryn Mawr English professor.

"That's better. Save the shuck-and-jive act for the honkie rubes."

"And what do you think you are, then?"

"I'm no rube. Not anymore," I allowed. "And if I'm a honk*ie* does that make you the honk*er*?"

"Mister Chris, nobody say honkie anymore," she answered, a hint of the old Cajun flavor slipping back into her accent.

"Cracker?"

"Only *really* old black folks call white folk cracker anymore."

"Well, then what—"

"You don't want to know. Now, about this job—"

"Hey, did you hear about Stephen Hawking saying that we could blow up the entire universe with a particle accelerator? Something about quantum tunneling and catastrophic vacuum decay."

"Prob'ly because of that supercollider they jus' finish in Okla . . ."

There was a heavy sigh at the other end of the line. "Don' change the subje—"

"Don't *want* a job, don't *need* a job," I interrupted. "I've got more money than I know what to do with. And, right now, I'm out and about. So: case closed."

"What you know 'bout Pandora's Box?" she asked before I could end the call.

I was hungry and the clock was ticking. And yet I was letting her bait me into an extended conversation, probably hoping to entice me into doing something ill-paying and incredibly risky.

And arguing with her was just going to eat up my phone minutes . . .

"It wasn't a box, it was a jar," I answered, surrendering to the inevitable.

"All the legends call it a box," she argued.

"What's your source material? The Little Golden Book of Greek Mythology?"

She ignored the gibe and waited, counting on my professional know-it-all temperament to kick in.

I sighed. "The original myth story of Pandora was taken from Hesiod's *Works and Days*. The gods gave her a pithos—a large jar— that contained all of the evils of the world. *Nice* wedding gift, by the way. The whole 'box' misunderstanding seems to have started around the sixteenth century—probably with Erasmus of Rotterdam who translated Hesiod into Latin. Pithos was transcribed as *pyxis* which is Greek for 'box.' Then you have Rosetti's famous painting of Pandora back in the nineteenth century. That probably cemented it."

"Mister Chris, how you know this stuff?"

I glanced back in at the naked, writhing woman. "I've always had an interest in comparative mythology. I taught a course in it a few years back. And ever since the scarier myths started showing up on my doorstep, I've tried to keep up on my research." I shifted the phone to my other ear. "Is this topic germane to anything?"

She hesitated: *not a good sign.* "I'll let *her* tell you that when she finds you."

The naked, handcuffed woman in the bedroom moaned.

"Uh huh, if whoever *she* is can *find* me: I'm not at home right now," I said. "Gotta run; my food's getting cold!" I ended the call and then turned my phone off completely for good measure. I didn't need the distraction and my groin didn't need any more stimulation. I turned back toward the bedroom and my . . . prey.

First things first. I glided around the room, repositioning the candles that seemed the likeliest fire hazards. I moved one away from the edge of the dresser, another from the drapes adjacent to the windowsill. The stage had been set hastily but the candles were almost more impressive than the handcuffs and the nudity.

Tonight's meal moaned again, pulling my attention back to the bed. More specifically, to the fleshy writhing that promised a double feast. "Oh my God!" she sighed, "you—you're a vampire! What are you going to do?"

Unfortunately the question didn't sound rhetorical and so some sort of response was expected. I fought the urge to do a bad Lugosi version of "I *vant* to *suck* your *blood!*"

"You know what I am going to do," I answered menacingly as I crawled onto the bed. My timing was off: I was still dressed and that was either going to be messy or inconvenient—whichever way this ended up going first. "Look into my eyes and tell me what is going to happen . . ." I fumbled with the first button on my shirt.

Her eyes grew wide and she did a little lip licking, herself.

"You—you are going to drink my blood!" she gasped.

"Yesss," I hissed—half at the second button that was proving to be uncooperative.

"You are going to bite my tits!" she moaned.

Um, what?

She was back to panting. "You're going to sink your teeth into my breasts and suck me until I scream for mercy!" Her labored breathing was turning her perfect bosom into twin, cherry-topped snow cones of delight.

I rocked back on my heels. "Um, okay, Randa." I took a breath. "They're very . . . lovely . . . and they look great. But one of the reasons for that is why they're off-limits."

She hadn't given up on the panting and now she was—well—*pushing* them at me. "I don't know what you mean," she whimpered. "I'm helpless! And I cannot stop you from biting me . . . anywhere!"

I growled. Sort of. "You have implants, Miranda. The slightest puncture would be bad news for you. And I know that I certainly wouldn't enjoy it."

The panting faltered. "They're not silicone. They're saline: It would be safe."

"No."

"Please!"

I sighed and pulled the dental appliance holding my "fangs" out of my mouth.

"Please?" she repeated mournfully.

"I don't believe this . . ."

"*You* don't believe this?" She used her thumbs to trigger the safety catches on the steel bracelets. The "novelty" handcuffs popped open and released her wrists. She sat up. "Why can't you do this for me?"

Why couldn't I do this for her? "It's . . . um . . . outside my comfort zone . . . ?" I tried.

"You don't want me," she said flatly.

Oh boy.

"I do—uh—want you. Just not in that way . . ."

"Which way?"

"The . . . ah . . . biting. The whole monster-predator dynamic. The Fifty Shades of Red roleplay . . ."

"And the sex? Or am I just a big ole bag of blood to you?"

Wow. Just . . . wow.

She shifted around to better face me. "You understand it's not the money," she said. "It's never been about the money . . ."

"Miranda, I—"

"Don't you have *any* feelings for me?"

"Of course I do. I'm very fond—"

"Fond?" The stressors in her voice were anything but subvocal.

"Well, this started as a business arrangement . . . and I've come to care about you a great deal?" I was working my way through a verbal minefield, trying to pick my words carefully, and my voice slipped upwards at the end, changing my last sentence from a declarative statement into a question.

She smiled but her eyes showed her hurt. "I'm sorry. I'm just feeling . . . a little . . . used . . . here . . ."

"Oh, Randa; from the very beginning I've tried to maintain a clear understanding as to what this was about. We had a deal—"

"In the beginning," she agreed. "But things change. This isn't the same as going to the blood bank and getting refrigerated packets to go."

"Boy, howdy," I said, rubbing the back of my neck.

"I don't mean for you. I mean for *me!*"

I turned away and sat on the edge of the mattress. "Which is why I pay you a great deal more than a blood bank would for making a similar donation."

She moved to sit next to me. "There's nothing similar about this!"

I hung my head. "I know."

"Do you?" she asked. "Do you really?" She huffed. "And don't say 'donation.'"

"Okay. Exchange?"

"You mean: you give me money, I give you my blood? That kind of exchange?"

"Well . . . sure. I suppose . . ."

"You suppose." It was her turn to sigh. "'Similar.' There's nothing similar about this and getting takeout from the local blood bank."

I flashed an obvious and appreciative leer at her, waggled my eyebrows, and said, "I'll say!"

She was not amused. Or driven off-topic.

"Look, it's obvious what this means for you: fresh, hot, living blood instead of that plastic-tasting refrigerated crap nearing the end of its shelf life. But do you know what it means to me?"

"You get paid extremely—"

"I hope you're *not* about to suggest that I am some sort of whore!"

I shifted mental and verbal gears. "You get to indulge in the ultimate vampire fetish."

Her fist smacked against my shoulder. "Well, you *are* a vampire."

"I'm not." Though it felt more and more that my transformation from man into monster was closer to the endgame than from where I started out . . .

"Well, the next best thing! You need blood to survive!"

I looked down to avoid her gaze. "The biting was your idea." I suddenly realized that I was staring at Miranda's contentious bosom and looked away.

"You had those . . . those fangy teeth before you met me. They're not cheap Halloween, costume props." She moved behind me on the bed and her hands slid up my back to rest on my shoulders. "They're very real and very sharp and they fit your mouth like a very expensive dental appliance. You've used them on others." It was not a question.

"Our arrangement—"

"Yes, I agreed to the transfusions in the beginning. But it's not the same for you as it is for me. You're *getting* the blood. I'm *giving* it. The direction it flows makes all of the difference in the world! All you know is that it feels good for you. That it is more life pouring into you. It doesn't hurt on your end."

I turned to her. "I'm sorry. I took every precaution with the needles—"

"It isn't the needle that hurts, you jerk! Have you ever been on the other end of a blood transfusion?"

The memory hit so fast it was like a bolt of lightning, dazzling my vision, chased by rolls of thunder echoing inside my head.

The fire . . .

 . . . the barn . . .

  . . . the thing in the darkness drawing life from my veins . . .

   . . . and infecting me with the darkness from its own . . .

"Yes," I whispered.

"The first time might be a business arrangement," she continued, seeming not to have heard. "But, after that, it's an intimacy! An intimacy that grows each and every time you take something out of me and into yourself." She reached out and touched the side of my face. "You may think that cold, steel needles and plastic tubing reduce such an exchange to an act of mere mechanics." She shook her head. "They don't. They clarify the need for the human touch in such intimacies. Intimacies require an embrace."

The edge of my mouth quirked. "A *vampire* embrace?"

The caress turned into a light face smack. "Don't you mock me. Maybe we started out with your 'business' agreement but you've accepted my renegotiation of the terms a few months back. I remember you being very enthusiastic on more than one occasion."

She was right: It was an intimate thing. And taking her blood—separating it from her flesh—only "worked" on the most basic, pragmatic level. In every other way, separating her flesh from her blood didn't really work at all. Her flesh was very much a part of the exchange: The undead were very clear about this aspect of the hunter-prey gestalt.

I had foolishly thought I could hold onto the remains of my humanity by intellectualizing the process and turning it into a business transaction.

Despite my best efforts, I was still turning into a monster.

"I'm sorry," I said. "It bothers me to fetishize your gift to me like this."

"It's not a gift," she grumbled, "as long as you're paying me."

Now I was totally confused: Were we discussing a business transaction or not?

"We need to take the money out of . . . the equation," she said softly.

And there it was.

Miranda wanted something that I could not give her.

I just couldn't.

And the clock had just run out for me, for the second time this night. There were only two choices here.

I would either have to strip away any illusions that her feelings might be reciprocated.

Or provide her with a new set of illusions.

Coward that I was, I took the easiest route. "Look at me," I said. "I want to tell you something very important."

"What?" Sudden reluctance.

"No, I'm serious." A little non-corporeal push. "This is important. Look me in the eye."

She studied my expression. Her eyes met mine. And held.

Now she couldn't look away.

"Miranda, who is Janos Skorzeny?"

Her brow furrowed. "You are. You are Janos Skorzeny."

"No," I said, fighting the impulse to shake my head. It was important to maintain eye contact. "Janos Skorzeny is the name of the vampire in the first *Night Stalker* movie."

"Night Stalker?"

"Carl Kolchak."

"Who?"

"Never mind," I said. *Oops: That might cancel the hypnotic command altogether.* "Just remember that Janos Skorzeny is not a real person. Janos Skorzeny doesn't exist. Except as a character in *Kolchak: The Night Stalker.*" I paused. "And it was the name of the Chuck Connors character in the *Werewolf* TV series."

"Werewolf?"

It took nearly all of my fraying, frazzled willpower to *not* say, "There wolf; there castle."

I cleared my throat. "Janos Skorzeny is not a real person."

"Then who are you?"

"I am *no one*," I answered. "I *don't* exist. You will *forget* all about me tonight. Just like you've forgotten about me every month until just before my next visit. Only this time there will be no next visit."

"You—you're going away—?"

"I was *never here* to begin with. And all of that money—that cash that's been mysteriously turning up in your purse? That's from your luck at the casinos."

"My gambling wins . . . ?"

"Except that you've decided to stop gambling now. You're feeling like your luck is *changing* and you don't want to risk losing after such a lucky streak."

"No more gambling . . ."

I looked for my reflection in the dresser mirror: If I concentrated, I could almost see it. The dark hair and the slightly Slavic cast to my features.

"And you're feeling the need for *other changes*, as well . . ." I instructed.

The whole vampiric mind-control power is a very iffy thing.

It's not something that every fully transformed undead can pull off. Even the ancient ones who can pass through walls and pour through keyholes like weighted mist find this particular brain mutation to be a rare and unpredictable result in the nosferatu sweepstakes. Given the fact that I was still "technically" alive, I shouldn't be able to impose my will on another sentient being, but fate, the universe, and undead genetics had a wicked sense of humor. I had been gifted with a "knack" that was spotty, at best. Theresa Kellerman had proven immune to my various attempts to "push" her thoughts while Walter "Spyder" Landon had gone from a scary genius geneticist to a guy who struggled with the complexities of late-night custodial work thanks to my attempts to bend him to my will.

Miranda had been one of my uncertain success stories.

And was becoming a little more uncertain of late.

After carefully researching and selecting Miranda Moore—research librarian, vampire enthusiast, between relationships, clean bloodwork, ninety-minute drive from my home and conveniently near the highway that I took for my monthly assignations with my accountant—I had approached her with the initial proposition of selling her blood. At ten times the reimbursement rate of the Shreveport blood banks. Of course I had also done a little mental manipulation—after her freely given consent—to ensure that I was "out of sight, out of mind" between my monthly visits.

Somehow there had been a bit of slippage over the past few months.

First there was the "let's do away with the needles and plastic paraphernalia" suggestion on her part. Evolving up to the whole *Debbie Does Dracula* roleplaying scenario that had spun out of control tonight. The candles, the handcuffs—hell, the nudity and writhing—were unexpected and signs that my control was more than just "slipping."

So the whole *you'll forget all about me, throw out your vampire romance novels, and start developing an interest in blond, blue-eyed cowboys* reboot might be just as destined to fail in the long run.

The smart thing would have been to drain her dry, knock some candles over, and eradicate any possibility of a back trail with an accidental fire.

That was definitely the *smart* thing.

But the part of me that was still human was trying to hang on to my soul for as long as I could. It was an aspiration that seemed doomed to fail and had already given me a reputation as an idiot in the eyes of the others who shared the Dark Gift. Most of them were surprised I had survived this long. The rest were amazed that I could tie my own shoes.

So, shortly after tucking Miranda into bed for a long night of (hopefully) forgetful sleep, I was headed back down the interstate. Still hungry, more than a little frustrated, and potentially a lot more vulnerable than when the evening started, I was trying to not think about how this meant that I was back to a diet of that plastic-tasting refrigerated crap nearing the end of its blood bank shelf life.

As I pulled into the travel plaza to refuel for the final leg back home, I reminded myself that bad luck usually comes in threes.

Of course, my credit cards were declined and I had left the last of my cash in Miranda's purse as a farewell gift.

Chapter Three

Call it paranoia but I was certain that someone had crawled under my SUV and cut my fuel line while I was bartering for a tank of gas to get me home.

I knew it instinctively as the engine began to cough and I realized that I had gone through a full tank of gas since leaving the travel plaza thirty minutes earlier. I didn't need a flashlight check of the undercarriage: The math was convincing all on its own. My gas stop was some twenty miles behind me and home was another hundred and some on down the road.

And it had been timed to happen around half past midnight. Forget the old saying that "bad luck comes in threes," I'd just been bumped up to quadratic equations.

Another lifetime ago I might have chalked it up to coincidence— before I died for the first time and awoke with the shadow of immortality in my veins.

You would think I wouldn't be so unique. Thousands had died over the centuries with vampire slobber on their throats. Hundreds had been granted a second unlife because their fangy sires mingled their blood, bringing both viruses into play. You see, bite-work alone does not a vampire make.

And then there's me. No bitey: no saliva, no secondary virus. Instead, a sloppy, in-the-field transfusion had loaded my bloodstream with Virus A. But no Virus B. Hence, no super-virus.

So . . . not undead. But not so alive, either. And just unique enough to put me on the iniquitous Hit List of The Damned.

And I couldn't exactly turn to the "living" for allies: They were likely divided between the superstitious put-a-stake-through-his-heart or the scientific what-might-vivisection-tell-us-about-the-biological-anomalies?

So, as they say, it's *not* paranoia when everyone *is* out to get you. I wasn't so "Brad and Janet" anymore: Belief in dangerous coincidences was one of the first things to go.

For the moment the darkness was a mixed blessing. On the plus side, I had maybe three hours to go to ground. After that, sunrise would inflict an arcane pyromancy that mere tinted windows could not forestall. But the pine-latticed night skies of northern Louisiana—which might buy me another thirty minutes of cover come sunrise—also concealed me from the eyes of potential Good Samaritans. The predatory gaze of creatures who could see into the infrared and ultraviolet spectrum would not be so obstructed. And all of the nearby towns would be small, locked down, and closed up for the night.

So I was alone. But probably not for very much longer . . .

Final champagne bubbles of gas got me to an off-ramp. Unfortunately no amount of coaxing could get my chugging, gasping SUV all the way up to the top where the side road slid off into deeper darkness. It died with a great shudder just off the main highway.

The nearest cone of sodium-vapor light was distant enough to screen me from the casual motorist but I still offered a dim silhouette to anyone actually looking for me.

I glanced at my watch to check the time and saw my naked wrist. I'd had to hand my Breitling Navitimer over to a pimple-faced high school dropout in exchange for a tank of gas. If the kid was actually smart enough to get it properly appraised, he'd be able to buy a new pickup truck with customized mud flaps. It didn't seem an equitable trade for thirty-six dollars worth of gasoline, but waiting past sunrise for the banks to open was so not an option.

And now this.

I unbuckled my seatbelt and rested my forehead on the steering wheel. *How much longer?*

My phone played the first few measures of "Clair de Lune" in my pocket and I pressed the answer button without checking the caller ID.

"Baby, what are you doing?" Lupé's voice asked.

I sat up. "Nothing."

"Shouldn't you be doing something?"

"What? I don't—what do you mean?"

"You're in trouble, aren't you." Her voice made it clear that she wasn't asking.

"How did you know?"

"By the pricking of my thumbs . . ."

Something wicked this way comes.

". . . You're always in trouble these days," she clarified.

"That's because you're not here," I said. "You know what happens when I'm left to my own devices."

Like becoming a big, insensitive, predatory jerk.

She laughed but sounded sad. "You know how much I want that but it's just not possible right now."

"I know," I said. But I didn't think I did any more. *Damn Sídhe . . .* "How are the others?"

The hesitation in her voice was even more telling than Mama Samm's.

My left hand clenched the steering wheel. "They're starting to forget, aren't they?"

She took a breath. "They don't want to. They're fighting it . . ."

I took my own deep breath. "They can't help it. They're in the Realm of The Fae: Human memory fades and the outside world recedes. I'm surprised that you still remember me . . ."

She laughed a sad little laugh. "Not completely human. Remember?"

"Better than human," I shot back.

She sighed. "I will hold you in my heart as long as I can, baby. And, when you come, I will remember you again. And so will the others. Which is why you've got to do things right."

I swallowed. "I've always tried to do what's right. I usually make a hash of it."

"Sounds like somebody is having a pity party."

"Not for me. I'm thinking of the body count."

"You're a warrior, Chris. Collateral damage is inevitable—"

"I'm not a warrior!" I bit back. "I'm an unemployed Lit professor who's stranded on the highway! Both literally and metaphorically," I finished lamely.

"So," she asked after a patient pause, "what are you going to do about it?"

I swallowed. "I don't know. I thought I'd sit here for a while."

"You can't do that, Chris."

"I'm tired, Lupé."

"A while longer, baby, and then we can all be together."

"I don't think I can wait."

"You know it doesn't work this way. Giving up is giving up, whether it is by your hand or another's."

"It's not the same this time," I insisted. "I'm pretty much out of viable options. And I'm out here all alone."

"It is only as a man puts off all foreign support, and stands alone," she said.

". . . that I see him to be strong and to prevail," I quoted with her. "He is weaker by every recruit to his banner."

"Is not a man better than a town?" she finished.

"You've never invoked Emerson before. I'd love to see the libraries you're frequenting these days."

"You know you're forbidden to come here," she said.

"As long as I am tied to the realm of mortal men and answerable to fate and destiny," I answered as if by rote. "And you and the others are forbidden to return, having been granted sanctuary by the *Daoine Sídhe*."

"Yes." Her voice was unbearably sad.

"So, how much longer am I condemned to exile?"

"Christopher, we are the ones in exile," she corrected gently.

"That's not how it feels to me."

"Liban and Fand have both said that you may . . . transition . . . soon."

"Really." I sighed. "You know that the Faerie have a different sense of time than the rest of us. Their egg timers measure in decades, not minutes."

"And, yet," she said, "you are the one who turned back the Wheel of Time and saved New Orleans from its greater fate."

She meant it as a compliment but it wasn't strictly true and it didn't make me feel any better. Funny how the saving of tens of millions of lives had not erased the guilt for the thousands still lost the second time around.

And it was pointless to argue who had really unwound the mainspring of history's chronometer and turned Hurricane Eibon into Katrina. An ancient, alien astronaut, worshipped as an elder god, had returned to its own dread dimension, folding space and time in the process of facilitating a launch window. My part in that affair and the repercussions that followed fell somewhere in between the flap of a butterfly's wings and having a sure steersman's grip on the tiller of the SS *Fate*. Responsibility and blame, like beauty, lies in the eye of the beholder. And now, years later, I was still locked out of the place between worlds where the Fey Folk had taken my friends and family for refuge against the Greater Darkness.

Porched. On a cosmic scale.

"Christopher . . . this is important."

My head came up. "What?"

"Liban and Fand were talking about you."

"That doesn't sound good."

I could hear the gentle smile in her voice. "Liban . . . still bears you much affection . . ."

"I'm just a curiosity to her. She's bored."

I could feel her nod a thousand light-years away. "There is that. She is ancient. And she appreciates your part in holding back The Darkness."

"Sure. I'm a chess piece with some value."

"More than a simple pawn," she agreed.

I smiled in return. "Certainly not a bishop."

"A knight!"

"In shining armor?" I made a rude noise. "Maybe a castle . . . Hey, I've been rooked!"

She laughed again. And sounded more distant. As if she were receding into the sweet oblivion of lost memories.

"Lupé?"

"They were talking," she said. "And Liban said something. It seemed important: They were both worried. Does 'empusa' mean anything to you?"

I had to sift through odd bits of trivia in the back of my head. "Did they just say 'empusa' or '*The* Empusa'?"

"I don't know, baby. Does it matter?"

"Does anything?"

"Are you giving up, Chris? You know we cannot be together if you . . . you give up."

"Acknowledging the inevitable is not the same as giving up."

"It is if you don't go down fighting. And you are a fighter, Chris. You've always fought for the right things. And now, tonight, *you're* the right thing. The rightest thing I know! I need you to do this! The others, too. We need you to fight for *you!* Promise us!"

"I'll . . . try . . ." I said reluctantly.

"Do or do not," she growled in a curiously ancient voice, "there is no 'try.'"

I laughed despite my sour mood. "God, I miss you."

"It won't be forever, baby. Unless you break The Rule. Now hang up so you can hurry up and get your ass out of there."

"You're the best, Lupé."

"And you're my Sweet Baboo."

And then the call went dead.

Just like my heart.

The question of empusa or "The" Empusa nagged at me a little.

In Greek mythology, Empusa was the daughter of the goddess Hecate and the dark spirit Mormo who preyed upon children. Mormo was one of the mythic precursors to the vampire legends that would develop around the chthonic deities down through the ages. Empusa was possibly the first *prosopopoeia* of those legends.

She was said to be beautiful—in outward form, at least. Flaming hair, alabaster skin, a divine face and form that enabled her to seduce multitudes of young men. Not only did they fall under the spell of her beauty, they were ensorcelled with a form of sleep paralysis, as well. And this demigoddess would then feast on them while they were thralls to her magic. Drinking their blood, even devouring their flesh, she was transformed, in time and mythology, to an entire race of vampiric creatures—spectres, actually. These empusae were Hecate's minions and would devour unwary travelers on lonely roads. They were cited throughout literary history by such varied scribes as Aristophanes, Lucius Flavius Philostratus, Johann Wolfgang von Goethe, and Rudyard Kipling. F. W. Murnau, the director of *Nosferatu*, gave the name *Empusa* to the ship that his undead Count Orlok traveled on.

So were Fand and Liban talking about the Greek demigoddess? Or the monsters that closely paralleled the Greek lamiai? Some of the latter would be more difficult to spot as they could take on many forms, even those of animals. As for a certain beautiful, red-headed siren? Later accounts of her legend suggested that she either had the leg of an ass or an artificial leg made out of brass. Well, brass or ass, we were into shorts and short skirt weather so picking her out of a lineup would be a good deal easier.

In the meantime, I needed to move.

I didn't think too much about the fact that I had to turn my phone back on to speed-dial my business partner while I organized my emergency kit one-handed.

"After Dark Investigations," she said, answering on the first ring.

"Olive," I said, "I've got a problem and I've got to move fast—"

"This is Moira, Mr. Cséjthe. I'm afraid Ms. Perdue is out sick tonight and it's just me covering the phones." Moira had been on the job for a whole week, now, and still couldn't pronounce my name properly. Most of the time it came out sounding like a half-strangled Chinese oath. This time she managed to make it sound like a cross between a cough and a sneeze. "Is there something I can do for you?"

"*Chay*-tay," I corrected absently, checking my rearview mirrors for movement of any kind.

"What?"

"Call me Chris," I sighed, and gave her a barebones explanation of what had happened and what I wanted. As she wrote down the highway and the number of the closest mile marker, I asked her to arrange for a tow truck and look up taxicab or Uber numbers for the nearest towns.

"Aren't you going to wait with your car?" she asked.

"Um, no."

"Why not?"

Why not?

Because there are things that want me dead—dead again, dead for the third time—that you can't imagine in your worst nightmares, little girl . . .

"Because someone slid under my wheels while I was inside a busy, well-lit truck stop and cut my fuel line while I was trying to figure out why my plastic is only good for bookmarks, shims, and door jimmies all of a sudden."

"Gee, Mr. Cséjthe, sounds like you're not having a very good night."

I fought the urge to lean forward and bang my head against the steering wheel. "I don't think you grasp the seriousness of the situation. Someone with that kind of skill and planning didn't arrange for me to be stranded by the side of the road—in the middle of the night, far from assistance or witnesses—just for shits and giggles. They're either going to show up right soon or send other sorts that I'd rather not wait around to meet."

I reached under my seat and pulled my handgun, a Glock 20, from its hidden carrier. Why was I having this conversation? It was wasting precious time that I needed to be putting distance between me and my vehicle. Using Moira as an excuse to get myself killed would be a technical violation of The Rule as Lupé and The Others defined it.

"You're kidding, Mr. Cséjthe—" It was official, now: The new intern had discovered more ways to mispronounce my name than any three people I knew. "—who would want to harm you?"

I shoved a magazine in the grip of the handgun and put three more in my pocket. "Moira, you wouldn't believe me if I told you."

And if I told you, they'd *have to kill you.*

I squirmed about, trying to meet all of the conditions of my concealed carry permit as I reseated the Glock in my fanny holster. Louisiana summers are hell for dressing comfortably even without trying to keep a weapon the size of both of your fists out of sight.

"I need you to be making those calls now," I said. *Instead of slowing me down with a bunch of unnecessary questions.*

"But—"

"Gotta go!" I terminated the call, ending any further protests.

I spent all of two seconds thinking about the sawed-off shotgun and the semiautomatic assault rifle secreted beneath the hinged back seat. Better to travel fast and light, I decided. And if the opportunity to hitchhike materialized down the road, I didn't want to lessen those already slim odds by looking like an extra from a Schwarzenegger movie. I grabbed the flashlight out of the glove box and the astronomy pointer out of the compartment beneath the armrest. A little larger and longer than a penlight, the laser pointer was a bit long for my shirt pocket but the teargas and pepper-spray pens as well as the colloidal-silver atomizer kept it snug and upright.

All I needed was a king-sized, nerd-worthy, tooled-leather pocket protector.

I was reaching for the door handle when a pair of headlights came up over the hill behind me. Was this someone making their move? Or just another late-night motorist bound for Monroe or towns and cities beyond?

Neither, apparently: A red and blue lightbar bloomed above the disembodied headlamps as it pulled onto the exit ramp behind me.

Against all odds, there was a cop around when you needed them!

I started to reach for the door handle then remembered the Glock. I tugged the semi-automatic out of my fanny holster. Reopening the glove compartment, I swapped it out for my vehicle registration and proof of insurance, then closed the compartment and locked it.

I was hunting through my wallet for my concealed carry permit when the patrol car's spotlight came on. As the beam traveled around the perimeter of my vehicle, I turned on the interior dome light.

My father had taught me how to handle late-night traffic stops.

Cops don't believe in vampires or werewolves or alien intelligences that inhabit a shadow dimension pressed smack dab up against ours. On the other hand, they know that with the dying of each day's light there is a shift in this world's balance. The majority of the good, the decent, the hardworking, go home. The majority of the hooligans, the troublemakers, yes, and even the occasional human monster, come out to "play." There are still good people out and about, but you don't have to work in law enforcement to know that your chances for unpleasant encounters continue to rise as the hour grows later and the landscape grows darker.

"There's no such thing as a routine traffic stop until it's over," my old man often told me. "Every time a cop approaches a stopped vehicle, he wonders: 'Is this the one? Will this guy have a pistol? A sawed-off shotgun?'" (Good thing both of mine were well stowed.) "So let me tell you something, son," my father said—this old man who had toted his own badge and gun back and forth to work for nearly forty years. "When a man is walking toward you with his hand on the butt of his gun, you don't want to do anything to make him more nervous than he already is. You get pulled over after dark; you turn on the dome light and sit there with both hands in plain sight on top of the steering wheel. Not just for his sake but for yours."

So I did. I sat there with the dome light on and my hands in plain sight long enough to wonder if my license plate had thrown a flag in the NLETS database.

Eventually a door was opened and the flash of the patrol car's interior lights revealed four silhouettes: two cops and what had to be a couple of perps in the caged backseat getting a detour on their trip to the Ouachita Parish lockup.

The PA speaker crackled to life: "Driver, please step out of the vehicle, keeping your hands in plain sight."

I sighed. No doubt Lieutenant Ruiz had flagged my license plate in the computer network—an invitation for her fellow officers to give me grief if the opportunity arose. Ruiz was two years gone—transferred down to New Iberia Parish—but the National Law Enforcement Telecommunications System had deep memory banks.

I opened the door and stepped down onto the gravel shoulder, shielding my eyes against the glare of the spotlight with my right hand. As I realized that I was still holding my flashlight with that hand, both officers stepped out of the car.

The driver had his hand on the butt of his service revolver. The officer riding shotgun was—well—carrying a shotgun. He held it a bit awkwardly, as if he didn't quite know what to do with it. All other details were lost as they stepped in front of the squad car's multiple light sources and became silhouettes.

"Please keep your hands where we can see them, sir," ordered the driver.

Damn Ruiz; I should be getting roadside assistance, not a little ill-timed payback for back when those corpses kept turning up in my yard . . .

"Mr. Cséjthe, our records indicate you have a gun permit . . ."

I gestured with the flashlight, flicking it on and pointing it over my shoulder, back at my SUV. "It's locked in the glove compartment." The silhouettes visibly relaxed and I silently thanked my old man's counsel: climbing out of my car, armed, to greet two officers of the law . . . well, just no way that would have gone pleasantly, even if they were professionals . . .

Professionals who pronounced my name correctly just from reading it off of the little computer screen in the squad car . . .

"Are you sure that we've got the right guy?" Shotgun asked the driver. "He don't exactly look like the Bogeyman."

And now the back doors were opening on that squad car. Since there are no interior door handles where the arrestees sit, the doors were literally kicked off their hinges. One of the doors went surfing across the road and median and into the opposite lanes.

The "perps" emerged.

I brought the flashlight around and illuminated the "cops" as their "prisoners" joined them. Their uniforms were hastily put together and haphazardly buttoned. Dark stains cascaded from the collars where the former occupants had had their throats torn open. The pretend cops smiled, their parted lips revealing the predatory Vs of elongated incisors.

Vampires.

Dressed up like the long fang of the law.

"I've got the camera," announced one of the "perps," likewise a vampire.

I spoke without thinking: "Camera? You guys are what—fans? I can't believe you cut my fuel line for a photo op!"

"Fuel line? Oh, this just gets better and better," the driver said. He jerked his head at one of the perps. "Check it out."

The thing that looked like a man moved with inhuman speed. He was back in less than a minute. "The tip was solid, Dwayne. It's been nicked in three different places. Can't tell if it's deliberate or some kind of damage from road debris."

I looked at the driver. "Dwayne?"

He looked at me. "What?"

I shrugged. "Guess I should know better by now. But I still expect vampires to have names like Boris or Vlad . . . maybe Heinrich. But Dwayne?"

Taunting the undead carries risks. Particularly if they have the advantage and outnumber you four-to-one. I was reminded of that as his handgun was out of its holster, now, and pointed at my midsection. Goading your assassin into pulling the trigger could be interpreted as breaking The Rule—but then I really had no chance of getting out of this alive unless I could provoke these guys into making a mistake. It was a fine line in terms of inevitability: There were four of them, any one of them stronger, faster, able to take more damage and shrug it off. My only chance was to make them careless. Careless and stupid.

"And the camera?" I continued, looking past his shoulder. "Makes you come off more touristy than menacing. Unless you're paparazzi, in which case I should point out that Britney Spears is from Houma." I pointed to the southeast. "Another five hours thataway. I hear the sunrise on the Gulf is to *die* for."

"I thought he was supposed to be all clinically depressed and borderline catatonic," the one with the shotgun murmured.

"We need a record for the Demesne," the driver answered me, "in case you discorporate."

I raised an eyebrow. "Discorporate?" He meant getting turned into a human-shaped pile of ash but I was more interested in why that was an issue.

"Issues of succession. No body, no evidence of successful termination. The leadership of the New York demesne remains in question until your primacy is fully resolved."

"Heh," I said. "Primacy. You guys are really serious about the legalese. Could've planted a bomb under my car instead of cutting the gas line and jumping through all the extra hoops."

They all smiled now. *Way* too many pointy teeth!

"If someone cut your gas line, it wasn't one of us," said Perp One.

"And it's not just a question of corporeal evidence," Perp Two said with some emotion. "It's a matter of payback." He produced a machete-like sword. "A lot of people owe you a death . . ."

I nodded slowly. "Couldn't agree more. You just trot on back to New York and tell the rest of the UV-challenged that they're welcome to die the second death and feel free to start without me."

"What?"

"He used to be an English teacher, Vern," Perp One murmured. "You shoulda said '*he* owes a lot of people a death' instead uh the other way around." And proceeded to draw a longish, Ren Faire–looking sword from behind his back.

"Whatever happened to the good old days," I groused, "when the undead just crawled out of their crypts and bit people?"

"We're not stupid," the one with the shotgun answered. "We know your touch is poison and your veins are toxic. And we aren't about to give you a chance to bloodwalk."

"Oh, darn!" Apparently the reputation that kept most of the undead off my back was finally facilitating a learning curve for the rest.

Vampires are stronger and faster than humans so they tend to be overconfident. Being longer "lived" makes them arrogant as well: They presume the advantage of time makes them smarter and wiser. It was that kind of arrogance and overconfidence on their part that had kept me alive in the face of overwhelming odds so far.

That and plain, dumb luck.

It appeared, however, that I was out of plain, dumb luck. Or handsome, smart luck, for that matter.

Vern the Perp furrowed his brow. "Maybe he's on drugs. That would explain why he ain't all suicidal . . ."

I smiled. "Don't need artificial chemicals in my system, boys. I've banished the doom and gloom of these past two years by finding my Happy Thought!"

"Happy thought?" Vern questioned.

"It's like from *Peter Pan*," the other sword guy muttered from the side of his mouth.

Vern looked blank.

"Helps him fly."

Vern's expression slowly morphed from *huh?* to *Omygodhecanfly?*

The other sword guy just shook his head.

I looked around. Even this late at night there should have been some traffic. "So, how are we going to do this? Do you shoot me or run me through?"

"Nothing so quick," Dwayne answered.

"Car," Shotgun announced.

"I've got it," the other sword guy said. He stepped toward the road.

After a good thirty seconds the hill behind us acquired a luminescent corona from approaching headlights. It was another full minute, however, before a car came over the concrete horizon. The headlights wobbled a bit as if the driver was having a momentary spasm, and then settled out as the car went streaking past.

Impressive.

Vampiric mind control is tricky enough in a small room where you can get the victim to look in your eyes. Projective telepaths who can sense minds a mile or more away and put the pay-no-attention-to-the-man-behind-the-curtain whammy on a moving target? I was outnumbered, outgunned, and outbrained. "Careless and stupid" hadn't been a viable edge to begin with and now it was so in the rearview mirror.

"All clear," Shotgun announced.

For the moment. My only chance would be to make my move when the next vehicle popped up. The distraction would probably cut the odds down from one in a thousand to one in eight hundred and fifty-two. Best case scenario: I could probably take one of them with me before the others "resolved my primacy."

I believed in focusing on the positives in any given situation.

"Anything else?" Dwayne asked the vamp with the shotgun.

He shook his head. "Not yet. We're clear to three miles out."

Dwayne turned back to me. "Now, where were we?"

I shrugged. "Something about payback . . . blah, blah, blah . . . slow and painful . . . blah, blah . . . but nothing about who's going to hold the camera, who's going to watch for cars to mind-wipe, and whether there's enough of you left over to take me down." I smiled and blinked expectantly. "Blah."

"Won't be a problem," he said, gesturing with his gun. "We shoot you in the knees so you can't run and then take our time and take turns with the blades."

I had to force a grin. "Well, that sounds messy."

Shotgun cocked his head. "He don't seem scared, Dwayne. Why ain't he scared?"

"Happy Thought," I offered.

"He's scared, all right," Dwayne answered. "He's just trying to hide it."

I raised my hands a bit. "Oh, I'm afraid, all right . . ."

"See?"

". . . scared that after going *mano a monster* with zombies, werewolves, master vampires, and creatures from the Cthulhu Lagoon, after facing down an immortal Nazi, an ancient Babylonian demon, a six-thousand-year-old necromancer, and a couple of Great Old Ones—I'm terrified that I'm going to get capped by evil masterminds from the Jerry Springer universe. It's a good thing that you're going to kill me because I wouldn't want to live with that humiliation! Too bad your plan totally sucks for you."

"Yeah?" the driver scowled, "How's that?"

"You said it yourself: the Rites of Succession."

"So?"

I shrugged. "Once I'm dead, the Throne of the New York demesne is totally up for grabs. And tradition usually recognizes the assassin of the old Doman as the new successor. Except your plan is pretty much going to muddle up who actually kills me!"

"If *we* kill you then our *Sire* becomes Doman," Vern's sword-toting buddy answered. "What we do, we do for Clan and Family, not for personal advancement."

"When, not if," I corrected.

"What?"

"You meant to say *when* you kill me, not *if*. Or maybe you're not so confident of the four-to-one odds."

"You really *are* some kind of English teacher," Vern said. I couldn't tell if his tone bordered on awe or astonished annoyance.

"A professor of literature," I corrected. "Though I can play the grammarian if the situation warrants. Benjamin Franklin said, 'Reading makes a full man, meditation a profound man, discourse a clear man.'"

"Yeah?" Vern's sword buddy raised his blade. "Who said big-ass swords makes a dead man?"

I shook my head. "No one. The Book of Matthew, however, says that he who lives by the sword shall die by the sword. But then I'm guessing you guys aren't all that big on the New Testament."

"All right," snapped the driver with the gun, "Enough with the quotage. Unless you have any last words." He smiled. "Aside from the screaming and begging for mercy."

I casually moved my right hand toward my shirt pocket and pulled out the astronomy pointer. "How about the pen is mightier than the sword?" It still looked more like a mini-flashlight than a writing implement but it was dark and I kept my hand in motion. "As for any last words?" I turned sideways and struck a fencing pose. "*En garde!*"

The two with the swords started to step forward, grinning, but Dwayne swept them back, holding out his arms on each side. "There won't be any on-guarding! Just a bullet—"

He shrieked as the glowing, green line of light slashed across his face. His eyes burst into flaming balls of goo like campfire marshmallows lit for grotesque s'mores.

I ignored the swordsmen for the moment, making the firearms my first priority. Shotgun was quicker than I thought, slide-cocking the Remington 870 while throwing it up in front of his face. Another eye shot was momentarily blocked so I directed the laser pointer where he was gripping the stock, shining the beam on his right hand.

A typical red laser pointer for classroom use is rarely able to push much more than a single milliwatt. As a weapon, they can do a little retinal damage but are pretty useless otherwise. I wasn't brandishing a typical classroom pointer, however. I was wielding a five-thousand-milliwatt green laser pointer whose weaker cousins were used for outdoor distance scopes. They can also pop balloons, light matches, and sear human flesh at some remove. Shotgun was a good deal closer and not human. His sun-sensitive, preternatural flesh was especially vulnerable to an amplified yet concentrated beam of coherent, high-frequency light.

His hand burst into flame.

"What *is* that?" Vern screamed as the Remington shotgun clattered to the asphalt. Fire began crawling up his companion's arm.

I smiled with my teeth. "Not as clumsy or as random as a blaster . . ." I swept the green, threaded beam across the swordsmen's faces, ". . . a Jedi's lightsaber is an elegant weapon . . ."

Vern ducked and the other swordsman lost only one eye but it was enough. His sword joined the shotgun on the pavement as he shrieked and clutched at his face. Dwayne had fallen to his knees, flames flickering from back of his empty eye sockets like a candlelit jack-o'-lantern. Shotgun was trying to beat out the fire on his right arm with his left hand and now both arms were aflame.

Vern had better reflexes. He hurled his sword at me and turned and ran for the squad car, sliding into the driver's seat. By the time he realized that he didn't have the keys for the ignition, Dwayne and Shotgun were man-sized bonfires and the other swordsman was running blindly down the ramp, his head fully ablaze like the Ghost Rider sans motorcycle. As he passed into a patch of greater darkness he seemed to transform into a will-o'-the-wisp bobbing away into the distance.

Vern looked up, his expression a mixture of fear, fury, and awe as I walked up to the broken-out driver's side window. "They said it would be easy!" he sobbed. "They said you was gone over!"

"Gone over?" I squatted next to the door.

"They was saying you had lost your mind. That you'd started drinking like you was still alive and wanted to be dead!"

"That or the other way around," I said.

"They said you had a death wish . . ."

I smiled. Too bad my teeth weren't naturally pointy. "What? Like *I* want to die instead of sending all of your New York, undead asses into the Great Beyond?" I leaned against the door's sill and aimed the laser pointer at his face. "Now why would I want to do that?"

Resignation and hopelessness filled the vampire's eyes like rising floodwaters. "Because . . . they said . . . they said . . ." His voice faded to a whisper and he closed his eyes. ". . . I don't know."

"Go ahead, Vern. What did they say? Tell me what they've said about me."

"That you're The Bloodwalker. The Daybinder. That . . . that you used to be human and that you . . . never were. That you went insane after your family was killed—"

I held up a finger in front of his lips and he stopped talking.

"They weren't killed," I said quietly. "They were taken to a safe place outside of this world. They're still alive. They're just not . . . here."

His eyes peeked open. "See, man; that's just crazy-sounding. I mean, it's just another fancy way of sayin' they died . . . leaving this world."

"They didn't die," I insisted, sounding a little crazy to myself, now. *What am I going to say? That they had been taken into the Realm of the Faerie?*

Or was Vern talking about the crash outside of Weir, Kansas all those years before that marked the first *passing of my wife and daughter?*

And me . . .

I bowed my head and took a shaky breath. "Look, let's say everybody's right and I do have a death wish. I can't just stand around and *let* you kill me. It's as good as committing suicide—which we all know is a big theological no-no. So it all requires a good faith effort on *your* part. Capisce?"

He closed his eyes.

I reached through the window and grabbed his arm. "Pay attention, Vern! I'm getting really, *really* tired of this!"

He shrieked as the silver-laced alkaloids in my epidermis seared his undead flesh. I pulled my hand back but an angry red palm print remained and his arm smelled like rancid pork tossed on a hot grill. "I—I'm sorry!"

"Sorry isn't good enough, Frakula! You and all the others! Just keep coming down here! You just keep coming and coming and you *still* can't do it right! What is so freaking hard about this? I'm just one man! And now I'm all alone! And yet you still can't figure out how to make it happen!" My voice caught and I couldn't yell any more. "You let me down tonight, Vern . . ."

"Let you down?" He wanted to rub his arm but was afraid to touch the burn.

"You and your friends. All of you. And the rest . . ." I shook my head. "I'm tired. And alone. And yet you still can't seal the deal."

"I-I don't unnersstand what you're sayin'."

"If you can't be Twilight pretty could you at least be Chris Lee smart? I'm saying bring your A game or stay the hell home. It's worse than annoying, it's a tease. You get me all excited about laying down my sword and shield . . . and then you don't come across. Plus, now I have to kill you. Really, what's the point?"

"Oh God . . ." His eyes pinched shut and the sound of his ragged breathing was surprisingly loud as he struggled to get enough air into his lungs.

Vern was a newbie. Like all of the recently turned, he had trouble remembering that the dead didn't actually breathe. Except to talk. And, as far as I was concerned, Vern was done talking. Then scarlet tears began to slide from beneath his eyelids like cherry Kool-Aid and I thought—just for a moment—about letting him go.

Let him run back to the New York demesne with the news of how another quartet of fanged assassins had been beaten by just one half-dead, still nearly-human guy. The tale would grow with the telling and so would my boogieman rep.

Which side of the death wish debate would that fall on?

If I let him go was it an uncomplicated act of mercy on my part and a stratagem to discourage future attacks? Or a Machiavellian ploy to provide the enemy with additional intel and up the ante? According to the M*A*S*H Theme, "suicide is painless" but managing a so-called death wish was giving me migraines.

"Don't kill me, man!" he pleaded. "I don't wanna die!"

"Jesus, Vern; you're a vampire. You're already dead! You've just been getting by on borrowed time. And being a very naughty boy in the process!"

"I'll do anything, man!"

I sighed. "Anything?"

"Yeah! Anything!" he promised.

"Call your boss."

"What?" Fear had bested fury, now befuddlement was climbing into the ring. "Dwayne's dea—"

"Your *Sire!* The one you bozos were going to elevate to Top Bat by punching my ticket! Get him on the phone!"

"I—ah—" He fumbled about. "Don't have a cell phone."

I pulled mine out, hit SPEAKER, punched in the New York City area code, and handed it to him. "Reach out and touch some . . . thing."

Vern looked conflicted. Apparently calling that far up the food chain was not going to be a good thing for him. On the other hand, angry boss-man was thousands of miles away and big bad boogieman me was about to turn his wheels into a personal crematorium. He punched in the remaining seven numbers.

"Who is this?" a familiar voice snapped after nearly a dozen rings.

Vern swallowed. "Mistress . . . I . . ."

I took the phone from his shaking grasp.

"It's after midnight, Carmella," I said quietly. "Do you know where your children-of-the-night are?"

"What? Cséjthe?" When she spoke again her voice was oozing calm. "How I've missed you!" Were I merely human her vocal subharmonics might have mellowed me into a compliant sheep-like state.

Knowing how that worked just annoyed me all the more.

"Yes," I said, "yes, you have. I could say you've missed me four times on this particular occasion alone."

"Darling Christopher, you misunderstand my gesture. I didn't send them there to kill you . . ."

"What's she saying?" Vern whispered.

"That she didn't send you down here to kill me," I whispered back.

"That ain't true!" he said, forgetting to whisper this time.

"Well, of course I *told* them to kill you," she said.

"Torture and kill," Vern corrected. "She said torture and kill."

"Christopher, I hope you will send *that* one back to me. It sounds like he's not yet properly trained."

Vern's eyes became very expressive. The primary expression looked like "just kill me now."

"Carmella," I said, "I don't need some undead newbie to tell me what the Le Fanu twins are plotting. This isn't the first assassination squad you've sent after me."

"But the fact that I told them to kill you . . ."

"Torture and kill," Vern mouthed.

". . . doesn't mean I actually *want* them to. I just want to get your attention."

I sighed. I seemed to be doing a lot of that lately. "Okay. You've got my attention: What?"

"The New York demesne is in disarray. We need strong leadership. There are things—forces—"

The normally smooth and unflappable Carmella La Fanu sounded rattled.

Interesting . . .

"—powers, if you will . . ."

"And principalities?" I coached.

"Don't mock. Something bad is coming. We need our Doman!"

"During the short time I was there everyone was trying to kill me."

"Not everyone, darling. If you'll remember that one night in your bedroom—"

Vern's eyes widened.

"Nothing happened, Carmella," I said through clenched teeth.

"Only because your thralls were there to interfere," she murmured seductively. "Now that they're gone—"

Up until now I was just pissed on general principal. My anger, which had been running cold suddenly flashed white hot. "You're right, Carmella, I *have* been away too long."

"You wouldn't have to feed your bloodthirst with cold packets of leftovers from the blood bank. Bethany misses you."

"Stop!"

"We could . . . we could rule together . . ." Her subharmonics faltered along with her sudden hesitation. Maybe she was picking up on my subharmonics now.

"When I come," I said, "it will be to end this dance, once and for all. And I'll be sure to look you up."

"Christopher . . . I—"

"Because I have something special planned for you, Carmella. Very special." Grief and anger combined, fueling a rage that seemed to overflow my physical body, radiating out from me like an invisible pulsar. "You know the old song, 'I've Got You Under My Skin'? You might want to learn it. The lyrics are quite . . . you know what? Just wait until I get there. It will be soon. And then I'll teach you the meaning of every word."

There was no answer at the other end, snappy or seductive.

"Can you *fear* me now? Good." I terminated the call and shoved my phone back into my pocket.

Vern took advantage of that split second of inattention to snatch the laser pen out of my other hand, tuck it under his chin, and press the ON switch.

Once again, I had looked into The Abyss and The Abyss had blinked first.

I put my SUV into neutral and pushed it on up the hill to get it out of the likely blast radius of the burning cop car behind me. My strength wasn't that of a full-fledged vampire but I could still move a two-ton weight on wheels up a mild incline without popping a sweat.

Well, not much of a sweat. Even north Louisiana was humid this time of the year.

Just as I hopped back in to set the parking brake, a little red sports car came roaring up off the highway and up the exit ramp. I popped the glove compartment and retrieved my handgun just as the two-seater MG squealed to a stop right next to my open driver's door.

The top was down and the driver was blonde, windblown, and looked all of sixteen. She leaned toward me, reaching out with a many-braceleted, multi-ringed hand and said, "Come with me if you want to live!"

Well.

Huh.

This was a no-brainer.

High school cheerleaders don't cruise the interstate, looking for strange, older men to offer rides to.

Not in classic, two-seater, British sports cars.

Not at one o'clock in the A.M.

And since my quartet of vampire assassins had no reason to lie about cutting my fuel line . . .

I slide-cocked the Glock and pointed it back at her. "Aren't you out past the Curfew for Jailbait, sweetheart?"

The gun didn't seem to impress her. Maybe she was aware of my track record with firearms. She started to say something else but it was drowned out by the roar of a large engine. The interior of my car filled with light. Light coming in through the rear window.

I looked just in time to see the burning cop car explode as an 18-wheeler plowed through it at high speed.

Headed right for me.

I had an extra second or two to register that the truck driver was a woman. And, sitting next to her in the high cab, was Moira, the new intern at After Dark Investigations.

Just a second or two.

Not enough time to get clear as the ten-ton truck tore through my SUV as if it were a tissue box and killed me.

Again.

Chapter Four

Forget the WWE or whatever those spandex-wearing, steroid-chugging, testosterone-poisoned prima donnas of the wrestling world are labeling their "sport" these days; the Ultimate Smackdown took place some six thousand years ago. According to the Old Testament, dude named Jacob got involved in a wrestling match that lasted all night. He was prepared to go longer but, when the dawn came, his unnamed opponent pulled a bogus move and dislocated ole Jake's hip. Time and duration alone would have made the event worthy of the record books but that's not why it's remembered to this day . . .

The author of the Pentateuch is a little ambiguous about Jake's opponent, calling him a "man." The prophet Hosea later said Mr. Anonymous was an angel. Jacob, however, ups the ante by stating afterwards, "I have seen God face to face and lived."

Maybe the tale grew with the telling: I can't figure The Big Guy taking all night when an ordinary angel would have you in a sleeper hold before you could say "Samson does steroids!" And I could say that with some authority because I was getting my butt kicked. Or, for purposes of anatomical accuracy, my fist slammed back against the bar.

Don't ask me how I wound up in this silvery-white . . . room? Space? Everything was indistinct and hazy . . . including how I got detoured out of my tunnel to the afterlife and into this generic, white space/waiting room with a—black bar? Counter top? Crossing arm?

Whatever it was, it had a flat surface a foot across and appeared to be infinitely long, stretching into the distance to my left and right until it was swallowed up into the diffused milky distance.

Distant landscapes, however, were less important at the moment than the immediacy of my predicament. The angel wasn't releasing me. My hand was swallowed up in his fist, my fingers lost in the ivory, ham-sized hand that kept me pinned at an uncomfortable angle. He leaned in close and hissed in my ear, "*You* shall not pass!"

I grimaced, wondering which was worse: the pain in my arm and shoulder or implications of this being some kind of supernatural roadblock.

"So what are you saying, Mikey?" I grunted. "Mama Cséjthe's baby boy is destined for 'warmer climes'?"

The angel I knew as Michael shook his head, his eaglelike visage flickering like a distant thunderstorm. "It is not your time, yet."

"Could have fooled me," I grunted, pushing back: I couldn't really win; I was just trying to keep my shoulder from being dislocated. "Ten-ton truck comes out of nowhere and flattens my SUV with me inside . . ."

"You are not fated to die by accident."

I shrugged. Half a shrug, actually, as my right arm and shoulder were effectively paralyzed. "Figured it wasn't an accident when she came barreling up the off ramp at ninety miles an hour, though a flaming cop car, and kamikazied my wheels on the shoulder. Especially with Moira the Suspiciously Clueless Intern in the cab." I shook my presumably ectoplasmic head. "Got to hand it to her. Timing the gas leak, rerouting the Agency calls to her cell phone and getting me to reveal my whereabouts, tipping off the available fangs to take me out—or at least slow me down and soften me up—and then using an eighteen-wheeler like the world's largest sniper bullet."

"You speak as if you approve of your own murder."

"I admire the style and execution—no pun intended. Not too simple, not too convoluted. It beats undead doofuses—doofii?" I shook my head again. "It beats vampires of questionable intellect brandishing firearms and cutlery." I grinned. "And you just used the phrase 'your own murder' in reference to me."

"Nevertheless," the glowing and glowering entity insisted, "you shall not pass."

"Wowsers," I panted, pressing back into his grip a little more vigorously. "Your delivery needs some work. You might want to check out *The Fellowship of the Ring* DVD. Sir Ian McKellen in the Mines of Moria really knows how to sell that line."

He sighed. It was a most un-angelic sound. Not that I'd know: Mikey was the only angel I had ever met and my previous encounters had been brief and unenlightening. I didn't even know which side he was working for or whether I was his *pro bono* freelance project.

"Look down," he said.

The fog around my feet rolled back and I could see straight down into the ambulance.

"Hey," I said, "an emergency vehicle with a sun roof!"

"And to think," the winged being muttered, "I actually shared the blood of the Elohim with you at our last meeting . . ."

"Is that what that white stuff was? I was guessing the milk of human kindness."

"Such a waste either way."

Below me the paramedic was holding cardiac paddles in his hands and looking for a couple of unbloodied patches on my torso.

"You're right," I said. "Just postponed the inevitable."

"You really do have a death wish," Michael growled.

"Why does everybody assume I have a death wish? I'm just a pragmatist. I mean I know I've survived some pretty heavy damage these past few years with no scars to show for it—"

"No outer ones," the angel muttered.

"You got something on your mind, Mikey?"

"Giving up is the coward's way of dealing with grief."

"Hey, screw you and the seraphim you flew in with! Nothing I do is going to make any kind of difference! Living, dying . . . the people I love are beyond my reach in this world. *And* the next!" I looked down and was surprised to see that I'd forced his hand back a good six inches. He looked surprised, too.

"You wanna bust my chops for my lack of enthusiasm? You go back and tell your boss that I've done everything that was required of me. I helped save the world but lost my wife and daughter. Twice. My unborn son. Lupé. Deirdre. Zotz. J.D. . . . ."

"It's not your time," he said. "And you still have a purpose—"

"Says who?" I snarled. "You? The Big Guy upstairs?" I looked around. "Or maybe down the hall? Enough with the enigma! What's the plan? Keep Cséjthe around to suffer a little longer because karma's a bitch? Or are you guys asking me to suit up for another End of Days Bug-hunt? Because if it's the latter, I've pretty much had it with being your cleanup boy! End of the world? Goody! My troubles will finally be over. Not the end of the world? I wasn't around for Hitler or Stalin or Pol Pot so I imagine you can manage without me!"

"A door is about to open," he said abruptly.

I stared at him. "A door," I said finally. "That's it? A *door* will open? What does that mean?"

He cocked his head as if listening for permission to elaborate. "You must close the door before it opens," he said finally.

"What does *that* mean? Close the door before it opens? Is that some kind of koan, like 'what is the sound of one hand clapping?' Because I know the answer to that one!" I demonstrated by snapping the fingers on my free hand. "See? So what is the sound of closing an unopened door? Or is this like when one door closes another window opens?"

He stared at me and his granite-like features seemed to soften. "You are angry because you are trying so hard to die now."

"The hell!" I growled, freshly enraged. "It's not a question of desire! At least not mine. And it's not a lack of will, either! It's Physics One-Oh-One! This kind of massive blunt-force trauma—there's no way to heal fast enough to stay ahead of the biological cascade."

"You are no longer human," he said. "You've survived worse than this."

I shook my head. "Maybe a couple of years ago. But everything's changed now. My nanites got nuked by Cthulhu's EMP-exit back to his own dread dimension. The necrophage has been compromised by my blood abstinence for most of these past two years." I tried to pull my hand out of his smothering grasp. "So, let's just get on with it. I'm tired. I want to go . . . home." My voice almost broke on the last word.

"You mean Heaven?"

"Home," I reiterated. "Where the heart is. Or belongs. What it yearns for."

His expression was enigmatic. In other words, redundant.

"Sailor, sea," I tried. "Hunter, hill?"

Below me the EMT had yelled "Clear!" and applied the paddles to my chest and side. I flopped "below" and twitched "above."

Michael smiled. Well, the corners of his mouth twitched upwards a fraction. "You're sparkling."

"What—?" *Sparkling wit? Sparkling personality?*

"Look down."

I looked. My stomach clenched and a wave of nausea rolled over me as I looked back down.

My bloody and battered carcass was sparkling like I'd been dipped in electrified glitter!

"Oh this is just *wrong* on so many levels!"

The angel released my hand. "Real vampires don't sparkle," he observed.

"Not. A. Real. Vampire," I muttered as gravity began to pull at my legs. "No. Nonononono! Beam me up, Mikey . . ." The wave of nausea was followed by a tsunami of dizziness.

I fell down into darkness.

When I dream, New Orleans is still the New Atlantis.

Submerged some thirty leagues south-southeast from the shores of Arkansas and a hundred and twenty feet beneath the green waters of the New Gulf of Mexico. It is not The Big Easy after its Catholic-style baptism by Katrina but Dead Easy as it was after the Holy Roller twist-and-shout, hold-you-down-deep-under-the-water burial by Hurricane Eibon.

In my dreams multicolored fish still pass through the turnstiles of the Aquarium of the Americas some twenty fathoms down. They swim about the floating remains of the humans that bob along the surface of the great captured air bubble at the top of its glassy rotunda.

Justice for ten thousand overfed goldfish.

There are nights in this reality—the new now— when the survivors of Katrina toss and turn in their beds. The years peel back and they dream of levees collapsing like mud soufflés and black waters up to their armpits. Eventually they awake to a city still on the mend, a city that may always be on the mend.

But in my dreams The Big Easy is still the submarine city where the French Quarter is invaded by the amphiboid Deep Ones and engaged by an army of drowned vampires sent by the resurrected Captain Nemo to oppose them. They skirmish in slow-motion silence while sharks and octopi glimmer at the edge of my vision like prehistoric revenants. Around them the corpses of buildings have begun to soften and dissolve like the remains of the city's once vibrant population.

And often, when I wake in sweat-soaked, tangled sheets, muddled with the nightmare memories of that other *timeline, I wonder . . . are these dreams true portals to that other/where and other/when? The one next door to this "here" and this "now?"*

Is there still a separate reality *where the clock was* not *turned back and New Orleans was* not *saved?*

Where it still lies deep and green and silent in the ocean's revised embrace?

If so, does the war beneath the waves continue on? Does Dakkar still direct his troops from the Nautilus with Irena at his side?

And am I there, as well? My doppelganger self on the other side of the looking glass, still trapped in Alice's Aquarium?

Or was that history completely unwound from the mainspring of Time, my sleeping visions nothing more than the random firings of misplaced memory neurons? Tattered hopes shuffled and patterned by my subconscious: the desire to redeem order from loss and chaos?

What of Lupé? And Deirdre? And the children—my unborn son and my reborn wife and daughter? Are they there as well? Do they play at hide-and-seek in the blue-green twilight behind curtains of foam and froth?

Or was Fand as good as her word, taking them between that world and the next? To that "deep romantic chasm which slanted down the green hill athwart a cedarn cover" that Coleridge described? Do they now dwell in wood and dale where sacred river ran to caverns of ice still measureless to man?

Or are they forever dead in this world and the next?

There has been no answer these past few years. All that I know is that I still have obligations. That, in the absence of answers, against the loss of love, in exile, there is still duty.

Till human voices wake us, and we drown . . .

"I think he's coming around, Doctor."

"Better not be. We've got at least four more hours before we can close and bring in the Ortho team."

"I'm seeing signs of arousal."

"Yeah, Jenkins, you'd be our expert on arousal."

"I'm serious. I think he's waking up."

"So he's sucking propofol like he's sucking blood? Christ! Twenty units of O-Neg in one hour and I don't know where the hell it's going! Give him some more."

"Blood or anesthesia?"

"Both!"

"I don't know how much more prope to give him! He's already had twice the optimum for his body mass!"

"Well, give him some more of something! Jenkins is right; he's definitely wak—"

The doors of memory reopen.

As always my dreams are not dreams but rooms of the past where I have lived and loved.

And lost.

Here is the barn where a forced exchange of blood with an ancient horror poisoned what was left of my life and infected everything that was to follow.

And there is the morgue where I awoke after the car crash that killed my family—awoke to see the remains of my wife and daughter on the tables beside me, a post-mortem family reunion.

As I take the familiar tour through this labyrinth of horrors, I pass windows that offer momentary glimpses of the Now and its fresh parade of indignities.

"—losing him!"

"Maybe you should call it."

"Not yet. Charge to two hundred. Clear!"

In this room I revisit the macabre puppet show orchestrated by a three-thousand-year-old necromancer against the people whose lives I loved more than my own.

"Nothing!"

"Charge to three hundred."

There's a high-pitched whine, like a gentle dentist drill. I feel tingly all over.

Sparkly.

"Clear!"

A buzz and a thump.

"What the hell!"

"Holy shit!"

"He's—"

In that room, the demon Lilith who had blazed a trail of death and destruction around the globe and across the centuries until her designs to bring about the end of the world brought her to my back yard.

Once again, I lost an extended family.

My first attempt at full consciousness put me in a front-row seat for the Marquis de Sade Show. A team of Torquemadas wearing surgical masks were twisting long metal skewers into my leg. They were assisted by a torture device that consisted of four concentric metal rings that encased my right leg from ankle to mid-thigh and the sharp, metal spikes on each ring's inner circumference were being driven through my flesh to anchor in my tibia, fibula, and femur.

It took longer than it should have for me to pass out again. Enough time to realize that sword-wielding vampires didn't seem like such a big deal after all.

A deathless Dr. Josef Mengele and his army of cloned Nazis were next on the Cséjthe Nightmare Memory Tour, his Frankenstein construct lumbering through my last home like a jigsaw juggernaut of unholy hatred and sadistic glee . . .

Then there were tubes down my throat.

More than one; less than five. It hurt to scream so I stopped right away.

A woman wearing scrubs and a surgical cap loomed in my narrow field of vision. "You're in Recovery. You're not supposed to be awake, yet."

I tried to apologize for waking up too soon. But there were tubes down my throat.

She wasn't paying attention, anyway. She turned her head and called to someone. "Can we get more blood, here? He's already out! Yes, agai—"

And, finally, the showdown with voodoo queen Marie Laveau and the mad monk Rasputin that sundered me from the last remnants of friends and family.

The supernatural storm that turned New Orleans into an underwater city.

And the departure of the ancient-before-time starship, carrying the giant, squid-headed alien god back to his own dread dimension, fracturing time as I knew it . . .

". . . monitors! I want this patient hooked up to every possible monitor, telemetry device, and alarm that ICU has on the board and then bring in anything portable with the volume turned up! And put a goddamned fire extinguisher next the bed! In fact, make it two—"

A woman appears in fresh darkness.

Ancient. Something between grande dame and crone.

She wears a maroon, long-sleeved, ankle-length dress with white laced cuffs and high collar. A purple wrap drapes around her thin shoulders and an ebony broach stares from her throat like an alien third eye. She sits like a queen upon a gothic Victorian armchair, her withered hands grasp the carved claws at the end of the armrests like twins to the wooden appendages beneath.

Her hair is so white as to be nearly transparent and she has kaleidoscope eyes . . .

"Come with me . . ." Her voice is the whisper of the wind from a thousand winters. ". . . come against The Darkness. . . ."

A great and terrible funerary urn appears at the heart of a maze. The seals on its heavy, ornamented lid are flaking and the cap trembles as if from some great inner tumult . . .

I turn and flee toward the light.

It is a mistake. Pain thunders through my body and lightning flashes and cracks inside my skull. There is a fire and I try to reach for the alarm but I cannot move my arm. Then I realize that I am The Fire.

I rampage like Godzilla and set everything around me ablaze.

The world burns.
Darkness returns in a rain of cinders.

When I awoke again I was in two-thirds of a room. The room was white and too bright. It hurt my eyes. I closed them and my left eye felt immediate relief.

My right eye continued to burn and throb like the dying heartbeat of some great, ancient beast.

One arm seemed heavier than the other. Which one? Sleep returned before I could decide.

Shirley Temple wears Dorothy Gale's pinafore and does not sing "Somewhere Over the Rainbow." W. C. Fields chews Emerald City scenery as The Wizard. A young Buddy Ebsen dresses up like Jed Clampett stuffed with straw—a true hayseed long before the Beverly Hillbillies. And Gale Sondergaard cavorts with the flying monkeys as a sexy Wicked Witch of the West—wrong and disturbing on more than one level!

Then another house falls out of the sky . . .

No.

Not out of the sky.

Comes out of nowhere.

Out of some otherwhere.

Gee, Toto; we're not in Oz, anymore.

The fields are green and gold and trees dance in circles, spaced out from the house like points on a compass.

There are three stories here, two there, and possibly a fourth hidden among the puzzle box facade that combines Italianate, Romanesque, Victorian, Neo-Gothic, and Châteauesque styles with towers, turrets, pediments, arches, cupolas, quoins, a couple of balustrades, a hodgepodge of ashlar and rustication faces, random lancet, sash, awning, and stained glass windows. A single, octagonal tower rises like an ancient Roman lighthouse above a sea of wheat and soybeans.

The windows are darker than the unlit interior might explain but the vaulted doorway is bright with light, haloing a strangely familiar woman standing within.

Jenny.

My poor dead wife smiles at me and I began to weep as if all that has come before was merely prelude . . .

✛ ✛ ✛

Someday the darkness would go on forever.

But not today, it seemed.

The darkness began to pulse and turned into a giant grey cell that proceeded to divide and re-divide, turning itself into multiple grayish blobs that oozed about and began to make noise. Gradually, the blobs resolved into hazed forms and fuzzed noise became articulated sounds.

I was in a hospital bed, in a hospital room, surrounded by monitors and IVs and machines whose purposes I couldn't begin to guess at. I was attached to a number of devices via needles and shunts and electrodes and catheters. Somewhere in the distance, behind the boops and beeps and humming sounds of the forest of electronics, I could make out two voices in a whispered conference.

"He's had another ten units this morning, alone!"

"He must be bleeding internally."

"If he is, we can't find it. His body just seems to be absorbing it like a dry sponge . . ."

I missed the rest as my focus was pulled to where my right leg used to be. It had been replaced by a giant, misshapen sausage that was suspended a few inches above the mattress by a couple of hanging slings. Surrounding the red, white, and purple monstrosity was a cage of metal rings and rods. Steel pins pierced my bruised and swollen flesh at frequent intervals and they should have hurt. The fact that they didn't was even more disturbing. I remembered the name of the contraption, now: an Ilizarov apparatus, an external fixator used for treating complex bone fractures.

I also remembered the name for the pair of steel rings holding my left arm immobile.

Handcuffs.

One ring was locked around my wrist, the other around the safety rail of my hospital bed. I pulled on it and it made an unpleasant clattering sound as it slid up against the reinforced crossbar.

A face appeared between the EKG screen and the computerized morphine dispenser. Blond, blue-eyed, and dimpled, he smiled pleasantly enough and said, "Christopher L. Cséjthe; you're under arrest."

I closed my eyes and submerged again.

✛ ✛ ✛

My sleep was finally dreamless and I awoke to a dream of peppermint.

Curvy peppermint.

The poke in my ear jumpstarted my attention and I refocused.

Red-and-white-striped jumper. Candy striper.

Taking my temperature with an electronic thermometer.

A scent of attar of roses and lavender soap.

Blonde hair. Grey eyes that strangely contrasted the smooth, lightly freckled features.

A veritable slinky chain of bracelets and arm jewelry that clinked and softly rattled as she puttered by my night stand. As I studied the ornaments that slid around her wrist she studied the two pairs of restraining bracelets that now cuffed each of my wrists to the stainless steel bed rails on either side of my mattress.

My fuzzy brain assembled the disparate images and compared the result to recent memories.

Maybe it was the five layers of pain that coated everything, including my eyelashes.

"You!" I exclaimed, remembering the nocturnal teen driving the red MG.

Actually, it came out more like a mumbled "yuh . . ."

An anachronistic oral thermometer was hastily produced and shoved into my mouth. She held it there so I couldn't spit it out.

"If you want to get out of here alive," she murmured, "you will do as I say."

I tried to give her The Look.

Unfortunately, having one's mouth pinched shut around a thermometer tends to undermine the intimidation factor. Plus, one of my eyes didn't seem to be working. Being handcuffed to the bed didn't help either.

"If you come with me," she continued softly, "you will live. For a while longer, anyway. If you stay, you will be taken into custody and probably not live long enough to see the inside of a cell."

Great: my would-be jailbait-rescuer from the night before was a government conspiracy theorist.

"If you come with me, you will have the chance to rescue your family. If you do not, this world may well fall . . . and the Daoine Sídhe will have no allies to resist the coming Dark."

Okay. She had my attention, now.

"I will get you out of here if you do as I say. Do we have an understanding?"

It wasn't like I had a lot of options for the moment: I nodded slowly.

"Good. Just relax for now but be ready to follow me when it's time to leave." She laid a hand across my throat as she withdrew the thermometer and made a pretense of reading it.

So what is your name? I asked.

Or would have asked if any words had actually come out of my mouth. There was a tingly numbness around my voice box.

"Is he really awake this time," another voice asked, "or is this just another bout of semiconscious eyerolling?"

I rolled my head to the side and looked at another woman seated in a visitor's chair by the window. She wore a dark suit over a white button-up shirt that was open at the collar. The side of her jacket was turned back just enough for me to see an inch or so of shoulder holster under her right arm. A leftie. Her whiter-than-white hair was layered in a short shag that was just two missed salon appointments away from an emerging mullet. Pale, ice-blue eyes gave the slight edge to pure Scandinavian-over-albino antecedents.

She stood up. And up. Long legs unfolded and she rose, clearing the five-foot mark while still bent at the waist. Five-four . . . five-six . . . five-ten . . .

Somewhere around the six-foot mark she stopped: a statuesque Swedish supermodel in a monochrome pantsuit.

Well, supermodel might be a bit overgenerous but she did have a gun and I felt it best to keep a deferential tone even if only in my own head for the moment.

She walked over to my bed and looked down at me. "You will live?" She almost sounded disappointed. She also sounded Swedish.

"Gee, I can't tell," I said sarcastically. "Seeing you, I thought I'd died and gone to heaven." Oops: this time words actually did come out of my mouth.

She smiled down at me. It was a nice smile until you noticed that it was totally disconnected from her eyes. "I want you to remember those words when the time comes."

What did that mean? I raised my wrists the whole three inches that either pair of handcuffs would allow.

"The one on your right wrist is mine. I don't know who cuffed your left."

I sighed and rolled my head to work out the beginnings of a serious neck kink. The TV swooped into view as I did a half shrug. Arnold Schwarzenegger was on the screen, standing behind a podium with the presidential seal on it. The set was a pretty faithful recreation of the James S. Brady Press Briefing Room of the White House West Wing but the dialogue seemed pretty dull for an action flick. "What are we watching?" I groused. "Comedy Central?" Getting killed and then waking up handcuffed to a hospital bed always puts me in a grumpy mood.

"Blame the previous reality star for amending Article Two of your Constitution. Perhaps you Americans would prefer to go back to electing lawyers for world leaders . . ." Stretch Blondstrong reached down for the bed's channel changer. "Tell me what you would rather watch."

Normally I would opt for the news but I had a feeling it would only make my headache a lot worse, right now. "I'm easy. How about switching it to Turner Classic Movies?"

She snorted. "Easy?" She shook her head. "And, I'm sorry, what kind of classic movies?"

"TCM." Maybe I was mumbling. "Turner. Classic. Movies." I enunciated slowly.

She stared down at me. "Sorry. Not familiar with that one. Though I am surprised you're a fan of the classics given your reactions to *The Wizard of Oz*."

"Funny," I thought, "and here I just had a dream about *The Wizard of Oz*." Then I realized that I had spoken my thoughts aloud. Again. *Damn painkillers.*

She shook her head again, muttering, "Painkillers . . ."

What? Did I say that out loud, too?

"I guess you were tripping pretty good last night," she said. Another smile. This one didn't touch her eyes, either. "It was on the television last night and you were critiquing The Wizard's performance. You were pretty slurry but, from what I was able to make out, you seemed to be less than pleased with a fair number of the cast."

Something cold and slimy slithered down my spine. "What?"

"You kept asking, 'Where's over the rainbow?'"

"Excuse me," said a slightly more familiar voice. "Who are you and what are you doing in here?"

The slightly more familiar voice belonged to the blond, blue-eyed man with dimpled cheeks who had presumably belonged to the other pair of handcuffs. His suit was nearly identical to the Scandinavian supermodel's, its major difference being the addition of an accessorizing dark tie. He was holding a Styrofoam coffee cup in his right hand so his reaction time was slowed as she turned and the flair of her jacket provided another peekaboo hint of a shoulder holster.

She got her gun out first, yelling, "Interpol!" while he chimed in with "Federal agent!" The coffee cup went flying but he was still several fractions of a second late in displaying his weapon.

Maybe it was steely nerves and professional reflexes. Maybe it was a mutual history of jurisdictional disputes. Neither one shot the other. There was, however, a protracted negotiation on how each other's free hand would retrieve their badge and I.D. There followed a carefully choreographed mirror dance until each was simultaneously satisfied as to the other's bona fides.

That settled, there followed an equally tense argument over who had jurisdiction over me.

Apparently the FBI was looking into my complex financial situation, expressing interest in my multiple identities and offshore accounts. Tax fraud? Terror funding? Conservative voting record? The I.R.S. was freezing all of my accounts and assets until they could fully investigate a series of anonymous tips that had come in over the past week.

Interesting . . . that undead learning curve had just become a parabola. The New York demesne had finally figured out that guns and swords and even semis weren't sufficiently deadly: Now they were going to whack me with government bureaucracy. It wasn't a bad strategy: I had bested every supernatural threat they had thrown at me so far.

The Internal Revenue Service was a lot scarier.

Hopefully Diggs was relaxing on a beach someplace where there were no extradition laws.

We were just getting to Interpol's stake in all of this when a killer nurse walked into the room.

There's a scene in Quentin Tarantino's pulp movie classic *Kill Bill* where assassin Elle Driver walks into a hospital room to murder the movie's heroine. Like that one-eyed member of the Deadly Viper Assassination Squad, my nurse was wearing the white cap, uniform dress and stockings, and matching white eye patch. The big difference was Daryl Hannah had still been a stunner at the age of forty-two when she played the role. My nurse looked at least forty-two years past the mandatory retirement age. And her eye patch lacked the sporty little embellishment of a tiny Red Cross appliqué—though it was a detail easily lost amid the seamed and wrinkled features of her dried-apple face.

She was holding in her right hand what, in the medical lexicon, is known as a "Big-Ass Syringe." She shuffled toward my bed and, for a moment, the movie memory of Elle Driver was replaced by Snow White's evil queen disguised as the elderly hag. Only a poisoned apple would be a lot less intimidating than the giant needle that seemed to grow an inch with every step that she advanced.

And it seemed all the more ominous as the room had gone quiet.

"Excuse me," a voice said finally as Nurse Leatherface closed within five feet. "But what's wrong with this picture?" It was Ms. Interpol.

She was answered by her armed and badged counterpart: "You mean the fact that all of the other nurses in this hospital are wearing scrubs?" Then he nodded at the girl on the other side of my bed. "Or that no one's worn a candy striper outfit like that outside of a bad porn movie since 1987?"

The syringe never wavered as it came closer and closer: Maybe the old woman was half deaf in addition to the eye patch. She reached toward the injection port on my IV as a hand fell on her humped shoulder. "Excuse me, ma'am . . ." FBI Guy said.

With a shriek, the ancient nurse turned under the blond man's arm and slammed the syringe into the center of his chest. As he stumbled backward with the force of the blow, the tube turned dark red with heart's blood and the plunger erupted from the end, sending gouts of crimson splashing across the room. He collided with Agent Sultry on his way to the floor and they both went down.

I tried to roll away as the old woman turned back toward me but the handcuffs barely allowed more than a twitch. Her fingers curled claw-like as she raised them in a menacing manner and her nails were long and ragged, thick as horn and discolored with great age. They looked like they could gouge through wood and sheetrock.

Another hand intruded. Caught the left withered arm by the wrist.

"Why, Deino," the candy striper said sweetly, "fancy meeting you here!"

The old woman's eye widened. "Σκατά!" she snarled.

Don't ask: It was Greek to me.

Then Candy Stripe punched Nightmare Nurse in the face and tugged the eye patch over to cover her good eye. The other eye socket was as empty as an ancient and endless cavern.

The old woman shrieked again—more panic than malice this time—and began flailing about.

Candy Stripe stepped back, pulled a bobby pin out of her hair, and went to work on my handcuffs. She had me free of the first pair just as the creepy crone got her patch readjusted. The Interpol agent was on one knee, now, her right hand pressed to the FBI agent's bloody chest, her left hand bringing her gun up to bear on his assailant. "Don't—" she started to say and was interrupted by the arrival of a couple of nurses, an orderly, and a doctor.

All of whom were wearing scrubs.

And blocking her shot.

The Wicked Witch of the Ward turned back toward me and rushed the bed.

Candy Stripe tripped her.

The old woman was tough; she stumbled but didn't go down. The girl jumped on her back and grabbed at her face. Crazy Crone went from shrieking to a full-on imitation of a tornado siren and flung her tormentor away. Serendipitously, it was in the direction of my bed where I was trying to figure out how to unlock the second set of cuffs while keeping an eye on the insanity around me.

"Here, let's trade," she said breathlessly, taking control of the bobby pin and dropping a gelatinous spheroid into my cuffed hand.

I stared down at the object.

It stared back.

I was holding the old crone's eyeball.

"The hell?" I asked, almost shrieking, myself.

"No, but close," she muttered, the pink top of her tongue peeking from the corner of her mouth as she moved the metal pin around the keyhole. "Would've been a lot closer if Enyo had showed up . . ."

"Wait . . ." I put my free hand to my head. *Concussion*? "Enyo? You called her Deino." I shook my head. Nothing seemed to come loose. "What are you saying? That she's one of the *Graeae*?" The eye seemed to roll in my palm as if to look over at its former owner.

"The operative phrase is '*one* of,'" she grumbled as the pin turned against something and the steel bracelet popped open. "We've got to go! Now!"

It was a lot to process in such a short time. And the meds weren't helping. "Give me a moment," I said.

Actually, considering my shattered right leg, I was going to need more than a moment. I began pulling out IVs and assorted shunts and ports.

While the downed FBI agent was hustled out of the room by staff reinforcements, a nurse and an orderly approached the blind hag who was still freaking out. The orderly went flying across the room. The nurse went sliding under my bed and came to a softer stop against the far wall.

"Hey!" I yelled. "Stop that right now!"

My command had all of the weight of a political campaign promise.

"Who wants to watch me squish this eyeball?" I asked more quietly.

The whole room went still. The crone, suddenly frozen in place, slowly turned toward me.

"That's better," I said. I waved off the blonde with a gun when she took a cautious step toward the old woman.

"Give me the eye and I'll let you go," Deino hissed.

"Yes you will," I agreed, "and you'll do more."

"Christopher Llewellyn Cséjthe," Candy Stripe murmured, "we need to leave before her sisters show up!"

I blinked. She knew my middle name? *No one knew my middle name!*

"Come on!" she urged. "The Liar, The Bitch, and Needs-a-New-Wardrobe will be here any minute!"

"I promise to let you go for now," the old witch elaborated, "and upon our next encounter I will give you a swift, merciful death rather than a protracted and painful ending."

"How about I just stomp on this thing and reduce the chance of our next encounter to just about nil?"

"Then you would have to go through us," said a new voice from the doorway.

Chapter Five

I thought Deino was old and hideous but she was practically Cinderella compared to the three old women trying to get into my room.

Talk about ugly stepsisters: All three wore wraps that looked like a cross between a dress and a toga: red, green, and grey, respectively. Once upon a time, all three appeared to have started out as "white" and achieved their current colors through an undercoat of rot with Jackson Pollack–like dousings of gore, phlegm, and excrement. All three wore giant, AARP-approved sunglasses but, thanks to the harsh fluorescent lighting, their eyewear did little to conceal their frightful countenances and the fact that their shriveled eye sockets were as dark and empty as craters on the far side of the moon.

And I say "trying to get into my room" because they were jammed together into the door frame having tried to all come in at the same time like an old Three Stooges routine.

Aggravating the situation were their three seeing-eye dogs. German shepherds would have been bad enough but the creatures straining against their guide harnesses made Rottweilers look like shaved Pekingese. Rather than cooperate in trying to untangle the jam, they snarled and snapped at one another like rabid beasts.

As did their service dogs.

"Okay," I murmured to the candy striper, "if that's Deino . . . and her sisters Enyo and Pemphredo are here . . . we've got one extra."

"Perso," she answered, trying to untangle my spam-in-a-frame leg from the two slings keeping it elevated.

"Haven't heard of her. All of the Greek myths name just three."

"Hyginus references a fourth. Called her Persis or Perso."

I felt my eyebrows rise—one of them, anyway. There didn't seem to be a whole lot going on on the right side of my face. "Gaius Julius Hyginus? Really? No one takes his *Fabulae* seriously. The only thing they're good for is suggesting older, lost material from the serious authors." I stopped and shook my head. It had to be the drugs. I should be focusing on the immediate threat—not discussing Roman revisionism of Greek mythology with a high school hospital volunteer.

Come to think of it, the idea that I was being accosted by the Stygian witch-sisters known as the *Graeae* suggested that I was still brain-deep in some hallucinatory fugue induced by trauma and industrial-strength narcotics.

Maybe I should just relax and go along for the ride.

Except . . .

Except that I had spent the last decade or so learning that my imagination—drug-addled or otherwise—was no match for the actual weirdness that was usually drawn to me like kamikaze moths to a bonfire.

Head back in the game, Cséjthe!

"Let's recap," I told the crones. "I've got your eye. You're blind. You want your eye. I want you to tell me what you want and then go away."

"You are in no position to bargain, *protathlitis*," rasped the "lady" in red. I was guessing Enyo.

"How about in the country of the blind, the guy holding the one eye is king," I offered.

They were through the door, now, and spreading out. The Interpol agent retreated toward my bed, her gun moving back and forth on a track to cover all four while her other hand rested on something just below her shoulder rig.

Candy Stripe was muttering under her breath and the "dogs" began to whine.

"What is it?" Green Gown asked. Pemphredo or Perso . . . I didn't know.

"Witch," Deino hissed.

"You're one to talk," I muttered.

The hellhounds yawned noisily. One lay down. The other two followed in short order and the crones had to release their harnesses or be pulled down with them.

"Who's there?" Enyo demanded. She was the aggressive one. Which was sort of like saying "the rabid one" in an attacking mob of pit bulls.

"Annwn, I thought," Deino answered, pronouncing it *An'oon*, "but too young."

"Daughter?"

"More like granddaughter."

"Great-granddaughter," Candy Stripe said.

Enyo smiled. She had one tooth. It looked like it had been filed to a point. "Two birds! Two baby birds!"

Grey Dress chimed in: "One stone . . ." She stepped forward. And tripped over her sleeping dog.

I meant to snicker; it came out as a giggle. Damned drugs. I cleared my throat. "Four to three," I told them. "Hardly overwhelming odds. We're a lot younger, have a gun. You're elderly, unarmed. And—oh yeah—*blind!*"

In response, each one produced a "cricket" from a fold in their garments. The folded metal toys made click-clacking sounds as they pressed and released the ends. Heads cocked, they began to move around, letting their sleeping dogs lie.

"What are they doing?" Interpol wanted to know.

"They're using echolocation," I said. "Sort of gives new meaning to the phrase 'old bats.'"

"Stop," she said, "or I'll shoot!"

"I wouldn't do that," Candy Stripe said. "You might make them mad." There was a crash cart next to my bed and she handed me the paddles from the defibrillator unit.

My hospital gown had a seemingly useless and tiny pocket over my left breast that was surprisingly perfect for holding a four-thousand-year-old eyeball: I pocketed the occultic orb and took a firm grasp of the insulated handles as she flipped a switch. There was a quiet whine as the charge began to build up.

"Give me the eye," Deino hissed as she approached the bed.

"No, me!" Enyo growled. Deino was closer but the Gray Sister known as The Waster of Cities was working hard to close the gap.

"It's my turn!" whined the one in the snot-colored dress.

It was nice to know that some things didn't change. Even after four thousand years.

According to Greek mythology, the hero Perseus had snatched their one, working eye and had held it ransom until the *Graeae* gave him the information he needed to complete his quest. They had fought over it then just as they were fighting over it now and Perseus slipped away to achieve greater fame and glory.

If it worked for him there was no reason it shouldn't work for me.

Except for, of course, my shattered leg.

And the fact that the Grey Witches hadn't shown up on Perseus's doorstep with a big-ass syringe, three hellhounds, and premeditated murder on their minds.

"I'll give you the eye," I told them, "if you'll tell me who sent you and let me leave." I caught the Interpol agent's eye and jerked my head at the wheelchair, folded and stashed behind a visitor chair on the other side of the room.

Deino reached my bed first and I almost used the defibrillator paddles on her but Enyo and the others were closing in fast. I scooted back against the far railing and ran the numbers through my head.

"Wait!" rasped the crone in the rotting shroud at the rear. "I'll tell you who sent us if you give me the eye!"

"I want safe passage," I reiterated.

"Your fate is sealed, mortal," Enyo snarled. "And we shall take Annwn's spawn to draw her out of the shadows. But give me the eye and I shall answer your question."

"You first," I snarled back as Interpol circled around the room to the wheelchair. If it made any noise as she unfolded and locked it into position, it was drowned out in the chorus of protests from the rest of the sightless mob.

"Nix!" Deino shrieked. "Nix! Give it to me!"

"That's not an answer," I said as the others lined up and grabbed onto the bedrail like a row of old crows.

"Maybe it is," Candy Stripe mused as I scooted toward my ancient assailants.

"Clear," I advised her as I checked myself to see that I was away from any part of the metal frame. I brought the paddles down on the metal railing where the clutch of their claw-like hands left enough room.

And I pressed the button.

Assuming Candy Stripe had turned the settings up all the way, I sent a jolt of some seventeen hundred volts through the railing.

It was like pulling the pin on a hag-grenade: Old women exploded across the room, two impacting the far wall with enough force to leave large dents. One smashed through a window and kept going. The last went headfirst into the television, adding some snap, crackle, and pop to the surreal scene.

"Quick! Into the chair!" Candy Stripe urged. Interpol positioned the wheelchair so that I could slither down off the bed and seat myself.

But not without a series of obscene displays aided and abetted by my uncooperative hospital gown. "What now?" I asked as I squirmed and re-tucked for modesty as much as for comfort.

"To the elevators!" Candy Stripe ordered Interpol. "And don't spare the horses!"

Getting out of the hospital was a bit of a blur.

Once I was out of immediate peril the adrenaline gave way to pain and the residual haze from the narcotics still in my system. And my head was spinning with a cacophony of questions. Who was behind these latest attempts to kill me? Vampires and werewolves were one thing. Siccing the Feds on me and hiring immortal Greek witches as assassins took the game to a whole new level.

At least with the Great Old Ones it wasn't personal.

After breaching the initial barrier of stunned hospital employees we bullied our way to the visitor's entrance using velocity and frequent badge and gun flashing to clear a path.

Outside, there was a Volkswagen microbus idling at the curb. Painted in garish, psychedelic colors, it looked like a pristine, Grateful Dead concert bus that had been parked in a collector's vault since 1967.

The side cargo doors opened, propelled by arms from within.

Candy Stripe joined Interpol in getting my chair over the curb and pointed toward the magical mystery tour bus. "Help me get him inside!"

The bump down to the tarmac jarred my leg and the steel fixator frame seemed to send its metal skewers even deeper into my flesh and bone. My adrenaline was exhausted, now, and a fresh wall of pain was rushing toward my head like a sizzling tsunami of angry hornets.

"Far out, man!" I whispered. And tripped out into merciful unconsciousness.

At some point I found myself riding along in a *Scooby-Doo* cartoon, seeming inked with overly vibrant colors. It was like being immersed under actinic lights in a marine aquarium and watching the hues blaze and bleed as we drove along in the Scooby gang's Mystery Machine. Fred was in the front seat, driving as usual. Scooby-Doo was riding shotgun. Velma and Daphne were in the back with me. Did that mean that I was Shaggy? *Zoinks!*

The blond and the Great Dane were discussing some sort of haunted house and I wanted to tell them that it was really old man Withers or Smithers or something, wearing some kind of glow-in-the-dark mask to scare everyone off so he could . . . what? . . . steal the treasure or find the map or get the land dirt cheap or something . . .

If there were any other variations on the cartoon plot tropes, they didn't immediately spring to mind. I thought about trying to make my mouth work again but decided it was victory enough that I wasn't drooling on myself for the moment.

Velma was wearing a candy striper uniform and fiddling with the metal bear trap that had snapped shut on my right leg while Daphne fiddled with her cell phone. I wasn't sure of her decision to dye her auburn mane platinum blonde. It made her look more severe.

She looked even more severe as Velma asked, "Is there some place we can drop you, Agent North?"

Her eyes narrowed. "You seem to be forgetting, Ms. Harkwynde. Mr. Cséjthe is in *my* custody. Where he goes, I go. And vice versa."

Velma had gone blonde, too, though the golden tones were a better choice in her case. Dropping the baggy sweater and eyeglasses had improved her appearance, too, though she looked nearly as intimidating as Daphne as she returned the focused stare. "Leaving aside the question of jurisdiction for the moment, what is Interpol's interest here?"

Daphne seemed to weigh her response. "Interpol has been tracking a person of interest for a number of years, now. His file is . . . old. Very old. He has been known to go to ground for years at a time, disappearing in one country only to resurface a decade later halfway around the world. His most recent appearances have connected him to Mr. Cséjthe, here."

"But Mr. Cséjthe's not accused of any crime?"

"Not as far as the international police are concerned, not yet."

"Then why handcuff him to his hospital bed?"

"Think of it as protective custody."

"Protection from whom?"

Daphne smiled one of those "that's-for-me-to-know-and-you-to-find-out" smiles. "Classified," she said.

"Really? Who is this person of interest?"

She shook her head slowly, her smile just as lazy. "Classified."

"What is his name?"

Daphne looked a little irked now. "Classified."

"And three times," Velma persisted, "*speak* his name to me."

Daphne shuddered. "Bassarab," she blurted. "Vlad Bassarab. Damn you, witch!"

"Vladimir Drakul Bassarab the Fifth?" Velma muttered. "Yes, the file on him would be very old."

"You are acquainted with The Impaler?" Scooby-Doo asked from the front seat. He didn't sound like the cartoon dog but his voice was surprisingly familiar. Yet still inhuman.

"Know *of* him," Velma answered, still staring at platinum blonde Daphne. "Got quite the family history. The Bassarabs were a great dynasty of the Vlachs. During their rule of Walachia they fought off invasions by the Mongols, Turks, and Hungarians back in the fourteenth and fifteenth centuries. Four of their princes ruled under the names Vlad: First through the Fourth. One was known as Vlad Drakul—which means Vlad the Dragon or Vlad the Devil. His successors, according to legend, were as bad or worse: Vlad Tepes is known to this day as Vlad the Impaler and Vlad Tsepesh was called the Son of the Devil—Drakul, with the diminutive 'a' added to the end."

"Dracula," Fred growled in a voice that was nothing like the cartoon character's but somehow vaguely familiar.

"Yes," Daphne answered reluctantly. "And Mr. Cséjthe gave him the gift of life when he was about to die the second death."

"So Count Dracula owes him?"

"Prince," I mumbled.

"What?"

"Prince . . . never Count . . ." I slurred.

"He looks more alert," Daphne said.

"He won't be for long if he doesn't get more blood in him," Velma said.

"Ice chest in the back," not-Fred said, swinging the van around a semi to pass.

"So . . ." the Great Dane in the front seat that was apparently not a dog after all, growled. "He is one of Dracula's minions?"

There was a long silence while we all contemplated that question. Well, they contemplated the question; I just wobbled around the edge of attentiveness.

"He wasn't bitten," Daphne said. "He was a donor by blood transfusion. There were—ah—anomalous side effects."

"Soooo . . . minion!"

"Didn't . . . volunteer . . ." I said, rousing and trying not to drool in the process. I glanced down at my chest. An eyeball stared back up at me from the pocket of my hospital johnny. "Eep!" I said.

"I'll take that." Candy Stripe Velma relieved me of my unsightly trophy and rummaged around in the Styrofoam box. She produced a couple of IV packets of blood. "Interpol seems to have a lot of unnatural intel on our boy, here." Producing a buck knife she shortened the tubing so I could drink out of the plastic pouches like squeezable sippy cups. I fumbled the first one and Daphne scooted over to help me. I don't know which surprised me more: that she seemed unfazed about my preference in beverages or the fact that Daphne was packing heat.

"Historically speaking," she said, "it is considered more effective to drink the blood of one's enemies than that of anonymous donors."

"Guess the gun's not so surprising after all," I mumbled.

She gave me a look and asked, "Where are we going?"

"His place, first," Candy Stripe answered. "He might want to pack a bag."

Back in 1726, Daniel Defoe wrote in *The Political History of the Devil*, "Things as certain as death and taxes, can be more firmly believed." More widely quoted is a line in Benjamin Franklin's letter to Jean-Baptiste Leroy in 1789: "In this world nothing can be said to be certain, except death and taxes."

Both were wrong. Defoe and Franklin, that is.

Death—not really so much of a sure thing. I had already died once. Well, twice, actually. Possibly three times, in fact; and my numerous undead assailants? Not exactly alive before I gave them their final dusting, either. So: Death, a slippery concept with more than a couple of loopholes.

Taxes? Not so much.

This is what I was thinking as I considered the notice of federal lien nailed to my front door. The red-gold light from the setting sun illuminated the crime scene tape and US Treasury seals, adding a festive effect to the proclamations that this was no longer my property.

I'd lost respect for the Grim Reaper in recent years. Truth be told, I considered him a bit of a bumbler. Even Blue Oyster Cult said, "Don't Fear The Reaper." (Though they could have said it with more cowbell.) No, the Beatles told us who to fear with the first cut on their *Revolver* album back in '66. Don't fear The Reaper but you gotta show some respect to the Taxman because, sooner or later, he's gonna nail your ass. Even the most notorious gangster of the last century was powerless before the purposeful audit. Public Enemy Number One, Al Capone, eluded the Feds on every conceivable criminal charge—racketeering, robbery, extortion, vice, murder—but was finally tried and convicted of income tax evasion. The best army of lawyers and accountants that money could buy couldn't save Capone.

I didn't have an army and Diggs had gone missing. Even if I could prove that I had a legal and legitimate need for all of my different identities and convoluted bookkeeping, I could be sure that all of my accounts would be frozen and my assets seized for the many, many years it would take my appeals to wend through the legal system. In the meantime, I would need to find a job and relocate.

Not to mention avoid being taken into custody.

Which could be tricky as Daphne had turned back into Special Agent North of Interpol and was standing right behind me.

"Well," she said, "are you to commit the entire document to memory or are we going to go inside?"

"I don't have my key," I mumbled, sullenly conscious of the fact that, in addition to losing my home, my possessions, my finances, and my freedom, I was still wearing my hospital gown and it was gaping down the back.

The front door suddenly opened, popping the Treasury seals, and a dead woman was staring at me. I stumbled backward into North and felt myself headed south as my legs gave way beneath me.

My last encounter with Elizabeth Bachman was in the basement of a condemned and abandoned hospital in Pittsburg, Kansas.

Some years back an ancient Egyptian necromancer had reanimated the corpses of my wife and daughter. Bachman was desperately playing the minion card for him when I showed up to object. My last memories of her were of her pale, beautiful face twisted by the cross-shaped cicatrix of hideously burned flesh where I had pressed a makeshift crucifix into her cheek. Before she could sink her fangs into my throat a gunshot had removed the top of her skull, turning the rest of her undead flesh into the contents of a knocked-over dustbin.

And now here she was, back in the flesh, looking all too human, and blocking my view of my living room ceiling. *And, oh looky: another dead person had joined her!*

Luis Garou.

Lupé's long dead brother.

While I didn't personally witness his death, it was described to me in stomach-churning detail by those who did. It isn't easy to kill a lycanthrope but Kadeth Bey had done it with his bare hands.

More than a decade in the past.

A discorporate vampire and a dismembered werewolf.

Looking down at me as if they hadn't suffered so much as a hangnail between them.

"So," Bachman sneered, giving me a quick looking over, "this is what we're going to all of this trouble for? He's not even a Practitioner."

"And we're needing Muscle, not Feeble," the barrel-chested man growled.

"Geez," I said, "I don't know whether to be hopeful that the hospital meds are this good . . . or depressed that my chemically altered consciousness chose to clean out the litterbox in my hindbrain."

Candy Stripe (who was apparently Annie Harkwynde and not a cartoon character named Velma) joined them in peering down at me and the hirsute man looked at her. "What is he talking about?"

"He doesn't know," she told him. "And neither do you. We'll catch everyone up later; right now we need to get the bus reloaded and reset for the next border." She turned to Bachman: "How far out did you set the wards?"

"I didn't have time. I had some trouble along the way. By the time I got here, disabled the alarm system and jimmied the back window open, you were pulling up the drive. What are you going to do about Stilts, here?"

I assumed that she was asking about Agent North (who wasn't really Daphne, either).

"Never mind her. Take the demon and do a full sweep. If we're not ready to go by the time you're finished, get eyes on the access road and report anything, *any*thing that even hesitates at the turnoff."

The dead people disappeared and only the teenaged girl was left in my field of vision. "Can I help you up, Mr. Cséjthe? We're on a bit of a tight schedule here."

I sat up with a bit of an assist. The girl was deceptively strong but she had to have had some help in lugging my semiconscious bulk into the house and depositing me on my couch. I eyed Agent North who stepped in and handed me my crutches. Naw. Probably "Fred" and "Scooby" did the heavy lifting . . .

I hoisted myself up and tried a few uncertain steps. My right leg was no longer swollen, purple, nor painful but it itched something fierce. I still didn't trust it. Plus, the fixator cage kept banging against my left leg. Any moment I expected to fall on my face. Maybe Agent North expected me to as well. She shadowed me as I gimped to the front window.

Outside, the Mystery Machine van of cartoon fame had turned back into the VW bus—although it seemed to be sporting a different color scheme than the one I remembered: lime green with a white roofline.

Luis Garou was repacking the roof carrier and Elizabeth Bachman was walking into the woods with something that was neither human nor anything resembling a talking Great Dane: My Scooby-Doo hallucinations had pretty much evaporated now and I was left to wonder—among many things—how I was going to tell Lupé that reports of her brother's demise were somewhat exaggerated.

I turned and crutched my way down to my bedroom, trying to put my growing list of questions into some sort of organized sequence.

The teenybopper had suitcases on my bed and open by the time I got there and was already packing the basics. I dictated a short list with locations for additional items, cash, and a portable arsenal. No one seemed to take exception to the excessive weaponry: A quartet of old, blind ladies who can kick your ass revises your perspective on "loading for bear."

The Feds had already been through the house once, bagging and tagging, removing everything that might have some evidentiary value. What they hadn't taken had been carelessly scattered in wanton disarray across floors, furniture, and any other horizontal surface to be had. Fortunately, they missed the hidden safe room where the real valuables were kept: data drives, IDs, passports, shrink-wrapped blocks of cash, go bags, emergency kits, portable coolers, and the serious firearms. And an extra fridge with a month's supply of whole blood.

I pulled two pocket protectors out of a drawer and started loading them with a fresh set of tools: two more green laser pointers, two more colloidal-silver atomizers, and a pepper-spray pen for any ordinary threats. Next to it I laid out what appeared to be two sets of brass knuckles with spring-loaded tactical knives modeled on the silhouette of the World War I M1918 trench knife. They retained the knuckleduster grips with the "skull crusher" cap extension while the spring-loaded blades were tucked inside the palm grips to conceal the double threat. I had picked up a dozen at a military surplus sale and arranged to have the blades and the finger rings heavily silvered.

Finally, I pulled out a shoulder rig and holstered a Springfield Armory 1911-A1 Government with a Rowland .460 conversion and filled the ammo pouches with silver frag-load magazines. While the Glock had seemed adequate for run-of-the-mill undead, it seemed I was deeper into unknown territory than I had ever been before. If the threat was bigger, I wanted to be able to blow a bigger hole in it.

At least that was my working strategy.

"Well, you're certainly prepared," my underaged rescuer said as she took in the contents of the room-sized safe. "This is a survivalist's wet dream." She was polite enough to not say *undead* survivalist.

"I learned the value of being prepared a long while back." I didn't feel as confident as I sounded: Even my experience and overactive imagination is helpless in the face of the weirdness that the universe conspires to throw my way.

"So," I said conversationally as I sat on the bed next to a cooler and began loading it with the four major food groups: A, B, AB, and O. "You didn't seem to be too amazed by a quartet of ancient Stygian witches from Greek mythology back in my hospital room . . ."

She smiled as she helped me rearrange the blood packets to make room for more. "An occupational hazard, Mr. Cséjthe, though I didn't expect them so soon."

I resisted the impulse to start frantically babbling a barrage of panicked questions. "If I understood correctly, one of them called you a witch," I continued with a studied air of nonchalance.

"Professional courtesy," she answered, her smile deflective. "You know, Mr. Cséjthe, if you're going to grab a shower, you might want to get started. We're kind of on a short timetable here."

"They seemed to know your grandmother," I persisted. If time was of the essence, maybe she would be more forthcoming if it would hurry me along.

"*Great*-grandmother." She stopped packing and turned her large, grey eyes on me. "The things that hunt you are hunting her, as well. And that is all that I am going to tell you until you are changed and ready to go."

Okay. Even arguing with a sixteen-year-old girl who *isn't* a witch is usually a pointless endeavor, so I retreated to the bathroom to regroup and lick my wounds.

Metaphorically speaking, of course.

As I eased out of my hospital johnny I became aware of an odd sensation. It took a few moments to place it as I hadn't experienced it in such a long time.

Excitement?

No, that was too strong a term.

Intrigue.

Yeah, that was the one.

I'd basically been limited to two emotional settings these past few years: "angry" and "who-gives-a-crap." Mainly the latter and "angry" was only a temporary distraction from the bone-numbing tedium. Maybe I didn't want all of the answers yet: Once the movie ends, the book is finished, the mystery solved, then The Boredom returns and The Rule seems less and less important in the grand scheme of things. This was the most alive I'd felt since the hairsbreadth Apocalypse in the Gulf of Mexico. Since the pressing of the reset button on Eternity's Stopwatch.

I ducked into the shower, planning on a quick rinse but stayed a good twenty minutes as the hot water felt great on my stiff and aching (and too cool) body. I didn't have to worry about getting a plaster cast wet as the fixator was all stainless steel. Still, it made strange, squeaky noises as I stepped out of the shower to dry off.

My surgical bandages were soaked through so I sat on the toilet lid and carefully peeled each off, mindful of incisions and adhesions. The ones that wrapped around my head and covered my right eye were the worst. My hair would grow out and cover most of them.

My eye, however, was gone.

Based on the scars that parted my eyebrow and intersected just short of my cheekbone, it hadn't gone easy. I should have asked Deino where she shopped for eye patches when I had the chance.

Underneath the other bandages I found cuts and abrasions but no serious scars or wounds and no evidence of stitches. Surgical glue? The fixator continued to squeak and now it began to rattle.

I looked down. The long screws were turning slowly as if invisible hands were making a myriad of adjustments. I expected discomfort but it quickly became apparent that the screws were loosening instead of tightening. I dried the rest of me slowly as I watched, fascinated.

When the first screw exited my leg the entry wound seemed to fizz with tiny black bubbles. Then they subsided and a tiny grey scab formed that quickly turned red then pink. And then another screw was pushed out.

It took another ten minutes for the last of the screws and stabilizing pins to be ejected and the frame became a useless metal cage around a pinker and stronger looking limb. I pulled the device off and gingerly tested my weight on my right leg. It took the strain, but ached enough that I was probably better off sticking to the crutches for a while longer.

By the time I was fully dressed and shaved and had made one last pass through my soon-to-be-former residence, it was fully dark outside. I leaned on my crutches in the middle of the room, shifted around and contemplated the furniture. My leg grumbled about remaining upright but my glutes were tired of being sat on for so long. Forget people: I couldn't even take a position that made all of my body happy.

And now what? I turned to gaze out of the large picture overlooking the front lawn. Six feet wide and four feet tall, it was one of the few windows in my home-sweet-bunker whose view wasn't obscured by a latticework of steel bars. The inch-thick layering of glass-clad polycarbonate could stop M16 or AK-47 ammo as well as small explosives so I'd almost learned to stop flinching when the occasional bird kamikazied against its deceptively transparent surface.

I couldn't stay here—despite all I had done to dig in and harden my fortifications over the past couple of years. The Feds would be back in a matter of days. Or even hours. So I had systematically and mindlessly packed for a trip as if I had somewhere to go.

But I didn't.

Unlike Vlad Drakul Bassarab, I hadn't had centuries to establish a network of safe houses. Hell, I didn't even have a timeshare near the beach. All of my friends and family were gone with the exception of Mama Samm D'Arbonne. And between her discomfort over that little "pheromone incident" and her exotic travels to get her mojo back, she had been pretty much absent these past few years. Besides: the trouble I was in? Not about to show up on someone else's doorstep with that kind of karma in tow.

Maybe it was time to go back to New York City, brace The Fangs once and for all, and go down in a blaze of glory! Screw Mikey and his not-your-allotted-time shtick. I wasn't going to last in federal custody. Never mind shivs in the showers or supernatural assassins: The first time they made me walk out under the sun . . .

And then it hit me: The sun had just gone down.

I had escaped the hospital in broad daylight.

My hospital room had windows and I had spent days—possibly weeks—exposed to killing doses of sunshine, minute after minute, hour after hour, day after day . . .

"Son of a bitch," I said. "They're back."

"Who's back?" Candy Stripe asked from the doorway.

Only she wasn't Candy Stripe anymore. She'd said her name was Annie and I was pretty sure that she was a witch.

Not that there were any such things.

Along with vampires.

And creatures out of Greek Mythology 101.

She had changed out of the peppermint uniform and into a pair of jeans and a maroon T that said something about the Spanish Inquisition and how it wasn't expected by anybody since 1970.

I wasn't particularly up for explaining how I had become infected with Nazi-designed nanites by Dr. Mengele's clones. "Long story," I said. "What now?"

She walked over to sit on the living room sofa and patted the cushion next to her. "I want to hire you."

"Really?" I moved to lean my crutches against the wall and picked up a large soup mug of gently warmed whole blood. Hobbling over to one of the easy chairs, I asked, "For what? Human pincushion? Senior center punching bag? Backless gown model?"

"Bodyguard."

"Yeah, right." I knocked back the contents of the mug like a man dying of thirst. Rebuilding a shattered leg and God knows what else required additional energy and more raw material than my bone marrow seemed equipped to keep up with.

She wasn't dissuaded.

"You've just reinforced the argument as to why you should take this job," she said. "You say you're recovering from major trauma? Of course you are. And it would have killed anyone else ten times over. But here you are and your body is healing so fast that it has already rejected the metal brace on your leg. Then there's the fact that you are a fugitive. I doubt you have any formed plans as to where to go and you certainly can't stay here. But if you come with me, I can provide you with all that you need for the time being—certain amenities, food, shelter, anonymity, and forms of protection that you cannot provide for yourself. And, as for some of those things that are chasing you? Well, that's going to bear a little more discussing but I know what I'm getting into. Better than you, in fact. I'm really making you an offer you can't refuse." She extended her arm, a scrap of black cloth resting on her open palm. "I'll even throw in the eye patch for free." She tossed it to me and I caught the piratical accessory one-handed.

It was all very nicely vague but I still didn't know what was in it for her.

"So, these . . . things . . . chasing me. You're going to help me run away from them?" I asked as I tied the eye patch in place and adjusted it.

Her lips curved slightly upwards and she shook her head. "Oh, no. I'm going to be running *toward* them. I need someone with experience. Someone who isn't afraid to run at them with me." She turned up the wattage on her smile as if she had just promised me a steak dinner.

My smile was nowhere near as encouraging. "You have the damnedest recruiting approach."

If anything, her smile grew in intensity. "Well, your audition and interview were better than anything that I had been led to believe. I need—for my grandmother, that is—a bodyguard."

"Grandmother or great-grandmother?"

"Sure."

"You're not serious."

"As a heart attack, Mr. Cséjthe."

"Good God, I hope not! Because if you are, you're either mad or have the worst case of attention deficit disorder that I've ever seen! I mean, I've just barely survived a near-fatal crash, can hardly walk, and nearly got my clock cleaned by a quartet of visually impaired old biddies. I'm the one who needs a bodyguard!"

"We're all going to need bodyguards," said a familiar voice from the doorway.

Chapter Six

If you were mad enough to actually seek a vampire's embrace you could do a lot worse than Carmella Le Fanu.

Think Cindy Crawford without the mole. Only younger and better looking.

I know, but try to imagine it anyway.

Other undead went bump in the night. Carmella was more of the bump-and-grind-in-the-night type.

Even the knowledge that she had a few centuries on me—and a couple of fangs she'd like to put *in* me—hardly ruined her looks. Thick waves of dark chestnut hair tumbled over her shoulders. A long-sleeved knit top and yoga pants hugged every voluptuous curve as if she had been dipped in tar and rolled in fuzzy lint. She looked like five-foot-seven of rollercoaster sex and I was distracted for a good two seconds before my cerebellum spasmed and I remembered that she was about to kill me.

Or not, as she threw up her hands. "Wait! I'm not here to kill you!"

I cleared my throat. "Torture and kill," I particularized. "According to Vern."

"Vern is an idiot."

"Was," I corrected.

She arched an eyebrow and shook her head slightly. "As I've tried to explain, that was just to get your attention. The last time I tried to get your attention I was unsuccessful as well . . ." She looked over at Annie. "Perhaps I should have dressed up as Catholic schoolgirl."

"I'm not Catholic," the schoolgirl deadpanned.

"You were saying something about bodyguards," Agent North prompted from behind her. It sounded more like a command than a question as the blonde moved the brunette ahead of her into the room.

Carmella Le Fanu turned and took in the statuesque Interpol agent. "Christopher, you have the damnedest tastes in acquiring minions."

North didn't say anything though her eyes narrowed at that last word. The woman was a master of the narrowed-eyes gaze; I could never pull it off without appearing squinty. Carmella took a step back. I didn't want to look at Annie's reaction so I jumped in with "Bodyguards? I don't need any help in handling you."

"Well, we'll never know unless you try." The arched eyebrow went higher. "And I do wish that you would. Try." The eyebrow came back down. At least most of the way. "But there's no time for that now. I came to warn you."

"I think you're confused. The last time we spoke *I* warned *you*. And told you that I was coming up there to . . . visit."

"That was over a week ago, my Doman. Since then I've received information regarding other players on the board. I came down here, at great personal risk, to protect you. You should be grateful." She did this thing with her lips and her eyes. "Very . . . grateful."

"Oh, ewww."

The vampire didn't even deign Annie with a look. "Be quiet little girl and let the grownups talk."

"So talk," I said. "But try to actually say something useful for a change."

"Yes, my Doman." She put her hands together and gave me a little bow. I couldn't tell if she was mocking me or being sincere. "It is as I have said. The New York demesne lacks leadership—"

"Kurt—" I began.

"He acts as your seneschal. He rules in your name. But his authority is secondary and not enough in your absence to keep the more politically subversive elements in line. Especially since stories of your . . . difficulties . . . have grown these past two years."

"You'd think with my 'difficulties' I'd be easier to kill."

"A point that your seneschal exploits endlessly to keep the

rebellious in line. Still, the political infighting has grown more bloody and other demesnes have grown bolder in their attempts to gain advantage. More of the recent attempts on your life have come from outside of the demesne than from within."

"Like the *Graeae*?"

"I don't know what that means. But there are non-demesne and non-vampire elements that are recruiting and your name is invoked regularly."

"Any idea why?"

"The politics are obvious for most nightwalkers. But outside motives are more obscure." She smiled. "Beyond your innate ability to just piss people off."

I smiled back. "I'm good with people. It's monsters I tend to rub the wrong way."

Her smile grew. "I'll bet you could rub me the right way."

"Oh. Eww," Annie repeated as I said, "Now cut that out!"

"Excuse me . . ." said Agent North.

"Anyway, why should I believe anything that you have to say seeing as how you just tried to kill me?"

"I told you, that was just to get your attention. You don't answer your phone; you don't answer your posts—"

"Won't friend you on Facebook," I deadpanned.

"Excuse me . . ." said Agent North.

"The bozos I sent down here had delusions of competence. They were merely a warning shot across your bow, so to speak. There's a bigger hit-squad headed your way and they've been recruited by something bad!"

"Some*thing* as opposed to some*one*?"

"Like a woman with the head of a jackal?" North asked.

Carmella blinked. "Why would you say that?"

North nodded at the window. "The new lawn ornaments."

We all turned and looked out the window. There was a vampire flash mob out on the lawn.

It wasn't like they were wearing capes or possessed of an obvious overbite and ridiculous widow's peaks. But a gathering of nosferatu gives off this giant soul-sucking vibe: I'd been privileged to experience it in close quarters and had the spiritual hickies to show for it.

Three or four neckbiters would be serious trouble. At a glance, it looked like we had at least twenty. Maybe thirty. Hard to estimate as we were focusing on the jackal-headed woman who kind of stood out—even though she had positioned herself toward the rear.

"Come out and surrender yourself and the others will be allowed to live," she barked.

You would think stuff like this would get old. For the Powers of Darkness, that is; I know it did for me. Which was probably why I didn't tend to panic so much anymore.

"Okay," I said after a moment. "This may not be as bad as it looks. Annie, Ms. North: there are a dozen flashlights in the hall closet. Bring six."

Annie gave me a questioning look. "I saw semi-autos and grenades in your safe room . . ."

I shook my head. "Maybe for a half-dozen Fangs—and even then your odds are fifty-fifty." I squinted at the leader. "I'd give one to Carmella for dealing with their boss but I'm not ready to trust her with a nail file, yet. Besides . . ." I looked back out at the jackal-headed woman. ". . . she looks like a real bitch. And, by the Laws of Similitude, Le Fanu should be able to handle anything she dishes out."

Carmella's response was lost as North and Annie returned with the blocky, extra-large flashlights.

"They're big," North grunted, dropping her three on the bed. "And heavy. I don't see the tactical value unless you plan to hurl them off the roof on your enemies' heads."

I picked one up. She was right: I had forgotten how heavy they were. "They're 'Ottow' mods," I explained, gripping the handle that ran along the top of the rectangular casing. "Dutch optics engineer named Ralf Ottow created this powerful flashlight-hack: The power supply has been altered to hold fifty-four nickel-metal-hydride batteries plus a ballast to regulate the current." I turned it so that the front was more visible. "Reinforced, heat-tempered glass and reflector with a built-in cooling fan." I pointed at the bulb. "Mercury-arc lamp. It turns on with a key for safety reasons. Keep it pointed away from your body. Aside from the obvious, if the design fails and the lamp shatters . . ." I shrugged.

"So you're going to dazzle 'em," Carmella snarked.

"The original design called for a special coating to the glass and reflector to trap and filter the UV radiation to keep it from scorching *human* skin." I smiled like a happy shark. "I left that particular modification out. Oh, and these babies pump out a thirty-eight-million-candlepower beam that will light up objects nine miles away."

"*Go hifreann leat!*" she swore, taking a step back.

I hefted a second flashlight in my other hand and I looked at Annie who was juggling her pair with considerable slippage. "You'll probably do better with just one," I advised. "Besides, you can turn the keys on mine when I get to the door." I reached for my crutches and then decided it would be less awkward to just limp.

North picked up two of the heavy mods with no apparent effort. Her deceptively slender arms were stronger than they appeared. As we moved toward the front door I heard Annie whisper, "Half a league, half a league, half a league onward . . ."

"What?" Carmella was perplexed.

"Charge of the Light Brigade. Tennyson," I said, grinning despite my best intentions. "Okay. Stay tight as soon as we're out the door. North to my left, Annie on my right. Keep the house at our backs and don't let them draw you out or get behind you."

"Anything else?" the kid asked as we reached the door.

"Yeah." I inverted the modified flashlights, bracing their butt ends against my shoulders. "Open the door a crack, key me, and don't cross the beams."

"What happens if we cross the beams?" North asked.

"Something very bad," I deadpanned.

"He's kidding," Annie coached. "You know: 'Who you gonna call?'"

Now North looked blank.

"Never mind." Blame the reboot. "Carmella?"

"I know. Don't go into the light, Carol Anne . . ." She shuddered.

I blinked. "Oookay. Let's go."

Carmella opened the door and stepped aside.

The interior light shone from the windows and the porch lamp provided enough illumination to make out the size and shape of the mob in general and the faces of those that were nearer.

A few of them started to move toward us before their leader called them to heel. "Wait! Bring me—"

Then the Mercury-arc lamps stuttered to life and the first two beams of light stabbed into the darkness. In this instance, the term "beams" was more akin to those slabs of steel used to frame skyscrapers than the dim glow generated by a couple of D cells and a fifty-cent bulb. The beams smashed into the mob of vampires like a pair of white-hot battering rams.

Since I'd never had the opportunity to fully field-test the mods, I was expecting something a bit less showy than my throw-down with the green astronomy laser. But what the mods lacked in focus and frequency modulation, they made up for in volume, raw power, and sheer force. Undead went down like wheat before the scythe. Others went flying backward like incendiaries fired from a cannon. Some were just instantaneously vaporized while others exploded like 20-die fireballs. What wasn't immediately disintegrated quickly flared like a book of matches tossed into a campfire.

By the time North and Annie had flanked me it was all over but the cleanup: They picked off the stragglers on either side who had already turned to flee. The light, so devastating to undead flesh, had no such effect on the woman with the canine visage. She shrieked, a cry of frustration and fury, and wings unfurled behind her. "You cannot escape your doom, Annwn Harkwynde! Time shall again be your master!" She leapt into the night sky and was out of sight in just seconds.

I looked over at the trembling girl trying to heft the oversized lantern in her slender arms. "I thought they were after . . ."

"As I was saying, Mr. Cséjthe: I am in need of a bodyguard for the next few days," she said in a small voice. "You have enemies. I have enemies. Perhaps we can watch each other's backs until I reach the Wyrding Circle."

"And then?"

"Then? I hope to be on Time's right side."

Carmella squeezed past Annie to stand next to me, carefully avoiding the side spill of light from the mods, and gawked at the smoldering remains of what had been a small army of vampires just moments ago. She shuddered and looked up at me with large, moist eyes. "Oh my God," she whispered. "I am so hot for you right now!"

And people wondered that I had a death wish.

✢ ✢ ✢

Bachman and Garou had been outside when the preternatural platoon had arrived. Had they been the vampire and the werewolf I remembered from a previous life they wouldn't have stood much of a chance. Apparently these versions were totally human. They were also totally drained, and—judging from their degree of inside-outness—totally dead.

Before I could ask the obvious questions, the not-so-obvious survivor caught my attention.

I stared at the oh-so-familiar bat-headed humanoid who sat atop the toppled VW bus, tending the numerous wounds that crisscrossed its dark-furred body. "Zotz?"

Its terrible, fanged visage turned toward me and I felt the weight of its predator gaze: measuring, cataloging, *pre-targeting*...

There was no warmth, no recognition in those gleaming black orbs that looked more like polished obsidian spheres than actual eyes. Its gaze shifted to over my shoulder as I heard footsteps come up behind me.

"Mistress," it growled in a strangely familiar yet alien voice, "I am . . . depleted. I must feed or else sleep for the better part of a fortnight."

I turned and looked at the kid who was looking at her watch and then the night sky. "How long do you need?" she asked.

"Likely an hour short of sunrise," it growled. "On the other hand, two or three humans . . . a cow . . ." it shrugged massive shoulders. ". . . I could be back before moonset."

She shook her head, her ponytail doing an impatient shimmy. "The Adjudication stands. You may only feed on the lesser beasts of the woods and field."

"I may need days, rather than hours," it argued. "This one's blood is a potent mix." It was staring at me again. "A single draught might sustain me for days. Like-ways, the Elemental. Lend one to me. I will try to not take a full life's measure."

I took a step back. "Darn tootin' you won't."

Annie folded her arms across her chest and shook her head again.

"Then give me the Deadling. She will bring you nothing but regret, that one. Her second death would serve your quest and ease her karmic debt."

"Hey now," came Carmella's more distant response.

Annie Harkwynde seemed to be giving the matter a little more thought. I took another what-I-hoped-was-subtle step back.

"We lack the time to serve your needs without our straying from The Path," she finally decided. "You have fulfilled the primary purpose for which you were geased: The Shadow Knight is in play."

It rose to its feet and physically expanded past its former frame, seeming to almost double in size. "Do not banish me," it said softly, almost sounding like the Mesoamerican bat god I had known before the Cthulhu debacle. "I can still serve."

"I'm sorry," the young woman said, seemingly fearless in the monster's black shadow. "This is too important and I can only divide myself so far. I rescind The Summoning. Camazotz, also known as Zotzilaha Chimalman and Lord Neckcutter, return to your cenote and slumber once more until there is either End or Need."

And then she said something.

It would not be accurate to say that she spoke actual words or uttered something in another language. Even a foreign tongue will register upon the ear and the brain, if only as so much gibberish or incomprehensible sound.

There was a sense of something composed of sound and syllables but it refused to resolve into an auditory experience—something that could be perceived as any kind of real-time utterance much less be stored in even the briefest flicker of short-term memory. I was merely left with a vague suspicion that something had been said . . . and the creature was suddenly gone.

No flash of light. No clap of thunder. Not even the cinéma vérité of a slow dissolve or fade to black. It was just . . .

Gone.

I looked around. So were Bachman and Garou's remains. I decided to not think about that beyond the immediate issues of convenience. When you're hemorrhaging humanity like an eviscerated cow in a slaughterhouse, convenience is a handy byproduct.

After a long moment I turned and looked at Annie.

"I know that you'd like explanations, Mr. Cséjthe, but right now we have more pressing concerns." She nodded at the crumpled remains of the microbus. "Like transportation. But I will tell you that the demon I just returned to his watery pit near Chichen Itza is not the Camazotz you knew in your timeline."

Great.

The only thing worse than unanswered questions were answers that raised even bigger questions.

"In the meantime," she continued, "I don't suppose there are any home-delivery, twenty-four-hour car rental agencies in your neck of the woods?"

I shook my head and did a visual sweep of the tree line on my property. No large infrared silhouettes came into view but the real threats could be cold enough to mask any heat signatures. "Not after seven and, no, there's no undead Uber, either," I told her. I looked over at Agent North who was fiddling with her smart phone again. "Hey, Interpol, who's your local law enforcement liaison? Can they help with some transport for a couple of hit-and-run vics, here?"

She shook her head. "No liaison. I am special agent-at-large."

"Oh," I said, "*Special* Interpol Agent-at-Large . . ."

"That is correct."

"I *see*," I said. Like I was finally getting it.

And I was. The question was whether I should let her know just how much I was getting.

"But I think your friend could probably give us a lift," she added.

And we all turned to look at Carmella Le Fanu.

As the vampress lowered her cell phone and the glazed look began to fade from her face, I turned to the teenager who had just imposed her will on a centuries-old nosferatu and said, "If you ever try to do anything like that to me, you'll pass from this world before you've ever had a chance to legally buy beer, vote in an election, or lose your virginity!"

She giggled. "Oh, Christopher—may I call you Christopher? You are even funnier than I had supposed!"

Yeah, the virginity thing was probably supposing too much, even at her age.

I didn't get the chance to course-correct before I had to intercept Carmella who had launched herself at Annie, apparently with the intent of carrying out my threat.

"He is coming with me!" Le Fanu hissed. "He is *my* Doman and his place is in New York where—"

"*Carmella!*"

Whoa. The subharmonics in *my* voice were even giving me a sudden headache. Everyone else looked like they wanted to pull an ice pick out of their foreheads. "I am *your Doman*, am I not?" The sub-vocals were still there but I was trying for a different pitch, now.

"Yes, my lord."

"And that means *my wish* is *your command—right*?"

Carmella took a deep shaky breath and licked her lips. "Yesss, my lord Doman. Command me . . ."

The others stared at me and I tried to not blush. "Okay, then. Command number one: no attacking the teenybopper." I looked at Annie. "Unless I command it. Or she tries to harm or mind-control me."

The teenybopper just smiled and dimpled.

"Number two: Your Doman is in need of transportation. As my loyal subject, I know that you are more than happy to loan me your wheels until we get things sorted out or can make some other arrangements. I apologize if the girl was a little . . . um . . . overzealous . . . in speaking on my behalf . . ."

She glared at Annie as a pair of headlights appeared at the far end of the road. "How far to your destination?" she practically hissed through clenched teeth.

So much for political blame-shifting.

"It's not so much a question of 'how far,' vampire, but when," Annie answered enigmatically.

"All right then," Carmella huffed, "how *soon* do you need to be there?"

"To the best of my calculations, eight days and we will be too late."

"So, seven," I qualified. "Shouldn't be a problem. God made the heavens and the earth in six."

"And all shall be unmade in one should we fail," the teenybopper added quietly.

Seemed a trifle dramatic. Until North stepped in with "And God was not hunted by more powerful beings than Himself while He labored."

Our ride turned out to be a Class B, RV travel van. A little over twenty feet in length, it looked like it could seat fourteen or sleep six. I looked at Carmella and asked, "How many?"

"Just two, my lord: a lycan and a human servitor. Security and someone to drive and handle the amenities while the sun is up."

"What? No entourage of eight? No retinue?"

"It's supposed to be a clandestine mission."

I looked at the oversized vehicle and back to her. "Seems like the vampire version of the short bus is a little much for just you and a couple of—what do you like to call them? Thralls? Or has 'minions' come back around in the lamia lexicon?"

She made an expression I couldn't quite interpret and gestured at the fancy travel bus. "I didn't know how many of *your* min—thral— *friends*," she decided, watching the expressions evolve on the faces around her, "you would insist on bringing along. Honestly, Christopher, you have always been so unpredictable in that department."

The driver's side door opened and her first "thrall" stepped out brandishing a shotgun. She was tall, athletic, and tan. Her sleeveless top revealed toned arms with a little more muscle than the fashion magazines like to promote as the feminine ideal. Her thick, honey-brown mane of hair was held back by a series of silver bands that were spaced in six-inch gaps to where I would guess it reached the small of her back.

Volpea.

Her eyes were still gold with flecks of brown but they held no recognition when they turned my way. "Mistress, are you under duress?"

"Good question, V." Le Fanu smiled at Annie, then me. "Am I?"

I smiled back at her. "Of course not. Can we drop you somewhere?"

Her smile was showing some teeth as she took my arm. "Can we talk? In private?" She half led, half dragged me over to the porch.

"What are you doing?" she hissed.

"Helping the kid out," I answered softly.

"Why?"

I just stared at her. The answer was complicated enough. Explaining it to Carmella Le Fanu, even more so.

"What? You got some kind of thing for little girls? Is that why you never gave me a tumble? You're some kind of pedophile?"

I opened my mouth and then closed it: Any kind of comment

would be pointless with her at this stage so I went back to just staring at her.

"Okay, that was out of line. When you're over three centuries old, all Warms and Breathers are children by comparison."

I continued to stare.

"Okay, my point is: you don't know anything about this little . . ." She frowned. ". . . person. Where are her parents? Where does she live? What does she really want?" She released me and put her hands on her hips. "Why isn't she in school?"

"I don't know," I finally said. "There hasn't been much in the way of opportunities to find out. But she helped me out of a couple of rough spots and I owe her for that. Plus, she's a Power. I don't know what kind. Or what kind of help she really needs. But I obviously can't stay here. And I have no place else to go. And, finally, I love a good mystery."

"What are you, Murder-She-Wrote? And you've got a place to go! The New York demesne! Come with me now and we—*you*—can rule and you can indulge all of your do-good instincts by postponing the Undead Apocalypse."

As ridiculous as it sounded, she had a point. My home, bank accounts, and assets had been seized. I was a fugitive from human justice. The New York enclave would offer a life, of sorts, with the chance to fix my karma before one of the inevitable assassination attempts caught up with me. It was logical and it didn't conflict with the damnable Rule that trapped me here, away from all that I held dear.

"Look, I have a debt to discharge," I said. *And some questions to get answers to.* "And once that's done, I'm yours."

Her smile became something frightening.

"You know what I mean," I amended.

Her smile didn't get any better.

Chapter Seven

Carmella's other thrall or minion or demesne version of a personal assistant was an adolescent girl nearly of an age to be high school locker-mates with Annie.

She had dark hair that should have been uniformly shoulder-length but was buzzed close to her skull on the left side. The other side had streaks of purple and she had woven a small portion into a long microbraid and tied it off with a small, fluffy feather that fell just in front of her right shoulder. She wore dangly earrings with amethysts bound in silver wire. They dropped from her earlobes but there were additional piercings from the outer helix to the inner folds of the tragus and concha, as well. Aside from her liberally bedazzled ears, her fingers were armored in a riot of rings—mostly silver with a scattering of crystals and stones of various shapes, sizes, and hues. Three more rings adorned her left eyebrow, right nostril and split the difference in her lower lip. As for any other piercings or adornments, I wasn't inclined to inquire or go looking.

"This is Stryfe . . . with a 'y,'" Carmella offered by way of introduction and ran down the list of everyone's names for everyone's benefit.

Stryfe nodded as names were appended to the people to whom they belonged. But she didn't take her large, dark eyes off of me.

Even after the intros were over and we began moving our luggage and gear into the outer storage compartments.

"I can help with that," the vampress offered as I carried a pair of twenty-liter canisters from the storage shed at the back of the house.

"No, you can't," I said absentmindedly, still trying to process future threat assessments based on hordes of undead led by jackal-headed, flying women.

"I'm stronger than you," she insisted.

"I don't want you handling this stuff. It's very old."

"Diallyl disulfide . . ." she read off of a yellowed, peeling label. "What's that?"

"It's an organosulfur compound."

"What does it do?"

"Generally?" I hefted the canisters into the storage compartment at the back of the transport. "Well, when it's highly diluted, it's used as a flavoring in food. The human body decomposes it into other compounds such as allyl methyl sulfide."

She gave me The Look as I turned back toward the shed for another trip. "That's it? You're packing along a dozen gallons of . . . *spice*?"

"Highly concentrated spice," I agreed, "but this stuff is also used in a couple of European nematicides, as well."

"Nematicide?"

"A kind of chemical pesticide that targets plant-parasitic nematodes."

"Pesticide?"

I nodded. "A number of nematicides have turned out to be highly toxic in the food chain which is why the European Union discontinued the use of Aldicarb and went in the direction of an Allistatin-based compound."

"You're doing nerd-speak to specifically annoy me."

I shrugged. "You asked."

"And why are you loading pesticide on our bus?"

"Because the kid wants me to help her get somewhere and she thinks we might encounter pests along the way."

I pulled out two more containers and a pair of backpack agri-sprayers. I started to relock the shed. Then I considered that I probably wasn't coming back and let the padlock dangle.

"Do you think bug spray is going to do any good against the sorts of pests that showed up tonight?" she asked, reaching for one of the canisters.

"It's not DEET," I told her, jerking the container away. "It's an antibiotic and a broad-spectrum fungicide with sulfur-containing compounds that kicks the crap out of serious microorganisms like staphylococcus and E. coli. You carry the sprayers."

"So," she persisted, following me back to the bus, "it's a medicine and pesticide. Why do we need gallons of it?"

"Because it's essentially a distillate from the genus *Allium* plant. The whole family is good for certain amounts of this stuff—leeks, shallots, scallions, onions, chives . . ."

All of the amusement drained from her face and she dropped the sprayers. "You're talking about . . . *garlic* . . . aren't you!"

I smiled and extended one of the containers toward her. "Why, yes I am. Still want to help carry?"

She danced back out of reach. "Are you crazy?"

I nodded at the delivery systems she had dropped in the grass. "Farmlite Pro-Series five-gallon, piston-pump agricultural sprayer. Ninety psi, twenty- to twenty-five-foot delivery height with adjustable brass nozzle for fan, flat or cone-shaped spray. Works off of a twenty-volt, lithium ion rechargeable battery. These bad boys can hose down acres of undead for over three hours on a single charge. When you see me break one out, you might not want to be standing downwind when I power it up."

She backed away, her eyes showing an uncharacteristic amount of white. "I always thought that harmless and innocent act was all for show," she whispered, "but you really are evil, aren't you?"

I smiled with my teeth. "Welcome to the twenty-first century, Carmella. Oh, and did you know that they make garlic-flavored jellybeans and bubblegum now? I've only packed one bag of each but I'm willing to share."

She turned and fled around to the other end of the bus.

The vampress kept her distance until all of the dangerous stuff seemed to be safely stowed. She understood the shoulder holster with the silver-loaded Glock but it seemed prudent to leave a few other issues off the list of talking points until such time as they might come up. For example, the green laser astronomy pointer that now hung on a carabiner clip from a belt loop on my left side and the two silver throwing daggers tucked into the ankle sheaths under my relaxed-fit jeans.

Taking one final look around the house I was struck, first, with the overwhelming feeling that I would never see it again. And then by the realization of just how much I had depersonalized my surroundings over the years. All traces of Jenny and Kirsten were long gone: erased by the fire that had consumed our home back in Kansas after their deaths. And, as much as I thought I had learned to love again, there was a part of me that was reluctant, paranoid even, about reconstructing any kind of investment in turning any subsequent house back into a "home."

Lupé and others being drawn into the Realm of the Fae had just confirmed those sentiments and, after all hopes of their return evaporated, I had carefully bundled anything that reminded me of their absence away from sight, from touch, from memory. Whatever the difference between the dumpster and long-term storage is probably the measure of hope ere its final extinction.

I nudged Carmella before we finished up. "Do I have spinach between my teeth? Or do I need to snap a selfie and text it to your girl Ringo over there?"

The vampress finally took note of her thrall's . . . um . . . enthrallment. "Stryfe, get on the bus. Mr. Cséjthe has already developed an unhealthy interest in one underaged girl. Let's not offer him any more unnecessary distraction."

As she complied—a little reluctantly, I thought—I turned back to Carmella. "Really? I'm not the one oozing the pervy vibe here. What's the deal with Little Miss Minion?"

The ancient creature in the form of a ravishing young woman shrugged her shapely shoulders. "She's new. She has abandonment issues. I'm still breaking her in . . ."

I stared at her in disbelief.

"Still breaking her in? You drove all the way down here with only two servitors who have access to you during the day when you are helpless and at your most vulnerable? And one of them is still an unknown cipher?" I shook my head. "You're slipping, Carmella." I shook my head again and walked away. "And I don't know why I even care."

No one wanted me to drive.

I suppose it had something to do with my newfound lack of depth perception, a recently shattered leg to work the brakes and accelerator, and chronic dehydration that had to be frequently quenched with blood or I would start to get wobbly with a full-on slide toward unconsciousness.

So Carmella drove, Annie rode shotgun to give her directions, and Volpea and Stryfe took the opportunity to catch a little rest on the beds in the back. Princess Piercings took one of the fold-down side-bunks and Volpea took off her clothes and climbed up on the large bed, doing a little *shifting* to get comfortable before the dayshift began.

It wasn't polite to stare so I tried not to. It wasn't so much all of the naked human skin—which was very fit and athletic and tan all over. I'd seen it before. Spent some time wearing it, actually—never mind: another story for another time if you haven't already heard it . . .

No, it was the sudden appearance of hair—fur, actually—sprouting *and* spreading as her body morphed from human near-perfection to lupine apotheosis that pulled at my attention.

And not because I'd never seen a werewolf before.

The last time I'd seen Volpea, I'd witnessed her transformation from human to therianthrope—or *falopexa*thrope, to be more precise. She had been a fox back then. Well, technically . . . no, not going there: She had been a were*fox*. Not a were*wolf*. So . . . a *falopexathrope*.

Yeah . . . let's just say "werefox."

Except she wasn't anymore.

And, as far as I knew, changing your meta-beast down the road wasn't normally an option. I should've thought about that more . . .

Instead, I was focused on the fact that this Volpea didn't seem to know me any more than the demon Camazotz had.

Perhaps both had drunk from the Well of Forgetfulness in Fand's realm and then found a way to return. If so, then perhaps she knew of a way back and I could squeeze through some sort of cosmic loophole to be with my family again.

Of course that wouldn't account for Luis Garou or Elizabeth Bachman and their own brand of Cséjthe amnesia: They were actually supposed to be dead and not just victims of Stockholm Seelie . . .

Annie looked back over the seat at me and said, "Christopher . . . Chris . . ."

It took a moment for me to set aside the distraction of this new possibility. I looked at her and tried to give her a portion of my attention.

She shook her head slowly with a regretful smile. "The Camazotz and Volpea you know still dwell in the land of the Fae" she said, as if reading my very thoughts. "The woman on the bed is not the woman who took you to New Orleans beneath her skin."

"And Bachman and Garou?" I asked.

"Ditto." She turned back and began another conversation with Carmella, truncating the inevitable follow-up questions.

I opened my mouth to demand answers and then shut it again.

What *was* my first question?

I had a list of "people" who were dead or exiled to another dimensional realm . . . and were suddenly back and yet *not* the people or undead or shapeshifters that they once were!

And I had a pretty good idea that trying to pry answers out of a teenager was likely to be a no-win situation for me at the moment.

And speaking of teenagers, Stryfe had bunched up her pillow so she could watch me from her bunk. Creeepy.

But she was the least of my worries for the moment.

I was currently fleeing my home *and* the Feds for an unknown destination with an ill-defined objective. Legions of undead and the Dames of the Damned seemed intent on spoiling my travel plans. Why? This didn't have the same—flavor? Of the political intrigues of the New York demesne or their assassins. In fact, nobody seemed to be who I first thought they were.

And, until I figured out what that really meant, maybe I would be better served by not calling attention to what and how much I didn't know and wait for someone to let something slip that they wouldn't have otherwise answered directly.

Yeah, that was a good plan: totally in the vein of making it all up as I went along. Which was how I tended to operate anyway. So I didn't plan to call any more attention to my rebooted history with Garou or Bachman or Camazotz or Volpea.

Agent North wasn't who she seemed to be either. But I didn't have a history with her so a little prodding was definitely in order.

She was sitting across the little collapsible table from me, watching me wash down my O-Neg smoothie with a little plasma as

I attempted to surf the internet on my laptop and ignore Little Miss Stares-a-Lot in the back. It was slow work as the cell towers were a little sparse along this section of road in northern Louisiana and my old 4G wireless connection kept losing connectivity.

"So," I said. "Special Agent-at-Large North. Do you have a name?"

She looked at me impassively. "It is North."

"Given that this is a road trip and you seem to be along for the ride, I figure on everyone being on a first-name basis. Carmella, Volpea, Annie, and Stryfe-with-a-y. You can call me Chris but I don't think it works to call you Special-Agent-at-Large. Unless we shorten it to an acronym. S-A-A-L? We could shorten it to Sal?"

Her mouth quirked. "Vanr—Vana."

"Vana North?"

She nodded curtly.

Did she think I was an idiot? Or illiterate? I sighed. "Okay. We'll leave the name thing at that. For now. So, how about telling me who you really represent?"

"I have told you. I am an agent of Interpol—"

"Special Agent-at-Large," I corrected. "Except you're not."

"I can show you my badge again."

"Anyone can go on the internet and order any kind of badge."

Her mouth quirked. "I could show you my gun."

"You could show me your Hello Kitty underwear but it wouldn't prove that you're a Japanese schoolgirl. But the whole gun thing sort of underscores my point."

"And that point is . . ." She deliberately shifted in her seat so that her jacket open to reveal the butt of said gun nestled in her shoulder holster. Riding just beneath the leather holster was a sizable knife hilt, protruding from a custom-made leather sheath.

"The ICPO or International Criminal Police Organization—widely known as Interpol—doesn't have 'special agents-at-large.' Interpol agents act as advisors to local and regional law enforcement organizations. They don't carry guns and they don't operate like secret agents-without-borders." I turned my laptop so that she could see the screen. "And this is what your badge should look like if it were legitimate."

"That Treasury agent seemed satisfied with my bona fides."

"Oh, please; he never had a chance to corroborate your story. And

I doubt he'd had any passing experience with Interpol outside of some European action flick."

Her mouth quirked again. "And you have?"

I shook my head. "No. But I've had a lot of experience with people and things that are not what they appear to be. I've learned to be suspicious and I've learned to do more than the reasonable amount of research." I tapped the laptop for emphasis.

She sat back. "So. It is strategy and tactics rather than prowess in battle that enables you to obtain victory after victory."

"Victory after—?" I sputtered, starting to redline again. "Lady, you really don't know shit about my life! Who the hell are you and what do you want?"

"Think of me as a scout. Or a recruiter . . ."

"I'd rather not."

"You haven't even heard my offer, yet," she said.

"I'll make you a better offer than she will," Carmella called back from the front seat.

"How?" I snapped. "By promising that you'll both go away?"

"Why would you want that?" she shot back. "Unless it's to be alone with Jailbait, here."

"Agent North," Annie said sweetly, "if you're not in immediate need of your firearm, I'd like to borrow it for a moment."

"Hey!" The van wobbled onto the road's shoulder for a second.

"Let me make you a promise," the woman who called herself North said. "I am merely along as an observer for now. I have neither plan nor motivation to interfere or compel you to do anything against your will. If the time should come that I were to offer an invitation, it would be for you to come with me of your own free will and volition. Is this acceptable?"

I stared at her. "I'm supposed to trust you when you handcuffed me to my bed."

The van made a sudden return to the shoulder.

"That was to prevent the little blond man from taking you into custody," North said. "He had already handcuffed you to the bed."

"He?" Carmella squeaked.

"*I* handcuffed you to keep him from putting you in jail."

"Yeah. Well, that kind of complicated things when the Grannies from Gehenna showed up."

"Who?" our undead chauffeur was firmly locked into question-mode now.

"See, this is the problem, Carmella," I told her as Annie placed a hand on the steering wheel as a precaution. "You think your vampire hit-squads are all wicked scary but I've moved up to the majors these last couple of years and you guys are just the farm team. The most worrisome thing out of New York right now is your driving."

"I want to help," she huffed. "How can I help if I don't know what is going on?"

"Good point," I said, turning back to "Special Agent" Vana North. "Who do you really work for?"

"As I said: When the time comes—"

I turned back to the front passenger seat. "Harkwynde, who is she and who does she really work for?"

The young woman shrugged. "I could guess but I don't really know for sure. She just showed up at the hospital and I'm still waiting to see if her goals are inimical to ours."

Carmella stared at her. "'Inimical'? Really?" She looked over her shoulder at me. "Not just jailbait, but nerdlinger jail—"

"Watch the road!" the rest of us yelled as a deer suddenly appeared in our headlights.

Vampire-quick reflexes saved us but just barely as we wove all over the road, spun around one and a half times, and suddenly we were headed back the way we'd come.

"Stop the car," I growled as Le Fanu slowed and made a U-turn, "I'm driving!"

"It's not a car, it's a Class B, RV travel van," she snarked. "And no one's letting you drive!"

"Like I could do any worse!" I leaned over her shoulder. "Now. Stop. The Class B. RV. Travel van."

Annie sat up a little straighter. "Don't," she said suddenly. "Don't stop!"

I looked at her. "What?"

She turned to me. "You need to trust me." She looked at North and then Le Fanu. "And we'll have to trust them."

Up ahead, a string of lights appeared in the distance.

"We need to hide Mr. Cséjthe," she continued. "Now."

The lights were growing in intensity.

"Let me pull over—"

"No! Don't stop. Drive normally," Harkwynde ordered.

"She means drive like other people." I elaborated.

"Where do you sleep during the day?" the girl asked, laying a careful hand on Le Fanu's arm.

"There's a compartment under the bed in back."

"Will it hold two?"

"Two? Two people?" The vampress started to smile. "I hope so. I plan on taking the Doman back with me and it's a long drive."

"Good."

I looked at Annie. "Good?"

"Get back there and climb in now," she ordered, unbuckling her shoulder harness.

"Why?"

"Because your life depends on it. Mine, too."

There was something in her voice that was suddenly convincing. I began unfastening my own shoulder harness as Le Fanu spoke. "Volpea, Stryfe, attend me! Help the Doman into my day compartment!"

The wolf was up and morphing before she had finished speaking.

"Listen to me," Annie said as the lights coming toward us became a series of headlamps, swaying to and fro above the pavement ahead. "If you're stopped in the next few minutes, play dumb!"

Everyone looked at Carmella.

"Hey, I'll have you know that I haven't survived for three centuries on my looks alone!"

"Well, if you truly value your Doman's life, you'll act like you've already been to his house to retrieve him."

"But I did go to his house to retrieve him."

Annie smiled. "See how easy that was?"

"Why not pretend that I don't even know him?"

"The best untruths are the little ones. You are known associates in some circles: Let's not risk that information being readily available. If you come across as uncooperative or deceptive in any way, you will be pressed."

"I've been *pressed* before," our driver said haughtily.

"Not by something farther up the food chain. Keep it simple. You drove down here to retrieve him. He wasn't home so you searched his house and found evidence that he is in federal custody." She moved my laptop aside as she climbed across the table toward the rear of the vehicle. "So you are headed back to New York because there's nothing more that you can do here."

"So I am driving to New York?"

"You're driving north," Harkwynde qualified. "New York by way of Little Rock."

"The sun will be up before then," she said. "Hope you like to snuggle."

"We'll resolve this before then," Harkwynde said, refusing to take the bait, "one way or another." She joined me at the back as Stryfe reached under the mattress and tripped a latch. The base of the bed opened to reveal a compartment that would sleep two but would require a great deal of intimacy if three tried to share the space.

I crawled in and tried to not think about my claustrophobic tendencies.

Annie slithered in next to me and turned on her side, facing outward. "We can spoon," she said as Volpea and Stryfe fitted the panel back in place.

"I heard that!" Le Fanu said as we were shut into darkness.

Even with what felt like additional insulation, the sound of the engine and the tires on the pavement beneath us were distracting. I was glad that I didn't have to spend my daylight hours trying to sleep in here. Of course, sleeping and fighting claustrophobia while you're awake in a confined space are two different things. And sharing said confined space with another person complicated it further.

"Don't worry about touching," Annie said as if she could read my mind. "Under the circumstances, it's almost impossible to not touch. I know you're a gentleman so I won't hold anything against you."

"Pun intended?" I muttered.

"Yes, Groucho." I could hear the smile in her voice. "I wasn't kidding about the spooning, though. We could probably hear better . . ."

"Hold on." I fished my cell phone out of my pocket. "If I can establish a connection to webcam and microphone on my laptop . . ." I depressed the ON button and the screen lit up, making our confined space all the more claustrophobic. I struggled to establish a connection as all other sound was drowned by the roar of multiple engines approaching our vehicle. By the time the thunder had slipped on by I was busy opening a series of protocols and establishing a link with my laptop.

Unfortunately, I was still stymied by the paucity of cellular service in rural Louisiana and the connection was elusive.

In the dim glow from the small screen, I saw a finger emerge from the darkness and trace a pattern around the plastic casing.

And I suddenly had—in the parlance of the old cyber-jockeys—a handshake with my laptop. The interior of the van appeared on my phone's display screen and I could see the interior of the starboard side of the van, including my vacant seat and half of the side door. It was dark out and the windows were heavily tinted to begin with, catching the distorted reflections of dashboard lights, and the laptop's screensaver bounced back at the webcam.

"They're turning around." North's voice, nearer the microphone.

"I see them." Le Fanu said, a little muffled but still discernable.

Who's "*them*"? I wanted to know.

"Here they come!" Stryfe called.

The sound of thunder grew behind us.

"Motorcycles?" I murmured. "Hell's Angels?"

"So to speak," Harkwynde whispered back.

The webcam offered little in the way of visual clues but the sounds of motorcycle engines bracketing us and the shaky maneuvering of the van, edging over and coasting to a stop on the shoulder, was eloquent enough. More light filled the interior from the front: headlights, no doubt, aimed through our windshield from more vehicles blocking our lane.

Though I could not hear the driver's side window being lowered, there was a sudden jump in the volume of both two- and four-stroke engines.

"Kill the motor!" a piercing voice shrilled, sounding like amplified nails down a chalkboard. Le Fanu must have complied as all vibration ceased after a brief shudder. A moment later the other engines died, as well.

A voice called but was too far away to be understood through the laptop mic.

"Vampire," the chalkboard voice answered. "Looks like a blonde and a were on board, too. Got any other passengers, girlie?"

"Who the hell wants to know?" Le Fanu snarled back.

There was the sound of a little scuffle with a lot of hissing thrown in—I couldn't be sure that it wasn't all one-sided.

Then the side door opened across from the laptop.

A couple of women stood framed in the backlight of motorcycle headlamps.

Both wore torn riding leathers with the slashes indifferently repaired with safety pins and staples. Both looked like sisters who shared things like car accidents, face trauma, and a marked indifference to cosmetology. Both had long, night-dark hair that was tangled and snarled only a little less than their lips when they spoke.

"Oooo, Achlys! Do you see what I see?"

"Yeah." The other one spat. "A *Chooser*. I think we're getting warm."

"Long way from home, Chooser. What brings you to these parts?"

"Might ask you . . . *ladies* . . . the same thing," North's voice drawled.

"You might want to watch your tone, Frostie. I see only one of you and there's a whole bunch of us!"

"I have sisters, too," she answered. "And, as a rule, no one sees us until they're dead."

The bikers suddenly looked up and then all around.

If they noticed Stryfe at the back of the bus, she didn't warrant their comments.

"We're looking for a guy—"

"Shut up, Nosos!" the other one commanded.

"Hey, she either knows or she don't. I'm guessing she knows something or she wouldn't even be here."

"You're right," North said. "And I can help you."

The biker chicks were scary but not all that savvy judging by their expressions.

"You want to find a guy?" North continued. "Wear some makeup. Use a little conditioner—scratch that—a lot, a lot of conditioner on your hair. Tweeze. And, for the gods' sakes, see an orthodontist!"

One of them lunged forward, bellowing, "*Nyx!*" It sounded like an oath.

The other one caught her, hauling her back. "She told us not to get sidetracked!"

"Sidetracked?" the first screeched. "I say we shove a rag down the gas tank and light this steel chariot up like the foundries of Tartarus! Ten—fifteen minutes! I'd hardly count that as being sidetracked!"

"Time is relative, sister. And I can't see the Choosers seeking to thwart our purposes. They have as great a stake in this as the rest of us."

The other one settled down a bit. "Is that right, *Valkyrja*? Are we on the same side in this?"

"You tell me, Κήρ: Just who is seeking to interfere with whom while we all waste each other's time in pointless bickering?"

"Are we not both Choosers? Do we not come to the same feeding grounds for our purposes?"

"The eagle and the carrion crow are both birds and they both hunt," North replied. "But they do not seek the same prey nor would one ever be mistaken for the other."

The angry one glared a moment longer and then whirled back into the night. The other stayed a moment longer, clenching her gloved fists.

"He's not there," North told her finally. "He's come and gone so you'll have to seek him elsewhere." A note of amusement crept into her voice. "You've heard the stories, I suppose. Are you sure that you really want to find him?"

A gloved hand came up to push the thick black hair out of her red-ringed eyes. With a start, I realized that the tip of each finger was long and pointed . . .

. . . and that there were only three fingers on each hand.

"By the black stars of eternal night, we have no choice!" she croaked in a less-than-human voice. "Even though he is more monster than all of us combined!" She flung herself back out of the doorway and a dozen motorcycles erupted in banshee screams.

Chapter Eight

Sometime after the van started back up but before it was deemed safe to come back out, I fell asleep.

Hunted by monsters and sharing a ride with people who weren't exactly human should have kept me awake and wide-eyed for the next forty-eight hours. Chalk it up to the physical stress of getting killed—again—and escaping from the hospital and tangling with Stygian witches, vampire battalions, flying jackals, and a motorcycle gang of The Fast and The Furies. I was exhausted and still running a blood deficit as I healed from the near-fatal trauma that the crash had inflicted. The last thing I remembered before darkness claimed me was the oddity of both Deino and one of the switchblade sisters uttering the archaic slang word "Nix" as if it held some sort of significance beyond the original meaning.

Awakening, I was surprised to feel Annie sleeping next to me. Maybe she was exhausted, too. That or it wasn't safe to come out, yet. Strangely, she was on the other side of me, now. I didn't know which was more mysterious: *Why* she had crawled over me to sleep in the back part of the compartment? Or *how* she had managed to do it without waking me up?

And . . . *why did she feel like she was naked*?

I found my phone and turned it on, lighting up the screen. There were three text messages waiting to be read. The light also illuminated the somnolent form of Carmella Le Fanu instead of Annie Harkwynde.

As naked bodies go, Carmella's was magnificent. The effect,

however, was somewhat ruined by the corpse-like rigidity of her flesh, the wide-open, staring eyes, and the knowledge that she was a soulless, selfish, centuries-old creature whose only interest in me was for my political value back in the New York demesne and the unique quality of my mutated blood.

I checked the time: six thirty-eight. At least I could count on being unmolested for a couple more hours while she lay unconscious in the deep, day-sleep of the undead.

Then I noticed that my shirt was unbuttoned and my pants unzipped.

Dammit! I started to wonder and then told myself that I really didn't want to know.

Besides, the silver alkaloids in my system would have turned any serious gropage pretty painful for her after the first twenty seconds or so . . .

So . . . I put myself back together, resisting the impulse to do a more thorough exam below the belt buckle, and turned my attention back to my phone.

The first message was from Lupé. "Be careful, darling," it read.

The second was from Deirdre: "We're waiting for you . . ."

The last was from Will.

My unborn son.

Assuming that I could trust the text's provenance.

And, if I could, what was the meaning of his reaching out to me after the years of silence from a parallel universe?

Was he now corporate in mine?

My sleep-addled brain was too muddled to go down that rabbit hole. Never mind *sub*text, the text, itself, was in Latin: "Tempus edax rerum. Tempus incognitum."

Tempus incognitum was easy enough: "Time unknown."

Tempus edax rerum was a little trickier. It shows up on the occasional sundial, translated as "Time flies." You probably think "Time flies" is *Tempus fugit* but that really translates as "Time *flees*." Close, I'll grant you, and interchangeable if you're not inclined to be precise . . .

But "Time flies" is just a lazy-assed distillation of *Tempus edax rerum*. A more accurate rendering is "Time is the devourer of things."

I was pondering both text and subtext of a message from a child

I was supposed to have fathered in an alternate timeline when I saw that I had voicemail, as well. I pressed play and held the phone up to my ear.

Before it was done, I was vomiting blood all over myself and the interior of the compartment.

Even after I had cleaned myself off in the cramped shower in the back of the van, I was still sick and shaking.

Annie Harkwynde didn't look much better, confirming that she had sampled a bit of the playback, as well.

Volpea and Stryfe just looked pissed as they continued to work at cleaning up their mistress and the interior of the underbed compartment.

North was driving.

"What just happened?" I asked.

"Something left you a message in R'lyehian," Harkwynde answered.

"Yeah, it sounded familiar. Had a chat with a guy named Gnarly-Hotep a couple of years back: nasty-sounding gibberish but it didn't try to rearrange my insides the last time I heard it."

"You had a . . . *conversation*?" Stryfe's voice started going up, in both pitch and volume. "With *Nyarlathotep*? And *survived*? With your *sanity intact*?"

"Well, 'intact' might be a bit of a reach," I started to say.

"Even when you can't understand the individual words, Mr. Cséjthe, a curse can still have its way with you," Harkwynde elaborated. "We were both fortunate to have dropped the phone before we could hear the message in its entirety."

I held my phone out at arm's length. It looked a little melty around the edges and the screen had developed a permanent haze. Time for an upgrade and a new data plan. As I set it down in one of the insulated cup holders, I saw a road sign flash past.

"How is it that we're still in Louisiana?" I asked as I finished buttoning up a clean shirt with trembling fingers.

"We stopped after you fell asleep." Harkwynde offered me a blood packet from the minifridge.

I shook my head and pushed it back at her. "I don't think I could keep it down. Why did you stop?"

"It wasn't safe. And you need the blood. Even more so, now."

"Seriously, I'm having spasms just looking at it. And what do you mean, it wasn't safe? Did Bitch Cassidy and The Sundress Kid make a return appearance?"

Harkwynde's face twisted into a grimace. "Nothing so simple as that . . ."

"Then what?"

There was a long silence.

Then Stryfe cleared her throat and spoke for the first time in my presence: "Every time you fall asleep we experience a reality-shift."

"Um, what?"

"Everyone in close proximity to you," Harkwynde elaborated, "is drawn across the event horizon of another space-time bubble."

"And it's seriously freaky!" Volpea added through clenched teeth.

"Do you remember your *Wizard of Oz* dream back in your hospital room?"

I turned and looked at my former candy striper. "Um, what?"

"The television set was on in your room and *The Wizard of Oz* was on at one point."

I raised a shaking hand to my forehead, remembering. "That would explain the dream. That and the drugs."

"Tell me about the dream."

"I don't remember much."

"Shirley Temple as Dorothy instead of Judy Garland?" Harkwynde prompted. "Buddy Ebsen as The Scarecrow?"

"Actually, funny story about that," I said. "Or not so funny, actually. A couple of decades before *The Beverly Hillbillies*, Ebsen was cast as The Scarecrow in *The Wizard of Oz*. Ray Bolger was supposed to play The Tin Man. Bolger convinced the producers to swap parts. Nine days in, Ebsen was hospitalized after being poisoned by the aluminum powder in his makeup. It almost killed him."

Harkwynde nodded. "Except it didn't. And they never swapped parts. No Jack Haley. No Judy Garland. No Margaret Hamilton."

I snorted. "Maybe in a parallel universe. The whole W. C. Fields as The Wizard and Shirley Temple as Dorothy casting? Just ideas kicked around by the studio before they found out that Fields was too expensive and Temple didn't have the vocal chops. And Gale

Sondergaard quit when the producers decided to 'hag' her up as The Wicked Witch of the West. She didn't want to lose her glamorous image."

Harkwynde gave me a long look. "Except, maybe, in a *parallel* universe."

I thought back to the disjointed images on my hospital room TV. "You're not going to tell me that Arnold Schwarzenegger is the President of the United States."

"Not . . . *here*. Not *now*."

"So . . . what? I suppose you're going to tell me that John McCain beat Hillary Clinton back in '08?"

She shook her head. "Barack Obama."

I blinked. "Who?"

"Oh, for the gods' sakes, seiðkonur," North called back. "Stop beating about Yggdrasill and just tell him that he is unstuck in time!"

"Like you," she added, after I'd had a moment for it to sink in.

"Trinity," she said. "1945."

I stared at Annie Harkwynde and finally said: "You're talking about the Manhattan Project."

She nodded. "More specifically, the first atomic bomb test. July sixteenth. The desert north of Alamogordo, New Mexico. Technically speaking, it wasn't so much a traditional bomb design as a gadget. That was their code name for it: 'The Gadget.' It was a plutonium implosion-type device and it released the equivalent power of nineteen kilotons of TNT. It was more powerful than the bomb that would be dropped over Hiroshima—sixteen kilotons—and only a little less than the one used on Nagasaki—twenty-one kilotons."

"You seem unusually knowledgeable about an event that took place over fifty years before you were born," I observed.

"Pfft." She waved a braceleted hand. "I know more about it than you can possibly imagine. Family history," she added at the sight of my raised eyebrow. "Anyway, are you familiar with the name Edward Teller?"

"Magician? Little guy who never speaks? Works with Penn Jillette?"

She gave me The Look. "You know better."

I had to rack my brain for old, cold memories of my American History homework from two decades back. "Wasn't he one of the founding members of The Manhattan Project?"

She nodded. "And one of the most controversial names attached to the development of the atomic bomb."

"Yeah. There was some sort of kerfuffle regarding his testimony on the Oppenheimer security clearance hearings and I think I read that he didn't play well with others."

She smiled sourly. "An understatement at best. But he was brilliant. So brilliant that the whole fission-based weapon concept began to bore him and he pushed for more research and resources for a fusion-based approach. He was ahead of his time, of course. And his people skills were abysmal."

I snapped my fingers. "Wasn't he the one who came up with the nutty idea that the atom bomb would set the sky on fire?"

She didn't answer immediately and, when she finally spoke, it was barely above a whisper. "He was misunderstood." The gathering darkness outside, offset by the orange glow of the dashboard instrumentation, lent a campfire quality to our conversation but it was her haunted expression and the hushed quality of her voice that made it seem as if we were telling ghost stories in a graveyard.

"Contrary to popular myth, Teller never suggested that the bomb would ignite the atmosphere like some sort of chemical fire. At least not in the way that most people think of a chemical reaction. He wasn't even thinking in terms of the physics of fission—at least not directly. You know how fusion bombs are detonated?"

I nodded. "Up until the recent advances in laser technology, you needed a fission reaction to generate the intense heat and pressure required to jumpstart a fusion reaction."

"Yes. Well, Teller was looking at various fusion theories and was haunted by the idea that setting off a fission bomb would jumpstart a fusion chain reaction utilizing the nitrogen nuclei in the atmosphere. From there, it would have been conceivable that the hydrogen atoms in the oceans would fuse in a similar process, turning sky and water into a gigantic fusion reactor, vaporizing the earth in between."

"Wait a minute!" Carmella's voice drifted from the darker confines of the underbed compartment. "Are you saying a handful of pencil-neck geeks rolled the dice on turning the whole fucking planet into a nuclear bomb?"

Harkwynde's face was grim. "You have to understand the desperation that most of the world was feeling after five years of war—"

"No! *You* have to imagine!" the vampress corrected as she emerged behind us. "*I* lived through World War Two, you weren't even born yet!"

"Well, technically—"

She glanced at me. "You shut up. I was there, even if I wasn't technically 'living' by then. I still had as much to lose as any Breather!" She looked back at the teenager. "The whole fucking planet? Really?"

The teenager looked at Le Fanu and cocked an eyebrow at the vampire's lack of attire but continued softly. "Oppenheimer was well aware of the stakes. He discussed it with another leading physicist, Arthur Compton. Compton himself wrote that this could prove to be the ultimate catastrophe: 'Better to accept the slavery of the Nazis than run a chance of drawing the final curtain on mankind!' he said."

"Damn right, Skippy!" Le Fanu backed up and began rummaging for clothes. At least I assumed that was what she was doing: I certainly wasn't going to stare.

"And, ironically," Harkwynde resumed, "this was the very reason that we beat the Germans even though they had a head start with their Uranprojekt back in 1939. Albert Speer, Hitler's Minister of Armaments and War Production, had a conversation with Werner Heisenberg and some of the German nuclear scientists as to whether a successful nuclear explosion could be kept under absolute control—or whether it might lead to a series of runaway chain reactions of growing intensity. According to Speer's memoirs, Heisenberg was uncertain . . ."

I almost smiled.

". . . and Speer recorded afterward that 'Hitler was plainly not delighted with the possibility that the earth, under his rule, might be transformed into a glowing star.' You can thank a madman's hesitation in the face of such odds for giving the U.S. the chance to jump ahead."

She turned away and looked out the window as the murky landscape crept off into the darkness.

"Hans Albrecht Bethe, the head of the Theoretical Division at Los Alamos, produced calculations to prove that such a thing could not actually happen. He was a brilliant theoretical physicist who later won the Nobel prize for his work on the theory of stellar nucleosynthesis. After the war, Teller cowrote a paper, 'Ignition of the Atmosphere with Nuclear Bombs,' with Marvin and Konopinski, producing their own formulae explaining why the heat-to-mass ratio would prevent such a catastrophic series of chain reactions.

"Still, so much was theoretical, so much was unproven. So much . . . unknown. The senior scientists at Trinity had a betting pool going right up to the last minute. Teller bet that The Gadget would produce nearly forty-five kilotons of TNT-like power. Oppenheimer was skeptical that they'd see anything over three hundred tons. Bethe was in the middle, wagering down to a mere eight kilotons. But all of them were betting that we wouldn't suddenly turn the solar system into a double-star system."

I cleared my throat. "Did Fermi have a known position on the matter?"

"Oh yeah. One of the most brilliant atomic scientists of his time offered to take bets on whether the test would just burn New Mexico or the entire planet."

"Nice," I said. "Thank God the pessimists were wrong."

Harkwynde's head snapped back around. "They nearly weren't!" she said.

"Uh, excuse me . . ." Le Fanu piped in after a moment of silence. "I won't pretend that the whole history lecture wasn't boring . . . and that I didn't get half of all the sciency stuff . . ." She leaned forward. "But the whole, turn-the-world-into-a-big-ball-of-fire thing? Pretty clear. And since it didn't happen—"

"It didn't happen because there was . . . an intervention," Harkwynde answered. "It didn't happen because someone was there, that day—July 16, 1945—in the Jornada del Muerto desert. A coven of the most powerful witches of all time joined hands and stopped it from happening."

My throat was suddenly dry. "Stopped what from happening?"

"The bomb?" Le Fanu asked.

"The sky from catching fire," Stryfe said softly.

Harkwynde nodded.

We were all quiet for a moment.

"Okay," I said, holding up my hand. "Say I buy into some sort of magic fire-suppression for the Trinity test. What about Hiroshima? Nagasaki? What about all of the nuclear testing that's been done since? Are you suggesting there's thirteen globetrotting spellcasters acting as a hocus-pocus hazmat team for every atomic event?"

"No." This time the silence stretched on as she turned and looked out of the window at the beginning of the moonrise. "That day, the day everyone says the world changed—" she said quietly, "—the world was *literally* changed in ways that no one would ever fathom. That day a . . . spell was cast. And the laws of physics were altered. First, in a bubble surrounding the White Sands Proving Grounds. That stopped the runaway chain reaction *that* day, in *that* place . . .

"But they knew that Pandora's box was now open." She glanced at me. "Figuratively speaking.

"So the spell was designed like a chain reaction, itself. Once loosed, it traveled outward like infinitesimal strings of dominos, each altered subatomic particle tipping the next and so on; encompassing the globe: the land, the oceans, the atmosphere."

I gaped at the concept, trying to envision any kind of a natural conversion process—never mind the deal-breaking concept of a "magic spell"—encompassing an area the size of New Mexico . . .

. . . never mind the whole freaking planet . . .

. . . and then I took a mental step back. "Did it stop there?" I asked.

"Who knows?" She shook her head slowly. "Perhaps the circle closed within days, surrounding this planet in a protective bubble that seals it off from that particular subset of physics in the rest of creation. Or maybe it continues, even now, spreading beyond the solar system, creeping across the cosmos, and it will go on, forever, to the very ends of the universe."

Le Fanu began to giggle. "Oh, ha-ha! A good one!" she brayed. "Atomic bombs and magic spells! Good setup! You're a master storyteller!" Her laughter grew and took on a manic quality. "But the whole 'witches changing the physics of the universe'? You totally lost all credibility, there!"

I nodded. "At least in terms of the solar system and beyond.

Otherwise, it would be snuffing out stars as it spread out. Starting with our own."

Annie put a hand to her mouth. "No one thought of that . . ."

I reached out and touched her arm. "Annwn. Your great-grandmother. That's how you know all of this," I said. "She was one of the Wiccans that were there."

Annie Harkwynde nodded slowly. "Annwn Harkwynde was considered the most powerful Wiccan in the known world. And she was the only one who survived the casting's backlash."

"So, she's still alive?"

"Yes . . ." Annie nodded again. "But she was altered, as well. The blowback literally dislodged her from the Timestream, much the way you were displaced by a dimensional ripple several years and uncounted timelines ago. And now she is hunted by things that would not only destroy her—but cause the destruction of the world once more! That is why I need your help! In six days she must perform another spell, a casting of such magnitude—" Now she shook her head. "If she fails this time, it would have been better if the world had burned to a cinder."

Chapter Nine

Okay.

Quantum witchcraft and a pissed-off visitation from the Greek *Moirai*. Ancient war spirits—a dozen or so on motorcycles and a distant cousin driving the bus.

And a teenage thaumaturgist who wanted me to be her bodyguard and help her great-great-grandmother . . . do . . . what?

Granted, I wasn't sure of any of this and each raised multiple sets of questions that I was bound and determined to start asking. But before I could open my mouth again . . .

"I did not leave the plains of Persia to treat with you, seiðkonur," North told Harkwynde. "I am here for him—if he is The One that is foretold." Her brow furrowed. "*Hvordan er han passere mellom sfærer og gjennom tiden?*"

I held up my hand. "Stop! Just . . . stop."

Everyone looked at me.

"You were supposed to be explaining what you meant when you said that I was . . . unstuck . . . in time. Instead, I get some kind of story about quantum witchcraft and the Manhattan Project. I gather that this has something to do with you wanting me to help you get to your grandmother but, seriously . . . why are we still in Louisiana?"

Harkwynde spread her hands. "Relative State Formulation."

"What?"

"The Everett interpretation." She said it as if it explained what she had just said.

"Sorry?"

"Universal wavefunction."

I blinked. "You're talking about the multiverse?"

"Well," she said, "a subset of the multiverse. Or metaverse, actually."

"What's a metta verse?" Le Fanu asked, finally getting the last of her clothing back in place.

"It's the concept of multiple 'universes' coexisting and even interpenetrating each other within a larger, all-inclusive cosmology," I said.

"You mean like parallel universes," the vampire said.

I blinked. I was half-expecting Le Fanu to take the term "interpenetrating" and run in a different direction with it.

"Not just parallel universes," Harkwynde elaborated, "but, yes; that's what we're talking about here. Alternative universes, quantum universes, interpenetrating dimensions, parallel dimensions, parallel worlds, alternative realities, alternative timelines, dimensional planes—whatever you want to call them."

"MWI," I said. "The Many-Worlds interpretation. The quantum mechanics theory of alternative histories . . ."

Harkwynde nodded. "Asserting the objective reality of the universal wavefunction but denying the actuality of wavefunction collapse. Up until Hugh Everett hypothesized Original Relative State Formulation back in 1957—" She paused. "It was '57 in this timeline, wasn't it?"

I shrugged. I really had no idea.

She shook her head as if to clear it. "Up to that point science had always treated history as a single, unfolding timeline or reality. MWI, however, brought the view that 'reality' is a many-branched tree—"

"Yggdrasill," North murmured.

"—where each and every moment creates multiple quantum realities. Parallel outcomes."

"I get up in the morning and I put on my socks," I said, visualizing the argument. "I put on the brown socks or the blue socks. It wouldn't seem to make any real difference except maybe one pair color-coordinates better with my outfit and it—er—improves my social life just enough so that—"

"You get lucky that night!" Le Fanu jumped in, proving that predictability trumped surprise more often than not.

"—maybe I end up dating someone who might have otherwise turned me down."

"And you get lucky down the road," she persisted.

"But if I put on the other pair of socks, maybe my boss thinks that I don't know how to dress for success. And I get passed over for that raise or that promotion. Either choice changes my life in different ways. Small changes that create an ever-growing domino effect in a multiplicity of outcomes."

"So there are worlds like unto ours in which the differences are very slight and others where the changes are so many that they do not resemble each other in the slightest," North worked out. "We call these 'realms' where I come from."

I started to ask just where *did* she come from but Harkwynde continued. "Yes, and those closest to us in quantum resonance—with the least fractal dissonance—are the closest to us in parallel placement."

Everyone else looked lost but I picked up the thread. "Sort of like the visible light spectrum." Now they looked even more lost. "Just as an example," I continued. "The red and the violet wavelengths are at opposite ends. But variations of, say, the yellow spectrum are lined up so immediately adjacent to each other that you can tune across multiple frequencies in the shift without even apprehending the difference for a bit."

Annie nodded. "If you were to move between parallel worlds—the ones immediately adjacent to one another—the differences would be so small, so slight, that you wouldn't necessarily know that you were. Especially since each new timeline reset your frame of reference so as to adapt to the gradual and gradated differences."

"And you're suggesting that this is happening to me?" I asked.

"Oh yes."

"Ever since I was born?"

She shook her head. "Everything that I have been able to divine points to a more recent divergence."

"How recent?"

"Less than a dozen or so years. Perhaps much less: Time is relative, after all."

I considered. "Cthulhu's departure . . ."

Stryfe's eyes narrowed. "You treat with the Great Old Ones?"

"More like trick-or-treat. Heavy on the 'trick.'"

"So you are able to time-travel . . ." Le Fanu mused.

"Um, no," I said. "I can't go forward or backward in time." I looked at Harkwynde. "Can I?"

She shook her head no.

"Right. Because, among other reasons, moving forward or backward in time—within the same timeline—would set up a cascade of paradoxes. That's Time-Travel 101. Moving across parallel timelines, neither forwards or backwards but . . . well . . . sideways . . . means I can't do the obvious no-nos, like killing my ancestor so that I can't even exist to alter history to begin with—that sort of thing."

Gee, that sounded so neat and rational: like skipping across parallel timelines was as logical and effortless as a simple game of hopscotch.

Her follow-up question was postponed as the van began to slow and North called from the front, "Do you think the soldiers at this checkpoint are familiar with these perpendicular waves of penetration that you speak of?"

"I have a bad feeling about this," North muttered as she pulled up to the border crossing.

I wondered which part troubled her. The fact that there was a border checkpoint right on the state line? The presence of reinforced gates across the highway? The armed soldiers looking at us like we were a Taliban suicide squad?

Or was it the elongated gallows just twenty feet off the road where a half-dozen corpses dangled from bent necks? Two of which looked like they had been there for more than a couple of days.

Even more disturbing: A variety of lights were positioned to light it all up like a roadside tourist attraction.

"No one speak a word," Annie said, crawling up into the front passenger seat, "let me do all of the talking."

North glided to a stop at the broad red line that transfixed the road. A soldier wearing a highway patrol uniform approached the driver's side while four more moved to surround our vehicle.

"Lower your window and smile," Harkwynde told North. "Without the teeth," she amended as North seemed to be struggling to impersonate a barracuda.

The captain also wore a state trooper's uniform but there was no mistaking the military mien in him, his fellow officers, their weapons or the overall setup of the checkpoint. The patch on his shoulder said TEXARKLAHOMA DIST.

"Papers and identification," he said. His voice was not unfriendly but his right hand rested on the butt of his holstered sidearm and his eyes swept the interior of the cab in a practiced manner.

Annie leaned across and smiled at him. "You don't need to see our papers and identification," she said.

"I don't need to see your papers and identification," he decided. He consulted the clipboard in his left hand.

"We're not on the list of people you're looking for," Annie added.

"You're not on the list of people we're looking for," he verified.

"You can open the gate and let us through," she suggested, her smile growing brighter. But there were frown lines forming between her eyebrows.

"Open the gate," the captain told his men. "Let them through."

"Move along," she murmured.

"Move along," he told us. "Move along. And have a pleasant stay in Texarklahoma, ladies."

It took a couple of moments to let us through and Annie's smile hardened as we waited, turning into a grimace akin to constipatory concentration by the time we were back on our way.

"Holy crap," I said, once we were another mile down the road.

"Well, yes," she sighed, finally starting to relax. "Pull over as soon as you see a rest stop. I think I will . . ."

"What just happened?" Volpea wanted to know.

The travel plaza was well maintained with manicured landscaping and a plaza of flagpoles adorned with rectangles and triangles of fabric that suggested a veritable fiefdom of governmental sectors and layers. The public restrooms that were so clean that the adjective modifier "sparkling" would hardly have qualified as the least bit of an exaggeration. The only bit of clutter was the dozens of wanted posters covering the walls inside and out.

The faces and descriptions varied in age, gender, and former political affiliations but all were wanted for "High Crimes and Treason" against the "citizenry of the United States and Confederated Territories of North America."

Some were familiar faces, many were not.

The ones I did recognize belonged to senators and congressmen prominent enough or possessing the political longevity to have stayed in the forefront of my increasingly distracted memory.

Two were "ex-presidents" that I had never heard of.

Okay.

We either needed to find a gas station that offered maps or road atlases for sale or a public library with a nonfiction section on recent American History.

Given that it was after nine P.M. in the Midwest, the libraries were all closed for the night so we found the gas station first.

I thumbed through the maps while Annie paid exorbitant amounts of funny-colored money for filling up the gas tank.

If there were any significant differences between the original ink on these maps and the ones in the glove compartment of my own car, several space-time continuums behind us, I couldn't immediately tell.

The *latest* layer of ink was somewhat telling, though. Someone had meticulously drawn new borders to various subsets of states, organizing them into regional collectives. Like the Texarklahoma District that we found ourselves in now.

I picked through the newspaper and magazine racks for more resource material before we departed but it wasn't until Harkwynde opened an odd-looking browser on her smart phone and handed it to me that I got the info I was looking for.

Apparently World War III had already come and gone and been a rather limited event. No nuclear weapons. No missiles. A few spotty bombings. Most organized military operations had been directed at pockets of civilian populations within their own borders. The geopolitical disaster had been an economic meltdown, not an actual military war.

Global terrorism had been rendered moot by the malfeasance of global banking.

Practically overnight any financial asset that wasn't actually possessed in the physical sense, appeared to evaporate. Any money that wasn't actually cash on hand, became inaccessible and, eventually, ceased to exist.

When people turned to their banks their accounts were frozen. Banks turned to the interbank market only to find insufficient capitalization. The interbank market discovered that the financial markets accounting was so much vaporware. And governments—from the civic to the state to entire countries—could not go to the cupboards for their cupboards were bare. Or worse than bare: The currency that they had been stockpiling for decades turned out to be promissory notes. Bundles and bundles, stacked to the ceilings of their warehouse-sized vaults.

Oh, and that "cash on hand"? Relatively worthless as the monetary system it represented was largely invalidated.

The inevitable followed: chaos, riots, looting, anarchy. Martial law. Then subversion. Rebellion. Revolution. And full-spectrum collapse.

In the aftermath: rebuilding—i.e. restructuring, i.e. revision, i.e. correction, i.e. justice, i.e. people's courts, i.e. kangaroo courts . . . which brings us to the prosecution and punishment of those held responsible for the financial destruction of whole nations.

The last vestiges of the old governments did what they always did: Politicians expressed outrage and sympathy while refusing to indict any of their own.

The people, however, were hungry and jobless so they had plenty of time on their hands to seek their own brand of justice. Stockbrokers and bankers were hunted down and murdered by angry mobs. Their appetites whetted rather than sated once this was done, "the people" turned their attention to those who had permitted the fiscal recklessness that brought about their ruin. And they were not in the mood for long-term political reform.

The new "authorities" issued subpoenas and arrest warrants for those government officials deemed collusive in what amounted to local, regional, state, and national Ponzi-schemes. Once-upon-a-time "treason" had become an abstract idea when applied to megalithic governmental machines. But when Treason became the blanket charge against those deemed responsible for stolen savings and retirements, lost jobs and homes, and, finally, the scarcity of food and utilities—decades of mistrust and out-and-out anger at unresponsive and often corrupt administrations boiled over. "Political Malfeasance" was elevated to High Crime.

Even now, many years later, it seemed that there was still a widespread appetite for the public execution of mayors, governors, senators, and congressmen. Presidents went without saying. Every town, every roadside attraction we passed now had its own gallows. And, as if the example set was potentially insufficient: the bodies were evidently left to rot until such time as the connective tissue between head and shoulders could no longer support the body's weight.

"Do they all get worse after this?" I asked Harkwynde as I returned her phone.

"All what?"

"The timelines," I said. "The ones between here and where we're going?"

"I do not really know," she said, looking out the window at the darkness. "I've been here and I've been there. But I haven't been everywhere. And, even as we discuss this, a million billion tributaries appear on Time's great river. But I can tell you this: If we fail to arrive on schedule, every timeline will be far worse than the one we find ourselves in now."

Why? I wanted to ask. Almost did. But considered how every Big Picture Question got rerouted through a nuts-and-bolts side lesson in weird history. And I got a brief premonition of something so huge and terrifying that it could only be glimpsed around the edges, else the gorgon-like first presentation would harrow up the blood and turn the intellect to lunatic stone . . .

I cleared my throat. "So, how do we navigate? How do we find the right temporal tributary?"

"Your displacement is more recent than mine," Harkwynde answered, "so, perversely, you're powering these quantum leaps instead of me. However, I can channel the raw power of each phase shift and— steer—us after a fashion. Not as directly as I'd like: Sometimes the best avenue available is something like a move in a multi-dimensional game of chess: jumping alternate squares, performing an *en passant*, or even 'hooking' and stair-stepping. Time, in all of its fractal off- and on-ramps, is not laid out on a linear plane. It's a constantly rotating Rubik's hypercube with endlessly replicating polytopes into infinite dimensions and, since we're dragging others along our event horizon, it is more difficult to maneuver as precisely as I might like."

"What if we jettison some extra ballast?" I asked, eyeing the vampress.

"Hey!"

Harkwynde smiled. "We're getting close enough. Besides, I had to come here first to pick up something we'll need."

"Something you couldn't get in a kinder, gentler reality?"

Her smile was a few shades off from reassuring. "Something like that."

That didn't sound good. "How long after that until we can jump?"

"You've only been up for a few hours," she answered, "so I doubt for a while."

"And I have to be asleep for this?"

She nodded. "Unconscious. The deeper under, the easier for me to steer."

"We could stop and buy some cough syrup," Stryfe offered. "Cold medicine. Three or four bottles might do the trick. Five or six if we want to make sure."

"No," the other teenager offered in a slightly reproving tone. "I have to meet someone, so we'll catch a movie and see if it helps Christopher relax a little."

"A movie?" I said.

"It's on the way," she answered.

I looked up at the faded but still gaudily lit marquee touting the JAMES MAITLAND HORROR RETROSPECTIVE! Then I studied the old brick building that had seen better days *before* the turn of the century.

Before the turn of the previous century, that is.

I looked at Annie who was attempting to parallel park across the street and a half block down. "Why?"

"Are you sleepy, yet?"

I shook my head.

"Well then, since we're stuck here until you go night-night again, we might as well catch a show."

"Not really into horror," I grumbled, looking back at the neon-bracketed "Now Playing" sign. I reconsidered my words in light of the past decade or so of my life: "For entertainment purposes," I clarified.

"But its James Maitland," the teenager whined unconvincingly. "He's the American Karloff!"

"Never heard of him," I said as she started to get out of the vehicle.

"Bet you have," she countered as she made the keys vanish. "Besides, since we're going to his house, you can count the stale buttered popcorn as part of the research."

"Is he expecting us?"

"Oh Christopher!" She laughed airily as I reluctantly exited the van. "He's been dead for years!"

"Like that really matters," I muttered.

She wasn't kidding about the popcorn.

The lobby reeked of stale buttered something-resembling-popcorn that helped smother the scent of mold and mildew and twenty-three flavors of rot that lurked in the dingy ceiling tiles, the bubbled velvet wallpaper, and the trenched carpeting.

"The American Karloff," I repeated as Harkwynde bought the snacks. An old, faded poster boasted a lithograph of a man turning into a wolf. Slashy-type lettering crowned the image with: *Werewolves of Wichita*.

At least it didn't say: *I Was a Teenage . . . or I Married a . . .* in the title.

"You're probably familiar with his early work," she said as she handed me a greasy bag of wrinkled popcorn. "*You Can't Take It With You, Mr. Smith Goes to Washington, Destry Rides Again, The Shop Around the Corner, The Philadelphia Story . . .* his pre–World War II pictures. Before he . . . went in a different direction."

I racked my brain as we passed through the double doors into the cavernous auditorium. The name "James Maitland" rang a distant bell in my memory but there was nothing in my film lexicon regarding an "American Karloff."

The lights were still up revealing maybe five hundred fold-down seats, only a dozen of which were currently occupied. The theater had not only seen better days, but larger turnouts, as well. There were several young couples slouched in the back, waiting so obviously for the lights to go down. Several mature aficionados were scattered throughout the first seven rows, apparently here for the movie, itself. And not, one could assume, for only the first or second time.

Well, it *was* a James Maitland Horror Retrospective . . . right?

We found our seats in the middle of a sea of empty red-velvet chairs. Annie was on my left, Carmella to my right; Volpea, North, and Stryfe were in the row behind, presumably where they could keep an eye on anything and everything around us.

I could feel Ms. Shave-in-the-haircut's eyes boring into the back of my head as if she were trying to read my mind.

I was surrounded by attractive women—albeit two underaged—who seemed disinclined to let me out of their sight. That might seem like a dream date at the movies for some guys but my track record with the opposite gender had been . . . let's say less-than-encouraging since Jenny had died. Carmella wasn't the only vampire to hit on me, she was just the most persistent, dangerous, and annoying one. There had been an ancient Babylonian demoness, a powerful voodoo priestess, a Celtic sea goddess, a reanimated corpse of many parts . . . It was like there was a dating service for the damned—maybe zombiesonly.com, edisharmony, or mangle—and someone had posted my semi-dead profile without telling me. If so, my "match" algorithms had taken a turn for the worse.

The *Graeae.*

The jackal-headed woman with wings and a small division of vampires at her command.

And the Hell's Belles motorcycle gang—talk about a bunch of harpies . . .

The lights went down just as the light went on in my head.

Harpies.

The projector was throwing an animated commercial for the theater concession stand on the screen while a different set of illuminated figures were dancing in my brain. The creatures wearing motorcycle leathers had some birdlike features but that didn't necessarily make them the personification of those winged creatures from Greek mythology.

It could, however, make them *close* family members.

Nix . . .

"Nix" was the key!

I turned to Annie Harkwynde but her head was turned away. Presumably to look at the man who was making his way down the aisle toward us.

He was elderly and navigated the row of folding seats with some difficulty. He wasn't tall to begin with and the weight of years had bowed his head and shoulders until he appeared to be no larger than a shriveled boy. The wrinkles on his face distorted the flickering light in the darkened theater creating a shifting panoply of shadows and seams across his visage . . .

Oddly, he looked familiar.

I stared all the more as he finally reached Annie and bent further to give her a hug. "Ah-noon," I thought I heard him say. "You're looking younger every time I see you."

"Jerry, you old reprobate," she said warmly, stretching up to kiss a seamed cheek, "I'm so glad you could make it!"

"You kiddin' me?" he said in a high, quavery voice. "A Maitland flick *and* my favorite godmother? Wouldn't miss it for the worlds! This one or any of the others!" He sank into the seat next to her with a grateful sigh. "'Course, I heard we're doing this so at least some of 'em 'll be safe."

She reached over and patted his hand affectionately. "Jerry, you might want to keep your voice down a little. There are others here to see the movie and they don't want to listen to a bunch of nutcases going on about The End of Days."

He shrugged but lowered his voice. "It's a Maitland movie, Ann; who's gonna notice? And don't call me Jerry; you know I hate that."

She leaned over and whispered conspiratorially, "If you call me 'Annie' I'll call you 'J.D.'"

The phrase "mental whiplash" seems inadequate at this point. I was still suffering the aftereffects of my voodoo voicemail and alternate-history lesson complete with nuclear deterrence via spell craft on the side. I was finally starting to reassemble the Rubik's Cube of *Graeae* and Nyx and what was starting to look like a bunch of Keres and all this brought me around again to Mama Samm's pop quiz regarding Pandora's "box." My skull had officially become a cognitive washing machine set to "full load" and "extra spin."

So, I was a little slow in connecting the dots between a kid who got himself undead in a Chicago back alley nearly a century ago and the living, breathing nonagenarian two seats over. Especially as said vampire J.D. got himself dusted a few years back.

In my timeline, I reminded myself as I deciphered the once familiar features through the curtain of withered flesh.

I started to open my mouth and then closed it again. What could I say? *This* J.D. didn't know me.

Unless he knew the me that inhabited this timeline.

Was there another me in this timeline?

What was I like, the other me?

What if we met?

Would we cancel each other out like some kind of matter-antimatter mutual annihilation?

Did the other me cease to exist as soon as I entered this timeline?

And would a gap be left behind once I passed out of this timeline and into the next?

Was I erasing multiple versions of Christopher Cséjthes as I traveled across the multiverse?

And speaking of time-travel, what would happen if and when we arrived at Harkwynde's destination? I mean, would I keep on tripping afterwards, trying to "hang ten" and surfing the universal wavefunction until I wiped out in some kind of temporal undertow?

"Do you have it with you?" I heard her ask.

"What? Are you seriously asking if I opened it up and popped the canisters into my pockets?" He shook his head in disbelief. "Last time I saw you, you said to 'keep it safe' and 'keep it secret.'" He shook his head. "You know how they are about terrorism around these parts. There are cameras everywhere and more than a few scanners, I'm bettin'. The message said: meet you here. After the movie we can go get it and you can do whatever you want with it."

"We are kind of on a tight schedule here, kiddo."

Kiddo?

"Aw, Annie; it's a Jim Maitland classic. I haven't seen this movie since I hit fifty," he whined.

"Ten minutes," she told him.

Interesting. The J.D. I knew from my timeline had developed an interest in the cinema of the macabre rather late in his—er—unlife. Like nearly a century after he was turned. Absent the distractions of being undead, this J.D. had turned cineaste somewhat earlier . . .

My musings were derailed by the sensation of a hand closing around my own.

I turned and looked at Carmella.

She offered me an open box of red licorice whips and cocked an eyebrow. "So, is this flick just a slumfest with werewolves or are we going to get any vampire action?"

I looked down at her hand resting atop mine on the chair arm. "Doesn't that hurt?"

She shook her head slowly and her smile was every bit as gradual. "I was wondering when you were going to notice . . ."

I slipped my hand from hers and held it up to my face. Of course there was nothing to be seen in the near dark of the theater—especially with a dim, nighttime scene playing out on the screen right now.

I refocused through the infrared band and observed that my body heat was a good twenty degrees below human norms.

Like always.

I strained to see something more and—just for a moment—it seemed as though my hand was swarming with fireflies, each the size of a pinpoint. I shivered, shook the offending appendage, and looked away.

Carmella laughed quietly and caught my hand in hers again.

"I think it's your nanobots, dear Christopher. They are neutralizing the silver in your flesh," she whispered.

Yeah. That made sense.

The sparkling effect in the ambulance when they were sending a thousand volts through my chest with the defibrillator paddles. Probably rebooting whatever remnants of my nanite infestation were still viable. And, oh goody: If they were replicating and mining my violated flesh for the silver alkaloids, what might they start cannibalizing next?

"Don't look so worried," Carmella breathed in my ear. "Now we can touch each other with no barriers. My skin on yours . . ."

Oh, this was just getting worse and worse.

"Carmella," I growled. "Aside from the whole 'silver is poisonous to both lycans and necrophages,' I think you're forgetting that, by touching me, you open the means for me to bloodwalk beneath your skin."

"Oh. I haven't forgotten, my Doman," she cooed, leaning in even closer than I thought possible.

I shuddered. I wasn't sure whether it was the faintest sensation of the tip of a tongue just north of my earlobe or the suddenly shocking image of a hideously scarred man emerging from the shadows up on the giant screen.

"I was just talking about skin *on* skin . . ." she continued.

What might have been the actor's once pleasant face was distorted into three different time zones of suffering: past pain, present anguish, and the promise of torment to come. It was a horrific visage, once noble and yet fearsome. The twisted slash of a mouth opened and The American Karloff spoke.

I could barely hear him over Carmella's murmuring in my ear: ". . . but if you want to come inside me . . ."

But it was enough.

I shot straight up in my seat and grabbed the back of the seat in front of me.

"Holy shit!" I yelled. "It's Jimmy Stewart!"

"James Maitland Stewart," J.D. said as we took the exit doors out through the back of the building, "had some moderate success on the stage before arriving in Hollywood in 1935. He was Henry Fonda's roommate and romanced Margaret Sullivan, Ginger Rogers, and Norma Shearer back when he was pretty much unknown. Then Frank Capra got a hold of him and *pow! Bam!* His career took off like a rocket!"

Outside the air had turned cooler and Annie took my arm as we headed for the sidewalk on the side street. "Sleepy yet?"

I looked down at her. "Are you kidding me?"

She shook her head with a smile. "He doesn't know you. He was never turned. Never walked the path that your J.D. did in your reality."

"I figured that," I murmured.

"Then the Japs bombed Pearl Harbor," J.D. continued. "Maitland already had a pilot's license. Had logged over four hundred hours in the air. Got himself enlisted to do the right thing but The Brass decided his real value to the cause was making training and propaganda films."

"Sounds like my Jimmy Stewart," I said, glancing over at Carmella who was glowering at Annie from over Volpea's shoulder.

North was somewhere to our "south," protecting our flanks in the darkness off of the main street. Stryfe, the riddle wrapped in a mystery inside a bad hairdo, was enigmatically absent.

"Yours fly in the war?" the old man asked.

"Yeah," I answered. "He actually got to fly real sorties over Nazi Germany before it was all over."

"So did Maitland. Yours ever shot down?"

I shook my head.

"Maitland was. Critically injured in the crash. Survived. Didn't get much medical attention in the POW camps. Big movie star who made some Anti-Axis films in addition to the romances and the comedies: The Nazis liked high-profile payback. Not all of the disfigurement came from the original crash. They marked him up on the inside as well as the outside." The old man shook his head, a flash of anger crossing his features like seamed lightning. "Years later they said Jimmy Stewart disappeared behind enemy lines in 1943 and the allies liberated James Maitland from Stalag Luft in 1945. Personally . . . I'm not so sure he ever completely left."

Somewhere in the darkness behind us North spoke: "It is easy to put a man with scars in a horror movie. Lazy, actually."

"Once, maybe. Or twice," the old man allowed. "But Maitland's legacy of nearly sixty films after the war is a testament—not of his face but what was going on behind his face. Chaney, Lugosi, Karloff, Price—no one could go from 'Aw Shucks!' to 'Oh Shit!' in ten seconds like James Maitland."

The normally taciturn Volpea finally spoke: "You sound like his biggest fan." Her tone suggested that he would get no competition from her corner.

"I dunno," J.D. said. "But it's like he reminds me of someone."

"Who?"

"I dunno. It eludes me. Always has. But it's like someone I used to know . . . but never have."

I turned to Harkwynde. "You wanted me to see Maitland/Stewart. Why?"

She shrugged. "I had to pick up Jerry and . . ."

I gave her the eye. "And?"

"Our final destination is the Maitland estate. It doesn't hurt to ease you into the next level of understanding."

I arched my eyebrow. Or tried anyways: It was the one above my eye patch and there wasn't a whole lot of feeling on that side of my face. Except for some weird itching where my eyeball used to be. "So I need easing now?"

She gave me a long, measuring look. "Maybe I've underestimated your tolerance for weirdness."

"Oh, he's pretty intolerant when it comes to weirdness," Carmella intruded. "Always yelling at the zombies to get off his lawn, always killing the romance in necromancy, telling the heads of all of the undead clans in New York to suck his—"

"Carmella," I hissed, "I will leave you in the very next available timeline if you do not shut up."

She glanced at the teenager's amused smile and mimed a zipping motion across her own suddenly sober lips.

"Maitland retired to a life of solitude, in the Midwest," Annie continued. "He spent his last years and much of his fortune collecting antiquities from around the world."

"Antiquities . . ." I echoed.

"As you can guess, from seeing the kind of career the man had—from imagining the kinds of torment that he had endured—his collection skewed somewhat to the macabre . . ."

I groaned. "Are we talking *Warehouse 13* weird or—"

"Trouble," Stryfe hissed.

We had drawn abreast with the intersection and were looking down the street to where we had left the van.

It was still there.

Along with a dozen or so miscreants.

Chapter Ten

The seven or eight young men comprising our reception committee slouched. Against our vehicle. Lampposts. A mailbox. A couple of sets of entry steps.

Like pouty male models for some back alley Dolce & Gabbana catalog layout.

Despite the cool night air, several had unbuttoned their shirts or misplaced them entirely to display their pale, spotty chests and torsos.

This was not a flattering look for them.

Most of them were smoking and most of those made an exaggerated show of dropping their cigarettes onto the pavement and grinding them out in a manner that cried out to be appreciated as bad boy behavior and full of wicked promise.

Their leader sauntered toward us. He had the insouciance of a self-styled predator whose confidence had never been seasoned by the experience of biting off more than he could chew. I could almost pity him.

Almost.

"So. Ah. You ladies. You like the werewolf movie?" he asked, flashing an impertinent grin. He wasn't good-looking to begin with and his lack of acquaintance with a toothbrush and dental floss wasn't helping any.

He continued to slouch as he approached, walking as if he was being pulled forward by his groin.

I turned to Annie. "Don't tell me: This is where I'm supposed to start earning my keep as your bodyguard."

She frowned. "I dare not expend myself before our next transition. And I mustn't tap any negative energies regardless."

"Uh huh."

"Hey!" Groin Walker sneered at me. "I'm talking to the broads here, man. Why don't you take Gramps, there, and bone out? These bitches look like they want to party with real men."

The old me would have laughed off the attempted slur of my manhood and verbally reprimanded the young punk for his vulgar language in front of the ladies.

Of course the old me would have been home with my wife and daughter instead of consorting with witches, weres, and vampires (oh my). The new me had preternatural predatory instincts: My hands involuntarily clenched into fists.

Which began to burn and tingle, suggesting my nanites were responding to a sudden buildup of stress hormones. My amygdala was triggering a cascade of catecholamines across the neurotransmitters in my brain and I could actually feel the levels of testosterone, norepinephrine, dopamine, and epinephrine racing through my bloodstream like a quartet of thoroughbreds in some kind of hormonal Preakness.

I glanced down at my knuckles: nothing. No spines, spikes, not even a ripple. Just what was this new generation of nanobots good for? Besides letting Carmella Le Fanu get too close?

The vampress laid her hand on my shoulder. "Relax, Christopher, a 'party' sounds like a wonderful idea after such a dull and boring movie. Go sit down please. Volpea?"

Uh oh . . .

I shook my head, feeling my anger fade into pity. "Come on, Gramps," I told J.D. "Let's go over here and sit on one of the cars. We don't want to miss the show."

Volpea pushed past us to confront our gathering of cretinous miscreants. She started unbuttoning her shirt. "I *like* werewolf movies," she purred.

Stud-boy stopped, blinked, and then remembered his grin. "I'll bet you do," he agreed happily. She shrugged out of her top and went to work on her belt and jeans with one hand while handing off her shirt to Carmella with the other.

The rest of our welcoming party exploded into a frenzy of

disrobing just moments later. I was already envisioning them fleeing like panicked Charlie Chaplins, trying desperately to run with their pants around their ankles.

Volpea got naked first: She had a head start and wasn't wearing any underwear.

"Day-yam, Mama! You got one bangin' body!" stud-boy exclaimed. "Ohhhh! And you want to do it doggy style?" he asked as she got down on her hands and knees. "Guess that werewolf shit got you really worked up!"

He looked back at his gang, the master of all he surveyed. Their response was to tilt their heads back and howl like the Werewolves of Wichita had done in the movie just a half an hour before.

"Well, just turn around and brace yourself . . ." he continued as he started working his own jeans down his boney hips.

But Volpea didn't turn around.

She just . . . *turned*.

The transformation from sleek *Homo sapiens* to fanged and furry *Canis lupus* was fairly swift; still it took Volpea at least thirty seconds to finish the process. Plenty of time for our pride of poseurs to start running.

Except they didn't.

They howled again.

And sprouted tufts of fur as their bodies contorted and began reforming into shapes not nearly human.

Who was overconfident now?

A lone wolf against a pack of human hoodlums was one thing—the rest of us could watch the show at our ease. A pack of shifters against Volpea meant that I, for one, was going to get bloody. Maybe the rest of us before the dust settled.

I reached into my pockets and slipped my fingers into the knuckleduster grips of the tactical knives I'd brought along from the house. My gun was on the bus with four or five shifting weres between me and the door.

Whatever the concealed carry laws of this or any future timelines, I vowed that I wouldn't be making *this* mistake again.

I took three steps forward, raising my clenched fists and triggering the buttons that shot the four-inch blades out of the spring-loaded grips. The silvered edges were still emerging as two of the beasties shot past me. I whirled, knowing that I was already too late to protect the others behind me.

And saw a pair of shaggy bodies crumpled at North's feet.

She held a broad-bladed sword in her hand nearly half as long as she was tall. Its wide runnel was bright red with blood but, for the briefest of moments, I thought I could see glowing, golden runes beneath the crimson. The streetlamp behind her surrounded her with a nimbus of light and, for a moment, she looked otherworldly. Ethereal but sharp and deadly.

"Hermaðr," she called, "say that you will go with me when your moment comes!"

Carmella shoved her aside and strode toward me. "Head in the game, Cséjthe," she hissed as she passed me. "Fight now, flirt later!"

I swung back around and joined her in the furry melee.

Volpea was giving as good as she got—better, actually: If these things were wolves, they were the runts of the were-litter. Still, she was outnumbered and they were working hard to surround and flank her.

Carmella was used to lycanthropes being submissive to vampires back home but, somehow, this didn't seem to cut any ice with this particular fang gang. Here the attitude and the numbers were working against her and she seemed out of practice at extended brawling. Several wolves went flying through the air, intercepting lampposts, stop signs, buildings, and the corner mailbox with sickening crunch sounds. But she couldn't keep it up.

If they were merely wolves, their wounds would have put them out of action for a long time to come. Lycanthropes, however, have that damnable accelerated regenerative factor that makes it hard to put them down and then keep them down.

She was going to tire out before they would.

As for me? If they killed me, then I got what I wanted without breaking The Rule. If they didn't, then I got to work off a whole lot of pent-up anger and frustration. I plowed through a welter of weres, punching with the knuckle-grips and slashing with the blades as I fought to protect Volpea's six. Like Carmella and her furry subordinate, I was outnumbered, too, and probably the weakest fighter of the three of us.

But I had silvered weapons, which the others didn't. When I hurt one of them, they stayed hurt. When I put one down, it stayed down.

And one more thing—which two of the weres discovered as one latched onto a leg and the other, a forearm. My blood was still laced with enough colloidal silver to discourage juvenile lycans: Jaws smoked and muzzles were scorched. I was promptly released and the howling now took on a decidedly less triumphant sound.

Why my flesh was still toxic to them and not Carmella was a question I didn't want to think about until later. Probably not even then.

But fight now, brood later: This latest round of howling suggested a call for reinforcements. We needed to end this as quickly as possible. I pressed forward, toward the bus, where the clusters of fur were thickest.

"Listen to them," I quoted in a mangled Lugosi accent, swatting a wolf aside and losing one of my blades in the process. "Children of de Night: what music dey make." I grabbed a tail and swung one of the smaller beasties around and into a nearby car. "Well, time to *face* the music, kiddies!" The car's alarm system started to bray, pulling my attention. Taking advantage of my momentary distraction, one of the larger wolves leapt at me and would have easily knocked me down except for the timely intervention of a small, teenaged cruise missile springing off of the roof of the bus and intercepting it in mid-jump. Stryfe punched it on the way down and there was a small flash of light with a popping sound. She got back up and the wolf didn't.

"The stories are true," she said, glaring at me with large, dark eyes. "You really do talk too much!" As her fist came up I could see that one of the gems in her rings had shattered and a wisp of smoke was threading out of the scorched setting.

I ran at her and shoved her with my empty hand, knocking her back.

Before Stryfe even smacked against the side of the bus two more wolves landed where she had been standing, snarling and snapping at the now empty air.

"Pot; kettle, much?" I asked her as I kicked one in the head and grabbed the other by the scruff of the neck. It bit me once and then quieted, whining. "Bad doggie!" I admonished, throwing it at a fire hydrant. I missed and the furry changeling scrambled to its feet and slunk away.

I turned to help Volpea but it was evident that Carmella was the one in need of rescuing now. There was probably a half-formed thought somewhere in the back of my brain—one that said I could solve a fair share of my troubles by turning my attention elsewhere. But I wanted to die more human than monster so I waded toward her.

I was up to my hips in fur, now, and the currents were unpredictable as they surged away from a slowly advancing Valkyrie with a Lite-Brite sword that seemed to do everything short of going "snicker-snack." A couple of more snapping and popping sounds behind me suggested they were learning to avoid Stryfe, too. Volpea had bloodied enough of them that they were now turning their attention to Carmella as the least intimidating foe in the mix.

All except two, it seemed.

A pair of wolves had morphed back to their human forms and, ransacking the discarded clothing all about, had armed themselves with switchblades. One of them was the leader of the pack and he was holding a blade in each hand.

This is why you bring a gun to a knife fight. Unfortunately, mine was still on the bus and these two were still in the way.

"North?" I called over my shoulder. "Could use a little help here!"

It suddenly got quiet.

Or "still" actually: Everyone stopped moving. There was even a wolf hovering in mid-flight! I wasn't sure if it was coming or going, leaping into the fray or knocked backward by an undead fist. Any further perusal was short-circuited by Vana North who stepped in front of me.

The white shirt and black pantsuit were gone, replaced by a breastplate of shining silver. The rest of her torso was wrapped in a sheath of white nanofiber and decked out with an intricate pattern of ceramic plates that offered maximum protection while allowing for maximum movement. Her arms and legs were relatively bare save for ornamented greaves and longish bracers that went from wrist to mid-forearm. A network of fine silver chains was woven into an intricate headband that did little to tame the platinum locks that swirled about her head and shoulders as if teased by an otherworldly wind. I checked out the furry boots and then worked my way back up to the fur-trimmed cape that fluttered back from her shoulders.

"Nice," I offered. "Not exactly Tony Stark but far more practical than a chainmail bikini."

"Our traditions are strong but we are given leave to adapt to battle wherever and . . . whenever . . . we seek our claims."

"Wow, you really know how to sweet-talk a guy! How about you let me borrow your pig-sticker there to even up my odds with these West Side Story rejects?"

"No man may wield Villieldr save another *óskmey*."

"I'm guessing that's a 'no.'"

"Tell me that you will come with me when it is your time," she persisted.

"How about you keep your finger on the big Pause Button while I go relieve those two odds of their bodkins?"

She shook her head, enhancing the otherworldly floaty effect. "I am not here to aid you in your quest. I am only present so that I may guide you to your greater destiny. All else is mere distraction."

I turned back to the two street toughs, thinking I might as well still make a move while nobody else seemed capable of making their own.

And stopped as I heard a sound like a crack of thunder.

Which was the cue for everyone else to start moving again. Or rather coasting to another kind of a stop while looking at something to my rear.

I looked back over my shoulder. The gun was very large and very old: which was why the cocking of the hammer was loud enough to be heard over all of the huffing and the puffing and the howling. The latter sounding like distant police sirens now.

The old man had taken a shooter's stance in front of Annie and Vana—who, oddly, was back to where she originally stood. It looked as if she hadn't moved at all. Either to engage after dispatching the first two weres or for our little intra-temporal tête-à-tête.

So the return to her original duds was, understandably, a little less of a surprise.

"I got enough silver loads in the cylinder," J.D. announced, "to put down six of you before I have to reload!" His ancient voice had all the gravitas of a castrato sitting on a vibrator—which spoiled the Dirty Harry schtick somewhat—but his message was more than a little convincing: "Maybe more if you line up just right!"

The members of the pack that were still up and fighting took a few cautious steps back, growling.

"Skedaddle!" he barked. And the gun barked once, right after.

Fortunately, Annie was close enough behind him to prevent the kickback from knocking him on his ass.

More fortunately, the still ambulatory members of the pack missed this as they were already off and running in the opposite direction.

"Everybody on the bus," Annie ordered.

The sirens were getting closer.

We made camp an hour's drive northwest of town, in a copse of trees near an abandoned farmhouse.

There was a dry creek bed that shielded us from the distant road and we built a small campfire ringed with stones where the light was least likely to betray us.

Tepid blood packs accelerated my healing where I had been bitten. These weren't my first werewolf bites and I had no worries about turning shaggy under the next full moon: I was on the path to becoming a different kind of monster. "They asked for it" seems a poor measuring-stick for determining guilt and innocence, and my lack of conscience over maiming and possibly killing adolescent shapeshifters was just one more clue to my current progress into True Darkness.

Carmella had been mauled a bit more than me but showed little evidence of it now beyond her shredded clothing. Instead of tearing into a blood pack or changing into something a little less titillating, she sat back from the fire with a dreamy look on her face and obsessively licked her lips.

"Broke the taboo, didn't ya, C?"

She turned her face to me, a flicker of guilt passing across her shadowed features. "What?"

"Tasted the forbidden fruit," I said. "You drank lycan blood."

She frowned. "It was self-defense . . ."

I spread my hands. "I got no beef: not my rules. But what will you do when you go back home? What happens when the others find out that you've acquired the powers of a Doman?"

She looked away. "I don't know that I drank enough—"

"This time," I pressed. "But you can already feel a difference, can't you? Is Volpea safe the next time you feel that urge to get a little more of the power?" I glanced over at our were who was still in wolf form, curled close to the fire and trying to heal under the waning light of the setting moon. "When your lust for power and the desire to rule makes the next time almost inevitable?"

She swallowed and glanced at Volpea. Forced herself to look away.

"Lucky you," I said. "And lucky me. You won't need me anymore. You can just go home and rule without having to seduce me and play second fiddle. You can just go—"

"I can't go!" she suddenly hissed at me. Her voice caught and she choked back a sob. "I can't . . . now. I don't know what's back there . . . who's back there . . . in *this* time! I don't know what will be back there after you sleep and it's the next time! Or the next! Or the next after that! There is no 'back there' now that I'm with you! And if I leave? Then I'm stranded . . . whatever or whenever or whichever *here* is . . ." She cradled her head in her hands. "My old demesne is gone. My clan. Valentine . . . my brother. You're the only demesne I have now . . ."

Oh.

The whole freight train of questions and suspicions inside my head suddenly ground to a screeching halt. It didn't immediately occur to me that I should have said something reassuring. Comforting. Maybe gone to her and given her . . . what . . . a hug or something?

Maybe I was just too gobsmacked by the realization that there really was no "home" to go back to, now.

It hadn't really sunk in for me because everything that I had once valued—my wife and daughter, Lupé, Deirdre, friends, allies—had already been stripped away from me well before now. Abandoning my property, being a fugitive and on the run from the government was just the final stage of letting go of any formal ties to a past and a place of belonging.

Or maybe I didn't go to her because I was finally the soulless, selfish monster I had feared becoming since that unholy transfusion in that barn so long ago.

Yeah, probably the latter based on the look that Stryfe was shooting me from across the shivering flames.

Volpea grunted and began to shift back toward her human form. North stood over her and held a blanket so as to offer her a few moments of privacy as she dressed.

I looked around. Counted heads.

"Where's J.D.?" I asked. Any port of distraction in a storm.

Harkwynde sighed and waved toward a smudge of greater darkness on the far side of the old farmhouse. "He's gone to fetch the package."

"The package?"

"Sammathea D'Arbonne reached out and tasked him with collecting a necessary component to help us seal The Portal."

"The portal?"

"It's why we stopped off here on the way to The Wyrding. Apparently, a lead-lined suitcase with eight lead-lined vials was too much for one old man to lug around on his own."

I set my jaw and leaned in to catch a little more heat from the fire. "It's time," I said.

No one made any reply.

"It's time to talk about what this is really about," I insisted. "What we're running to and what we're running from. Who's who and what's what. Why are we here and what are the stakes?" I glanced at Carmella. "No pun intended."

She managed a small smile.

"All right." Harkwynde came and sat down across from me so that I could see her face just above the flames. She waited a moment as Volpea joined us, fumbling at the last buttons on her shirt.

"There are . . . Things . . . that exist Outside of this creation . . ." she began. The light of the campfire animated the shadows on her face, lending her words the air of a clichéd ghost story.

"Vampires," Carmella murmured.

"Lycanthropes," Volpea whispered.

"The *ásynjur*," came North's rejoinder from behind me.

The teenager shook her head and the bracelets on her wrists chattered as she gestured. "Things that lurk in the Dark and the empty places between the stars," she clarified. "Creatures . . . abominations . . . there is no apropos word or workable concept for such anathema. 'Things' is such a generic term and yet may serve best as such . . ." She looked past us at the darkness just beyond the firelight as if searching for an approaching threat. "*Things* that do not bear much scrutiny because to consider *Them* at any length is to invite madness and worse. And They . . . *hunger*.

"These Things do not exist as you or I, creatures of flesh and blood consuming calories from protein and carbohydrates." She looked at Le Fanu. "You think you're fearsome because you drink the blood of others? I speak of Things that feed from unimaginable troughs and prepare Their repasts in unholy kitchens. And They most desire that soft kernel which is the human mind. And, yes, Vampire, you are human by comparison to these . . . Things . . . of which I speak. Any mind of complexity and higher thought is unbearably sweet to Them, with all of its juicy emotions and less tangible synapses permitting egress into the human soul. Such Detestations understand that the flesh is merely a pathway, its mortification the means to access veritable feasts of agony and terror. It is these psychic and emotional repasts for which They lust with unholy appetites.

"They know those sweetmeats, the heart and mind, are most savory when carefully and artfully peeled of their pulpy husks."

A stick at the fire's heart snapped loudly and the rest of us all jumped a little. Harkwynde didn't even blink.

"These ancient and evil Intelligences should not exist in our creation. They are not only abominations of logic and reason, but defy the very physics of our own space-time continuum. Nevertheless, They press up against the barriers between our reality and Theirs and . . ."

"They . . . *leak* . . ." I said. Mama Sammathea D'Arbonne told me that once upon a time. In another time. Another timeline. Back before the storm dark waters of the Gulf of Mexico closed over the city of New Orleans and turned it into a New Atlantis beneath the sea.

Harkwynde nodded. "Yes. Just as you and I are able to pass through parallel timelines or realities, there are Things that will enter this universe if They are not stopped before time runs out."

"Well, I suppose that would be bad for whatever time-thingy these Great Big Ones get into," Le Fanu decided. "But as long as Christopher here could jump into another time-thingy and get away . . ." She cleared her throat. ". . . taking us with him, of course . . ."

Harkwynde's eyes were fixated on mine and I could tell she knew that the very same thought had fluttered through my mind like a demonic moth.

"Christopher," she said, "you remember Hurricane Eibon." It was not a question. Before Slutty Vampire could open her mouth again, she continued. "As awful as the images of Hurricane Katrina were on your television screens, they were mere Shadows of what really happened."

I nodded.

"To understand *Katrina* as Shadow you must understand the allegory of Plato's Cave." She nodded to me, passing the narrative baton.

I gestured at the pattern of firelight playing cross the side of the travel van. "Socrates believed that all of the components of this reality are but the shadows cast by the Greater Reality that is beyond our perception, beyond our ken," I told them. "Look at a table and a chair. They seem solid, they seem real, independent and whole unto themselves. But Socrates posited that they are but shadows of the über-table, the über-chair that exists in the Über-Universe beyond this shadowbox dimension in which we dwell. This reality is but a shadow-show on the wall of a great, ancient cave . . . projections of a more substantial Reality and we are but ephemeral reflections of the Source." I looked at Carmella to see if I'd lost her.

"Hey, I know what 'ephemeral' means. And I know all this uber-talk isn't about a ride-sharing service."

"This is true of the animate as well as the inanimate," Harkwynde continued. "We see Reality's Puppet Show, but not the hands beneath the foam and cloth and buttons and yarn—hands or, perhaps, other appendages that reach through flesh and bone and viscera. We do not perceive the marionette strings, where they lead up—or down—into the true galleries of the Puppeteers. Katrina was but the vaguest Shadow of Hurricane *Eibon*. Not an umbra or even a penumbra, but the barest afterimage, the hem of Shadow's cape."

I sat up straight. "You're not just talking about these Things leaking into one of our timelines, are you?"

Harkwynde stared at me, the shadows from the firelight aging her until she seemed almost as ancient as the *Graeae*.

"You're suggesting They could leak into The Source, itself."

North nodded beside me. "And cast Their dark corruption into every realm of Creation."

No one spoke. Even the crickets had fallen silent during Harkwynde's story.

I looked up at the night sky and found that I was suddenly blind to the blaze of constellations and the soft glow of the Milky Way. As if for the first time I was seeing only the emptiness between the stars and wondering what looked back.

Annie finally spoke. "Christopher . . ."

"You want me to plug the leak," I said flatly.

She shook her head slowly, sadly. "No. I . . . have people for that. I just need you to get me to them on time . . ."

"And?"

"Make sure that we live long enough to seal The Portal."

"Before these Things start to leak," I finished.

"That's the thing . . ." She cleared her throat. "They already have."

Chapter Eleven

"Okay," I said, gently slapping my hands on the tops of my thighs. "This explains the *Graeae* and, I'm guessing, the Keres." Everyone except Annie looked confused. Well, I couldn't see North who was somewhere behind me and Stryfe had her face turned away but I know *I* was still somewhat confused. And I'd played "the dozens" with Cthulhu and Nyarlathotep just a couple of years back.

"Okay, in the beginning, the world was without form and void and darkness was upon the face of the deep . . ."

"Is this going to be a Bible lesson?" Stryfe interrupted petulantly.

"No," I answered with a sugary pleasantness, "so pay attention, missy, so you'll know what's coming for you just before it cracks open your marrow and sucks out your soul." I resisted the impulse to mutter "if you have one" and continued.

"Unlike the Judeo-Christian story where the Spirit of Yahweh moved upon the waters and brought the light, the Greeks held that The Darkness was an actual entity, one of the Protogenoi before all the Mount Olympus soap opera that came much, much later. They named it Erebus, son of Chaos, and said that all was Darkness for untold eons. But this Erebus wasn't alone: He had a consort, sister and wife, the Queen of the Night. Her name was Nyx . . ." I looked at Stryfe. "With a '*y*.'"

"That old crone at the hospital," North said, remembering. "She said something about Nyx . . ."

"Yeah," I qualified, "that was Deino. I was asking who had sent them, the *Graeae*, and she said Nyx. I thought she was refusing when she said 'nix'—kind of an old colloquialism but not as old as the *Graeae*."

"She was answering you," Annie said. "She was giving up her mother."

"And what a mother," I agreed. "After some uncounted eons passed, Erebus and Nyx decided to have kids. And Nyx bore hateful Moros, better known as 'Doom,' and black Ker—'Violent Death' to her friends and, I suspect, the leader of our jolly band of vampire assassins back at *mi casa*. And let's not forget Thanatos, Mr. Death. That's with Daddy Erebus."

Stryfe was staring at me like I was a demented oracle. Which maybe I was, doing a Cliff's Notes quotage of the Greek poet Hesiod.

"And again the goddess, murky Nyx," I continued, "though she lay with none, bare Moros—or Blame, and painful Oizys, nicknamed Misery. Also she bare The Fates whom the Greeks called the Moirai." I was ticking them off on my fingers now. "And then there was Nemesis whose whole *raison d'être* was to afflict the race of mortal men . . . and Apate—or Deceit . . . hateful Geras, the *nom de plume* for Old Age . . . oh, and here's something you might like, Stryfe: hard-hearted Eris. Her name translates as Strife. *I* instead of *y*."

Stryfe's eyes widened—a feat I had not thought possible. Then she jumped to her feet and ran off into the darkness.

Annie gave me a look and then got up and went after her.

I looked over at Carmella. "Hey, she's your thrall. How come you're not going after her?"

The vampire looked at me as if she'd been dozing and I'd just awakened her with a string of non sequiturs.

"What?"

"Stryfe?"

"What about her?"

"For God's sake," I sputtered, "she's your vassal. Do you know nothing about the care and feeding of minions?" I reconsidered her clouded eyes and blank expression. "She's not really your minion, is she?"

"What?" She started out of her fugue state. "Of course . . . she . . ."

"Where did you pick her up?" I demanded more than asked.

"I . . . uh . . . asked for a Practitioner . . ."

"And what?" I pressed. "Someone sent her to you? She just magically appeared?"

Carmella stared back at me as if she couldn't quite process what I was asking.

"Never mind," I said. She seemed to relax. I couldn't. This Stryfe was just a kid and maybe a tad unstable but she had infiltrated the largest vampire demesne in the country *and* had glamoured an Elder into believing that she should be brought along and treated as a member of her inner circle. She had jumped on a werewolf and punched it into unconsciousness. And she seemed to bear me some enmity so until I knew exactly what I was dealing with, I needed to pay more attention.

North joined us in the firelight. "You were just getting to Achlys and her crew," she prodded.

"Oh yeah, the Death-Fates: the ruthless avenging Keres. Sometimes known as the Erinyes, sometimes The Furies. I get the impression you know these harpies?"

She nodded, staring into the flames. "Achlys. Death Mist. Not my realm but they get around. Technically, they're not the same as the Erinyes who are vengeance daimons. Or Harpies, for that matter."

"Right, right. I remember, now: The Harpies were the daughters of Thaumas and Electra."

"And like The Furies," she continued, "they are agents of punishment and vengeance. The Keres, however, are The Fates' Death Squad. It is not about who deserves what. Their purpose is to kill any and all who are designated by their mother as requiring a permanent solution."

"Nyx? That bitch!" For a moment I was very angry. And then it hit me: On the hit-list of a Protogenoi goddess and immortal assassins looking to put an end to yours truly . . . the certain, almost inevitable outcome would mean I would finally get what I wanted without breaking that damnable Rule.

Maybe, I thought grimly, things were starting to look up.

"Tell me that you will come with me when the moment comes," North said softly.

I looked sideways at her, her pale face half hidden by the long fall of silver and white hair, the rest playing peekaboo in the shadows cast by the firelight.

"And go where?"

She tilted her head up and looked to the north. "There is a realm called Glaðsheimr. The name means 'bright home' in the Old Tongue. I will take you to the Valhöll where you may know a rest you have never known. You will know the company of men who understand honor and sacrifice, great loss and how great deeds may undo the great wrongs that cast shadows upon hearts and souls. You will be honored and celebrated and . . . looked after."

I sighed. "Sounds like a reward . . . but isn't it really a recruitment program? You and your 'sisters' are really just rounding up the best warriors to fill the ranks in the afterlife for the eventual Day of the Wolf. In the end aren't they all just Fenrir-fodder? Sounds like my kind of karma: trading one monster apocalypse for another."

"It—it's not like that. You—you think yourself a monster, unfit for heaven or happiness. But I can take you to a place that will honor you as you deserve! Where your cup will never be empty, your belly never empty—"

"Your bed never cold?" Carmella interrupted loudly. "You're poaching, whitey. Go peddle your Viking river cruise up somebody else's fjord!"

I put my head in my hands. Where was Anaplekte—the Ker of Quick, Painful Death—when I needed her? Maybe that had been Moira, my supposedly clueless intern who had ridden shotgun in the semi. Annie and Stryfe eventually returned to our little circle of uncertain light.

Now, in a complete reversal of her former behavior, she refused to look at me.

"Well," Harkwynde said as she tossed a couple of sticks on the dying flames, "where were we?" She settled herself back down on the other side of the fire.

"The motorcycle gang was actually these Greek death-spirits who've been ordered to kill Cséjthe for the goddess of Never-ending Night," Volpea answered from the shadows. "When they do, the Valkyrie here wants to take him home and get him eternally drunk until the Twilight of the Gods."

And now Stryfe was back to staring at me.

"Sleepy, yet?" Annie asked.

Actually I was.

And that's when the night ended abruptly.

Flash-bangs—the "soft" slang for flash grenades—do more than just cause temporary blindness. The loud, concussive blast adds temporary deafness to the whole sensory package. And they were especially effective in the quiet darkness that we had been enjoying before.

I was grabbed, forcibly pushed into the ground with my arms pulled behind me, and a moment later my wrists were pinched together with zip-tie cuffs. From the sound of it the others were getting a similar treatment.

Then I was hustled through the darkness to the road where a half dozen police vehicles were just arriving. I was bundled into the back of a patrol car and driven away.

I shook my head and yawned, trying to "pop" my ears but we were halfway back to town before I could communicate with any coherency. "Am I being arrested?" I asked, trying to shift positions to take the pressure off of my wrists and arms. "What are the charges?"

"You have to right to remain silent," answered a voice from the front seat. "Why don't you use it right now?"

I considered my options—beyond being silent, that is.

My last run-in with the "cops" turned out to be an undead hit squad and had contributed to my death by 18-wheeler. Considering how people had turned out to not be what and who they seemed this week, I had my concerns above and beyond making bail in a strange timeline.

I could try to *dominate* and control them with the ole look-into-my-eyes-and-obey-the-sound-of-my-voice shtick—but my success rate was iffy at best and probably not as effective if there were two in the front seat and I was only working with one eye now. That and the driver wasn't likely to take his own eyes off the road.

If I could relax enough and manage to concentrate I might be able to escape by *translocation*. Sadly, I'd never mastered the technique without leaving my clothes behind. And then what? Stranded by the side of the road, alone and naked in an unfamiliar reality with a fifty-fifty chance of my wrists still cuffed behind me?

Let's call that Plan D.

I had a more immediate problem right now: The adrenaline was wearing off way too fast.

My last sleep cycle had been disrupted by a little resorting under the bed in the travel van and a cursed R'lyehian voicemail as a wakeup call. Add one street fight with a bunch of shapeshifters and throw in a little temporal *pas de deux* with a Norse *dísir*, and I had all the makings of a melatonin meltdown.

The urge to just lay my head back against the top of the seat and catch twenty—or maybe even thirty—was getting stronger with every mile. But if I did, I would drift into another adjacent reality and leave the others behind given our current separation. I couldn't just abandon the others because I was up past my bedtime. At least not two teenaged girls and an old man . . .

I began grinding the heel of my right foot on top of the toes of my left and alternating the discomfort with a little tongue biting to keep me lucid the rest of the way into town.

Processing wasn't much different from my own timeline—having never been formally arrested, I based this on the accounts of my more dodgy acquaintances and years of watching gritty cop shows. A nocturnal lifestyle is not particularly diverse in the TV fare on basic cable.

Photographed, fingerprinted, divested of wallet, keys, pens, all pocket contents—including my spring-loaded blades, I was led to a smallish, two-bunk cell and told to behave myself. I looked at the cell's other occupant as the cops exited the lockup area and asked, "So they do coed in this timeline? How progressive."

Stryfe regarded me with a glum expression. At least I think it was glum: sort of the same sour expression she usually wore only with considerably less enthusiasm. "I told them that you were my father."

"Oh boy. Now I'm really in trouble."

She sighed. "We're all in trouble. This is a reality where werewolves are out. The authorities are armed and trained to deal with meta-humans and they don't take any chances. Two different cops tasered Annie and then worked her over pretty good. The old man got planted pretty well, too . . ."

"What about you?" I asked, still feeling the deep throb in the back of my own head where the baton had pressed my face into the ground while I was cuffed.

She gestured with her now ringless fingers. "Some bruises. Nothing special: Annie tried something, I didn't."

"Volpea? North? Carmella?"

"I don't know about the shield maiden; I think she split as soon as the goons showed up. These guys are more paramilitary than your average local-yokel fuzz. They tranked the wolf before she could barely start to turn. They know about werewolves and they know how to take them down . . ."

"Instead of bear, they came loaded for wolf," I mused. "It's almost like they were specifically looking for us."

"I'm betting the Beastly Boys turned informant as soon as the cops arrived," she growled. "Probably told them we were way more dangerous than we really are, just to preserve their street cred. As for your fuck-buddy, I don't think they know that she's a vampire. Or that such things are real."

"Whoa," I held my hands up, "language, young lady! And there's no carnal involvement there whatsoever, no matter what she'd like to believe."

"Yeah? Well. She acts awfully familiar for someone who's been set straight on boundaries." She peered at me in a deliberate manner. "You *have* set her straight . . . haven't you?"

I walked over and sat on the other bunk. "Multiple times."

"Maybe you weren't very convincing."

I stared at her. "Taking this whole 'daughter' role very seriously, aren't you?"

She looked away. "You're right. It's none of my business."

I cleared my throat after a moment. "So where is your father. The real one, that is?"

She seemed to shrink in on herself and still refused to look at me. "I said your personal stuff is none of my business. My personal stuff is none of yours, either."

"It's just that you seem a little young to be running around on your own."

She snorted. "Running around?"

"Infiltrating vampire enclaves, glamouring the undead, taking extended road trips with men of questionable morals?"

That got a ghost of a smile and she glanced my way.

"Aren't you a little old to be running around, unattached? Unencumbered by the domesticity of a spousal unit and several mini-me's?"

I blinked. Thought about saying something equally flip. Or withdrawing into the old, familiar hurt. But this kid seemed way overdue for something genuine so I answered her honestly. "I was married," I said, trying to keep my voice neutral without sounding defensive or totally divorced from still caring. "I had a little girl."

And I would have been fine if she had left it alone.

"So what happened?" she asked, unfazed by the news. "Who walked out on who?"

Normally I would have come back with "whom."

I didn't though because my wife and daughter were the one subject that I could never be flip about even after the spill of years. "They died," I told her matter-of-factly.

Even though I tried to say it unemotionally, even though I didn't act like her assumption was offensive and hurtful, given what had happened to them . . . the color drained out of her face.

"What . . . ?" she asked in a small voice. "She never said . . ." She looked away for a long while and I didn't spare her from her new introspection.

"How did it happen?" she finally asked, still unwilling to look at me.

"It was an automobile accident. I pulled onto the highway and didn't see the semi . . ." I was suddenly struck by the synchronicity of the two encounters with 18-wheelers: the first killing my family all those years before, the second killing me just days ago.

"How could you not see a semi?" she whispered. Her eyes asked the next question: *Were you drunk?*

"I had just been drained," I answered. "Infected with the Dark Gift and just starting to change. But I wasn't bitten. The necrophagic virus that is transmitted through the saliva was absent. I only caught the viral load that came with a crude transfusion in an old Kansas barn. So the change was different, incomplete. I was still suffering some PTSD and the aftereffects of Bassarab's mind control. I was driving disoriented . . . and . . ."

"So it wasn't your fault."

"It *was* my fault!" I snapped, my voice suddenly raw with long-suppressed emotion. "I *should not* have been driving! I was being macho, doing the 'man's gotta do what a man's gotta do' bullshit! And I got us all killed!"

I wanted to finish. To say the rest. But I suddenly couldn't.

Until she prompted: "You look pretty good for a dead man."

"Yeah. Lucky me. I'm still here. Even though I don't want to be. But life and the universe don't care about what you want. You'll figure that out someday if you live long enough." I was angry now. That was good. Because being angry was better than feeling the other thing. The awful thing that was pressed up hard against the other side of angry, trying to climb out of the black well of forgetfulness. And I was on a roll.

"I'm infected with one-half of the necrophagic virus that turns the living into the undead. So I'm still here. I should have died in that barn. The people who did this to me let me go because they thought it was a kindness. It wasn't a kindness. I should have died in that barn. Do you know what the last good memory of my wife and daughter is? Both of them screaming just before the truck hit us and tore everything apart! That's my last *good* memory! Because my next memory is waking up in the morgue next to their bodies. Next to what was left. Jennifer . . . my wife . . ." I felt a catch in my throat but soldiered on. "And my baby . . . Kirsten . . . she . . ." I tried to clear my throat. "All the king's horses . . ." *I couldn't clear my goddamned throat!* "I was denied the kindness of the embalmer's artifice. No postmortem magic was remotely possible. Maybe the closed caskets were a comfort to the others but I can never unsee what was dumped on those autopsy tables . . ." And suddenly I was inexplicably weeping again though my tear ducts had grown dry and desiccated all those years ago. "I. Should. Have. Died. Not them! Not them!"

I was hugging myself now, unable to talk about what came after or how their remains were further violated by malevolent entities serving an ancient necromancer. There are horrors beyond words that human thought can scarcely bear.

Suddenly there was another pair of arms around me and we were crying together. I didn't know why and for the moment I was beyond caring.

Except that there was comfort in another pair of arms and that all of the tears on my cheek were not exclusively my own.

And that my sorrow was strangely moving for an angry young woman who had apparently known losses of her own.

Of course a moment like this wasn't destined to last.

"Well, isn't this a pretty picture."

Stryfe released me like I was a hot stove. I swiped at my eyes and peered at the trio of men who had entered the cellblock while I was distracted and now stood on the other side of the bars.

One was a uniformed cop, presumably one of the local badges where we were currently incarcerated. The second, judging from his uniform, was military—or on his way to a costume party, masquerading as a full-bird colonel. The third wore a black suit, black tie, and a white shirt that was probably crisp eighteen hours or so earlier. Though he said nothing, the body language of all three made it pretty clear that he was the one in charge.

"You," the cop said, pointing his nightstick at Stryfe, "back up against the far wall."

She looked at me and I nodded.

"And you," he told me as the girl reluctantly complied, "turn around and back up to the cell door with your hands behind you." It was a reverse of my entry into the cell when they had snipped the zip ties off of my wrists. Now I felt the cold, steel press of regulation handcuffs cutting off the circulation below my wrists before the door was unlocked and I was spun and hustled out of the cell block.

We ended up in a small room at the back of the station. Cinder block walls, a couple of sturdy chairs, and a steel table. There was no glass, no one-way mirror that you would expect in an interrogation room. The cop pushed me down into one of the steel chairs and recuffed me so that my hands were trapped between the three metal struts running vertically up the back.

Then he left.

On his way out, he offered the colonel the handcuff keys and his nightstick.

G.I. Joe took the keys and waved off the wooden club.

That was the good news.

The bad news was that the man in the black suit reached inside his jacket and produced a gray, metal tube and snapped his wrist as the door closed. The rod telescoped out to three times its original length and locked with an ominous "click."

"I think it's time I either got my phone call or a lawyer, now," I said. It had already occurred to me that there might be guarantees of neither in this timeline and I felt my mouth growing dry before the last words were out.

"Terrorists," the man in black said in a calm and utterly reasonable voice, "don't get lawyers. Or phone calls."

And before I could finish processing the word "terrorist," the grey metal blurred at the edge of my vision and turned into a Fourth of July Christmas tree, complete with skyrocketing colored lights and spinning, whizzbang ornaments that exploded across my suddenly diminished vision. My head rocked back and I blinked before the pain rushed in to fill the sudden void in my skull. Vaguely, I seemed to understand that I was being spoken to but the sound hadn't quite caught up with me, yet. I tried to move my lips but nothing seemed to be working.

Black Suit leaned down and in. "I said, do I have your attention, now?"

I wasn't sure whether he'd broken my zygomatic bone or just opened my cheek down to the muscle. It hurt like hell and I had trouble focusing on his next words.

"Tell me about the uranium. What is the plan? Suitcase nuke? Dirty bomb?"

Uranium? I shook my head and immediately regretted it. Uranium might explain a lead-lined suitcase with lead-lined vials inside. But in asking my questions as to why we were being pursued by a Greek chorus of monsters, we'd only gotten as far as a history lesson on the first atom bomb test and the Everett hypothesis of Original Relative State Formulation. Then something about a portal (or *The* Portal) and the cosmic love spawn of H. P. Lovecraft's three-way with Arthur Machen and Robert W. Chambers. . . .

Questions were rolling around the pinball game inside my head, bouncing back and forth off of bumpers of throbbing aches and flippers of flaring pain. I didn't know why a long-dead vampire from my original history had showed up alive some eighty years later, in an alternate timeline, with a sample case of fissionable isotopes. And, even if I did, explaining the time-traveling, dimension-hopping, magical mystery tour with a teenaged witch was going to go over so well and insert-sarcasm-emoji-here.

Lest I seem like I was all logical and analytical and developing a carefully crafted plan of escape, the truth is that stuff was all spinning around in the back room utility closet of my brain like socks in a dryer set to Tumble Dry. Meanwhile, out on the front porch, I was all fight-or-flight and so not inclined to sit still for the next blow.

It wasn't just pain-avoidance. If Guantanamo Bob beat me senseless, I'd probably drift out of this timeline and leave the others behind. Maybe good for me in the short run but—if Harkwynde's intimations were true—a worse fate for me and the multiverse would be the result if the mission went off the rails now.

Whatever that mission specifically was. . . .

Instinctively, I dropped my head forward, shifted my weight as best as my cuffed arms would let me, and launched myself, chair and all, headbutting my tormentor while he was still leaning in close.

Had I been human, I doubt I could have done anything more than move just enough to startle him. Had I been a full-fledged vampire, I would have snapped my cuffs and made a couple of box lunches out of my captors. Instead I had just enough enhanced strength and reflexes to hit the man in black, full on, in the face.

There's this myth that the right blow can shatter the maxillary process, driving the shards of bone back and up into the cerebral cortex, either killing your opponent or lobotomizing him into a turnip. It's a bunch of hooey as the region around the sinuses is mostly cartilage. But a powerful blow there is pretty disabling: He stumbled backwards, his face a sudden mask of blood. He wobbled a bit, then his eyes rolled up in their sockets and he toppled over backwards, hitting the back of his head against the steel table with a loud clang.

Maybe I had killed him after all.

I know I had just given myself a mild concussion and it hurt like hell! Still, better than another hit from that steel rod.

Or a bullet from the M9A1 the colonel was unholstering!

Still crouching with the steel chair riding me piggyback, I tried to crab-step sideways and spin around to catch him with one of the chair's legs.

I missed but he danced backwards and I bought myself an extra three seconds.

Which probably wouldn't have done me any good if the heavy metal door hadn't suddenly slammed open and gone flying off of its hinges. It struck the officer a glancing blow and he fell to the floor, the pistol slipping from his grasp.

Carmella Le Fanu strode through the doorway and kicked the gun away before he could regain the sidearm. Then she kicked him. He was lifted off the floor, flying back and up to smack against the far wall. He flopped back down to the floor and didn't move after that.

She walked around behind me and nuzzled my neck. "I hope you appreciate how easily I could take what I desire," she murmured in my ear. Then she reached between my wrists and broke the chain holding them together.

I stood, rubbing some circulation back into my purpled hands and took in the vampire's disheveled appearance and redder-than-red lips.

"I'm guessing you would have been here sooner but you stopped for a snack," I said as I went to the colonel and searched through his pockets for the handcuff key.

"Two or three, actually," she agreed as I unlocked each of my metal bracelets. "But it was this new ability to pass through locked doors, that took a little figuring out."

"Were you able to keep your clothes on?"

Her look of astonishment morphed into a slow smile. "Why? Did you not want me to?"

"No! It's just that when I—never mind." Now was not the time to explain my sartorial difficulties with translocating.

"I thought you might want these," she smirked, handing me the envelope containing the personal effects the cops had confiscated during my arrest. The green laser pointer and the colloidal-silver atomizer were intact but the pepper-spray pen was missing. My wallet was devoid of cash but what I'd had was probably unspendable in this timeline or whatever might come after, so . . . .

"Do you want any of this?" she asked, picking up the bloodied man in the black suit and looking at him like an after-dinner apéritif.

The blood would accelerate my healing but we were "the bad guys" inside a police station so the clock was ticking and there were higher priorities. "I need to get Stryfe and the others out."

"You could leave her here," Carmella suggested. "I know she annoys you."

"Hey, *futue te ipsum!*" Stryfe said as she appeared in the doorway.

I went to her and gave her a hug, saying, "Language, young lady." And then glared back at the vampire. "You're the one that annoys me. She's just a kid with authority issues."

"Hey, you don't know me," the kid said, her voice muffled against my chest.

"Looks like someone wants to know you," Carmella snarked.

"Go suck yourself!" was the muffled reply.

"That's enough," I said. "So, do you have the keys to the other cells or do we have to wait for someone more responsible to show up?"

"Unnecessary. Just giving the furry one a chance to hotwire a car before we blow this joint." She sank her teeth into Black Suit's throat and began to feed again.

I looked at the broken door and the shattered lock in the frame. "So, I'm guessing they know how to handle shapeshifters and meta-humans," I speculated, "but vampires are an alien concept or not even a literary convention in this timeline."

Carmella dropped her latest meal and wiped her mouth. "Hmmm. That *would* explain a few things."

"Where is Annie?" Stryfe wanted to know.

"Opening doors for Volpea. They're both a little wobbly. I came to get you so she'd have time find us a ride." She shrugged. "I figured that it would save us an extra trip."

"So Annie's okay?" I asked.

Stryfe muttered something under her breath behind me as we walked to the outer door.

"She'll live," Carmella allowed, "though she's still pretty buzzed from the tasers. The old man, though; cops worked him over pretty good for an old geezer. Volpea had to carry him."

I nodded, remembering the werewolf's strength back when I'd gone all ride-a-long in her head a couple of years back. "What about North?"

"Haven't seen her. Pretty sure she decamped when the fuzz showed up."

I glanced at the two-hundred-year-old vampire. "Really? You used the words 'decamped' and 'fuzz' in the same sentence?" I should have been focusing on getting the hell out of Dodge instead of snarking at the walking corpse: I smacked into the edge of the doorframe and stumbled through a drunken two-step before falling to my knees. That steel rod had really rung my bell and my head was still vibrating.

Carmella knelt next to me and wiped the sheet of blood on my cheek with her thumb. "You really should feed, Christopher. Better your tormentor than an innocent and you are going to need the strength." She stuck her thumb in her mouth and sucked it.

It occurred to me that she should be writhing on the floor and screaming now as my blood turned her mouth into a smoking and blistered ruin.

Instead she smiled dreamily and went: "Mmmm . . ." in a blissful voice.

Slightly terrified, I grabbed the doorframe and leveraged myself back up. "Let's get the hell out of here."

Stryfe caught my arm in the hallway and helped steer me to the back door. Carmella opened it and I blinked as we exited into the remains of the night. Sodium vapor lights illuminated the parking area and a predawn glow was starting to limn the eastern horizon.

There wasn't enough room between the squad cars to walk two abreast—much less three—so I was pushed and pulled between two rows of black-and-whites to an all-black "paddy wagon" parked on the far side of the lot.

Volpea scrambled out of the passenger side of the cab just as the engine coughed to life. Running around to the rear of the vehicle, she opened the back doors indicating that we should climb aboard.

We were just three feet away when a voice behind us yelled, "Stop! Or I'll shoot!"

I turned and grabbed Stryfe. "All aboard, kid," I said as I lifted her off the ground and tossed her into the van. Volpea jumped in after her and turned back to assist her mistress in boarding. My expenditure of energy in tossing Stryfe out of the line of fire had used up what little reserves I had and my legs took on the consistency of old gelatin. Carmella had one foot on the bumper and one hand in Volpea's grasp as she turned back to me and grabbed my arm.

As she lifted me, somebody ran up behind me and whacked me with a ball-peen hammer. I was thrown against the far wall and whacked again as I slid down and rolled over. As bad as my head hurt, the hammer hurt more.

Only there was no hammer.

Just a lone cop, standing just beyond the back entrance to the precinct station, emptying his service revolver at us. The police van jerked into motion and the back doors flapped wildly as we picked up speed, leaving the copshop behind.

A sharp left and we were out of the line of fire save for one stray bullet that must have ricocheted off of one of the doors and whined past my ear.

Somewhere, maybe off my left shoulder but sounding a couple of miles away, I could hear a litany of curses from Carmella Le Fanu. She must have caught a bullet and it sounded like it hurt like hell. Vampires are used to thinking of firearms as a nuisance as they have an immunity to normal ordnance. But we were trespassing in a timeline where werewolves were out so I was guessing the cops were armed with silver bullets—which have nearly the same effect on undead flesh as lead slugs on humans. Not quite as deadly but a lot more painful with wounds that burn like tiny, flaming pits of hellfire.

My tolerance for silver kept me from experiencing the red-hot agony from the preternatural ammo. In fact, I wasn't feeling much of anything—which was not a good sign at all. I tried to roll over and get up but could barely flop onto my side. My legs were a distant memory, my arms seemingly disconnected from anything I wanted to do. Volpea sat on the floor of the van, leaning back against the bench seat that ran along the side wall. Red blooms stained the front of her shirt and she panted rapidly, her face twisted in pain and her features blurred between her canine and human aspects.

Stryfe was suddenly blocking my vision, bending over me and trying to sit me up as well.

"Are you all right?" she asked as I hung in her grasp like a rag doll. It sounded like she was talking in a tunnel.

I opened my mouth but the blood in my throat prevented me from talking. Lung. I thought. And maybe a kidney. I hiccupped a little and felt a crimson tide start to dribble down my chin.

Her eyes widened in horror and turned luminous. "Da-daddy?" She started to sob. "Puh-please d-don't die . . ." Her voice faded to a whisper. Or maybe that was just my hearing.

Nope. More profanity from Le Fanu as she bumped the kid aside and did a quick assessment of my wounds despite her suffering.

"You're dying, Cséjthe!" she said, looking a little more freaked now. "Why are you dying?"

Well, duh . . . shot . . .

Wait a minute . . .

Daddy?

"Why aren't you healing?" the vampire demanded.

Good question.

Nanites on the fritz?

Necrophagic virus at low ebb due to blood abstinence?

God finally letting me off the hook?

I didn't know and I no longer cared.

Except . . .

Daddy?

I coughed and felt my left lung fold like a meat origami.

"Kuh . . . kir . . . stin?" I murmured.

Stryfe was back, next to Carmella Le Fanu. "Don't die," she whispered. "Please don't die! I'm sorry I was so mad!"

I looked past the purpled hair and the punk/goth makeup. Past the once surly, now grief-shattered mask and saw . . .

My daughter.

The little seven-year-old girl who died with her mother at the intersection of 103 and Highway 69, just outside of Weir, Kansas.

Maybe a decade older now than when she died and I was launched into my second "life" and left straddling the worlds of the living and the unliving.

Kirsten.

"I'm sorry, baby," I whispered. And then had to turn my head and spit out another mouthful of blood. "I'm so, so, sorry . . ."

"No, Daddy!" Her eyes overflowed and she swiped at a trickle of snot that was running from her nose. "You can't die! Not again! Not when I've just found you again. Please! Please don't die!"

"You need blood, Christopher!" Carmella was talking now. "You need to feed to heal. You'll die if you don't!"

I just stared at her. Vampire blood might be tasty to other vampires under certain circumstances but it had no restorative powers: I could drink Carmella dry but it wouldn't save me and she knew it.

"Volpea," she said. Her eyes were nearly as luminous as my daughter's. Trick of the light: Vampires don't cry.

I rolled my eyes back over to the wolf lady.

Volpea was in bad shape. Dying, possibly.

Dying for sure if I took any more of her blood that was already pooling about her splayed legs and back.

"No," I gargled.

A switchblade appeared in Stry—Kirsten's hand and she bared her arm.

"Take my blood!" she pleaded. "Please!"

My heart began to hitch in my chest and I smiled a red smile, blood drooling down to my chin.

"Wouldn't. Be. Enough."

"Daddy!" she wailed.

"Sorry. Honey." I held onto my smile though I wanted to curse: God was playing His cruel game of cosmic keep-away all the way out to the end.

She whirled and began pounding on the wall separating us from the cab of the vehicle.

"Stop the truck!" she screamed. "Stop the goddamned truck!"

And then it stopped.

My heart stopped.

Everything stopped.

Chapter Twelve

There was brightness above and darkness below.

Silver and gray mists swirled around me and I felt lighter.

Released.

Barely tethered to the pain and the heaviness and the years of regrets and sorrows, I felt myself . . . not so much rising as gradually defying gravity—like a forgotten balloon from last month's birthday party adrift behind the sofa.

Vaguely, I was aware of the others: my daughter from another timeline, pounding on the forward wall of the van where it backed the driver's seat in the cab, her fist frozen in mid-strike. The vampire, raging at me in her impotence to find the blood that would save me and my refusal to save myself at the expense of another life. The look on her suddenly stilled features might have convinced me that she . . .

But I knew from past experience that the undead were incapable of any kind of love that exceeded their own self-interest.

Weren't they?

The werewolf was a hunched statue of petrified agony, her Lycan blood only hesitating in this extended pause between heartbeats before it would spill anew from her non-regenerative flesh.

She was dying.

As was the old man riding shotgun up front with our underaged witch at the wheel. He slumped on the edge of my peripheral cognizance like an ever-deepening bruise trapped in ice while the young woman beside him blazed like a bright, blue star in the growing darkness. The barrier between the cab and the rear compartment now seemed as insubstantial as my fading extremities.

At greater distance—an almost impossible distance, I almost imagined that I could "feel" the minds and hearts of post-mortal/postmortem family. Lupé, Deirdre, Zotz from a parallel Mesoamerican Hell, and my reborn children and my once and future wife. It was as if they were at the other end of the universe and yet the barest breath away, on the other side of Eternity's veil.

Soon.

I would be with them all very soon.

Sometime soon.

Eventually . . .

But nothing was happening.

The stillness—along with the darkness—went on and on.

"What?" I demanded, attempting to get up.

Nothing much came of it. Despite feeling all floaty, my body—or what passed for corporeal existence between the ticks of Eternity's timepiece—refused to do much of anything.

"Mikey?"

Neither he nor The Universe deigned to answer.

"Quit screwing around!"

The Silence was Cosmic.

"Oh, what! Did! I do! Now?"

No answer.

"Really? No Heaven? Not even a decent Purgatory? Sartre said: 'Hell is other people.' Did the entire Afterlife unfriend me? Oh, come on! If it's going to be Limbo, don't I get a horizontal pole and a little Caribbean music? Or some Chubby Checker?"

Nothing.

"Am I On Hold? Aren't I entitled to an endless loop of annoying music and automated voice messages?"

The empty Silence dragged on.

I sounded pissed but it was just petulance and whistling past the graveyard. The real anger kicked in the moment I finally caught my existential breath.

"Hey, God? Yahweh? Hello? Allah? Waheguru? Yoohoo! Paging

the Supreme Being! Brahman? Pangu? Any Supreme Being! Ukko? Jupiter? Or do you prefer Zeus? Maybe I'm personifying too much: Hey Universe! Fate! Destiny!" I shook my head. "Maybe I should ask for Janus, the two-faced god: That seems about right! Talk about a real dick move! Put the daughter I lost in another timeline next to me on a Whovian road trip and not tell me until it was too late! That's really fucked up!"

And now I felt myself at the edge of a really dark, deep abyss.

"I'm . . . really . . . fucked up . . ."

I pounded what passed for my chest in Oblivionville. "I can't even die now!"

I wanted to weep.

Or, at least, I felt like I should. But those tears had left the station a couple of lifetimes ago and there simply wasn't anything left. I shut the hell up and just floated.

And meditated.

Or I tried not to. I tried emptying myself of all thought, all emotion.

For a few moments—or whatever moments in timeless eternity actually may be—I seemed to be uncoupled from everything. The past, the present, any desire for a future . . .

But I just wasn't hardwired that way. My mind turned back to thoughts of my daughter . . .

Not the sullen teen witch who had manipulated vampire aristocracy and spent the last couple of days working through her angst for a father who abandoned her by dying in her timeline.

But the little girl I knew and remembered for those seven brief years from the day I held her in my arms as they cut the umbilical cord . . .

. . . to the day her life was cut short along with her mother's . . . and I awoke on a table in the morgue, next to their remains.

Kirsten.

Jenny.

Funny how, even after all of these years . . .

All of the attempts to tamp down those memories . . . those emotions . . . lock them away . . . bury them down deep . . . forget . . . try to move on . . .

Even learn to love again . . .

It was still my first family's faces that now came to me in the silvery darkness.

The little girl who asked her daddy to check her closet and under her bed every night for monsters.

And her mother who had married the guy monstrous enough to kill them both by being behind the wheel when he shouldn't have.

It was my fault. I should have been the one to die. And stay dead.

So what was the point?

I had asked myself the question so many times that it felt as if any answer would ultimately seem meaningless.

Yet, here I was, staring into The Void and The Void refused to make eye contact. Fuck you, Nietzsche.

A man dies. His wife and daughter lie mangled on stainless steel tables: the handiwork of an 18-wheeler and his own inattentive driving.

Maybe my resurrection was cosmic justice. Divine (or not so divine) punishment. Another life/sentence granted to atone for the two lives so carelessly lost in an irretrievable instant.

Over the years I had selfishly imagined that I served some greater purpose. Every encounter, every small victory over the greater darkness, had seemed to me a possibility that whatever Light existed in a universe filled with Dark, might need a catspaw, some sort of freelance agent who could operate on the fringe and go where angels fear—or at least do not deign—to tread. Neither cherubim nor seraphim, just a guy who could get his hands dirty in a just cause and (please God) be sacrificed like a pawn in a celestial chess gambit to serve some kind of meaningful—what? Non-life? Un-life.

Unreasonable.

Unbelievable.

Laughable, really.

If the Universe had a purpose for me, it was to drift through eternity, always failing, always losing the people I loved. Family. Friends. Complete strangers who had the misfortune to cross my path at the wrong moment.

If there was a Higher Intelligence—Michael's existence notwithstanding—it either had no interest in me or saw my best value as a diverting game of Kick-the-Can.

No.

I had no value.

No special, cosmic meaning in the greater scheme of things.

The only purpose in my existence was what I made of it.

Putting one foot in front of the other. Trying to do the right thing. Even as I'd come to understand that there was no bargaining with whatever Higher Powers might hold the keys to . . .

Salvation?

Happiness?

Peaceful Oblivion?

My only "Purpose" was what I could knit together out of the frayed edges of my unraveling existence.

Even if that purpose was nothing more than babysitting a couple of witches and whatever alternate timeline rejects that got pulled into my orbit.

Which was now just another unfinished task that had slipped through my fingers like so much spilled blood.

So *much* spilled blood . . .

A new voice spoke and it took me a moment to realize that it wasn't mine . . . or any other coming from inside my (metaphysical) head.

"I come in search of a doughty warrior. Art thou a pouty warrior, as well?"

I turned my gaze outward and beheld our recently missing Valkyrie.

She was all glowing light and shades of whiteness, floating against the gathering darkness that surrounded us. Her pale skin was luminous as was the barely-there samite gown that clung and gaped to remind me that the Valkyrie of legend were celebrated for their other services in Odin's Hall as well as their battlefield reconnaissance and retrieval skills.

"Well, look at you: Quippy Longstocking," I rasped, demonstrating a fleeting degree of willpower.

She smiled. "I do not know that name, *seggr*, but I know that tone. You yet defy The *Myrkr*."

I started to say that it wasn't like I had much of a choice but she floated right up to me and embraced me. Her ice-blue eyes were now inches from mine and a much more alluring distraction than the emptiness all about us.

Then her mouth was on mine, tasting of honeyed wine and

promising feasts beyond the trestle tables groaning with food in Valhalla. Thinly veiled flesh filled my hands and I was reminded that the ancient Norse description of "cup bearers" for the Valkyrie had double meaning . . .

I let her kiss me. I mean, it wasn't like I had anything else to do. And there might have been a little reciprocation . . . a hint of tongue on my part . . . but just a little. I didn't want to be launched into The Void with any more guilt than necessary.

The kiss seemed timeless. Whether that was because we were inhabiting a temporal null-zone between the frozen beats of my dying heart—or because it really was *that* kind of a kiss—it seemed to go on far longer than any oral osculation I could readily recall. It certainly went on long enough for me to run down the not-too-inconsiderable list.

At last her mouth moved from my lips to my ear. "Are you ready to come home with me?" she murmured.

I almost shivered: There *was* a little tongue.

"No," I murmured back.

"Then let us . . ." She stiffened in my arms. "What?"

"I'm not ready," I said softly.

She drew back and stared into my face, my eyes.

"I can't leave yet," I said.

"You cannot stay," she countered. "Your wounds are mortal!"

"Maybe. But I don't have to go with you," I answered, picking my tone carefully. "And you can't take me against my will." I wasn't really sure about that but I had to bargain with what I had. Which was essentially nothing.

"You have nowhere else to go!" she protested.

"Don't I?"

She pushed back and drifted a little more than arm's length away. "If you did, you would have gone by now."

"Maybe I want a little peace and quiet before I go . . . to my other destination."

A sly smile started to leak but slipped back into her lips' new impassive alignment. "Very well. I'll just keep you company until you are ready to depart."

I smiled back. "Sort of undermines the whole 'side-trip for the peace and quiet' plan." Then I frowned. "Unless . . ."

Her face subtly changed again: no hint of a smile this time.

"Unless," I repeated, "you've been deliberately blocking my transition. Holding me here against my will, making sure I will choose you instead of some other, less Twilight-of-the-Gods afterlife."

The look on her face confirmed it. God wasn't messing with me. Or even *a* god.

As usual, it was one of The Help.

Now I pushed back. And, to my surprise, I actually moved. Put a little more distance between us. "If this is how you're going to play it, you can forget all about my signing on for the *Ragnarøkkr* festivities. I'm betting that you can't hold me here forever: You and your spear-siblings have other jobs to do and one guy is not worth all the downtime that would be involved."

Her smile slipped in pieces. "Do you value yourself so lightly?"

"I value myself enough to not be taken for a patsy. I value myself to *decide* for myself. You may be one of the Choosers-of-the-Slain but you forget that the slain may want to make their own choices."

"And what choices do the slain really have?" she asked.

"I don't know. But the fact that you're blocking me tells me that I have options. And the fact that you are interfering in those options makes me want to *not* go with you over all other choices."

North—if that was her real name—just floated and stared back at me. Judging from her expression, this was the first time in thousands of years that she had encountered any kind of resistance from her battlefield pickings. Still, she was going down swinging: "I offer you the fellowship of heroes, a place of honor in the halls of the gods, the . . . companionship . . . that could sooth your weary heart . . ." She looked at me with that expression I've never been able to fully read in a woman. "And if you do not find me comely . . . I have sisters . . ."

I held up my hand. "All right. You don't have to sell the package. Compared to wearing white and sitting on a cloud for eternity or roasting like a marshmallow next to child molesters and politicians, it's a pretty sweet deal." I gave her my own look. "And you're comely enough, Vanir. But a little cold for my tastes. You'll forgive me if I've never had cause to think of you in that way. You haven't exactly been throwing me the 'come hither' vibe until all of a sudden I'm the next best thing to dead. Especially since you want me to come to Edda-world to fight for another hopeless cause." I took what felt

like a deep breath even though I was pretty sure my lungs were
vestigial appendages now. "Here's the problem. You're worried about
the Big Bad Wolf—"

"It is not Fenrir, alone!"

"Yeah, I know: *Jörmungandr*, the world-serpent and the giants'
Surtr and *Hrym* with all of their frosty *jötnar* kin . . ."

She let a frown slip out. "You treat the Doom of the Gods as if the
end of the world is an inconsequential thing."

I shrugged. "It's an end followed by a new beginning. At least
according to your *Vafþrúðnismál*." I saw the look in her eyes: *Yeah,
baby; after I figured out who else was riding the bus I did a little more
research on the web.* "It says that a new and idyllic world will arise
from the sea and will be filled with self-planting fields. You'll get a
new Adam and Eve—Lif and Lifthrasir—to reboot the human race.
Likewise, gods will be reborn: some old, some new. Wickedness and
misery will be banished from the new order. Nice for your realm.

"Meanwhile, back in Pandoraland, it sounds like we've got a
dimensional portal that's about to blow open. I've seen a couple of
things from the other side of that barrier and let me tell you: the giant
squid-faced thing would make Fenris his lapdog while the floaty,
tentacle horrors would eat your frost giants like so many popsicles on
a hot summer's day.

"And that may well happen because these Things leak! If They get
loose in one timeline, They'll eventually infect the others. Like stones
skipping across the waters, They'll launch Themselves in search of
new prey and drop down wherever the human cattle draws their
unholy hunger . . ." I shook my head. I was starting to sound a little
too much like Mama Samm. "They will spread, like a dark stain until
every realm that they can access is as black and mad and hopeless as
Their own dread dimension. And, make no mistake, they will come
for your realm before They're done."

Her eyes were pools of electric blue in her softly glowing face.
"And you think you can prevent this?"

I shook my head. "Not me. No. I'm in over my head. My money's
on the kid. Little Miss Witchy Woman and her friends. The ones
waiting at this Weirding thing that she wants me to get her to. And
her grandmother. Or great-grandmother . . ."

Or, more and more likely, faux grandma.

"Whatever. Point is, the fate of the universe—or a few square blocks of inhabited real estate—doesn't fall on my shoulders for once. I can't tell you what kind of relief that is. But I can't just walk away. Even if she's the key to the lock, I still have obligations—"

"To her?"

Those luminous eyes could drown a man but I clung to my metaphysical floatie and stared back. "To my world. My time. All of the times within my realm. And whatever realms might lie in the paths of Darkness if It isn't stopped. So, yes: to *her*. Ever heard of 'save the cheerleader, save the world'?"

She shook her head.

"Never mind. So. If I am already dead . . . if I can't go back and finish this . . . this . . ."

"Battle." She drifted a little closer.

"Yeah . . . mission . . . quest . . . whatever label you want to slap on my latest sucky internship in Fate's laundromat, then it's got to be something I can't—as usual—do anything about. The Universe, Itself, has to tell me: Game Over; Creation has decided to commit seppuku and my services are no longer required . . . desired . . . and I have no choice but to end up where I end up."

"Even if it's here?" she asked.

I tried to sigh. It felt like an act of some effort in a place where breathing was a lost art.

"What I'm trying to say is: I'm. Not. Running. Away."

"Accepting your reward—embracing eternity when your time has come—that's not running away," she protested.

I shook my head. "It feels like it. Something really, really bad is about to happen in my little corner of the multiverse. I had a job to do in plugging that leak. Even if I wasn't the guy to fix it, I was supposed to make sure that somebody actually got there and lived long enough to fix it. I'm not supposed to be the hero this time but if the hero fails and worlds die because I didn't show up? Eternity is going to suck big time. The world can expel me, reject me, totally kick me out but I'm not going quietly. It can move me away, along, on out . . . but I won't move myself. To turn and head toward the light when so much dark is gathering behind, feels like a weasel move. So, thanks but no thanks. I'm not moving or moving on until I'm absolutely sure that there's no way back in."

"Or something else moves you," she said.

I just looked at her without speaking.

Suddenly we had company.

Three more women faded into view over her white shoulders. The redhead had a spear and a winged helmet, the brunette held a great and fearsome-looking tapestry bobbin, and the blonde unshouldered a large water pot that she turned upside down and sat upon.

"What?" the redhead snorted. "This is the one that the fuss is all about?"

"Not now, Skuld," North hissed between clenched teeth.

"Skuld?" I echoed. "You brought *Norns* as your backup?"

"She didn't bring us, sweet cheeks," the blonde answered with a bit of a smirk. "She always sneaks off when she's going slumming."

"Let me guess," I snarked back: "Verthandi?"

"I am Verðandi," the brunette said, waving her spindle like a bastard-sword. "She is Urðr."

"Right," I said, pointing at the redhead, blonde, and brunette, in turn. "Skuld, meaning 'Debt' or 'Future.' Urðr, meaning 'Fate.' And Verðandi, which means 'Happening' or 'Present.'"

"Oh, clever for monotheistic infidel!" the brunette applauded.

"Sisters," North gritted, "I am working here!"

"Don't mind us," Urðr answered, "we're Norns; we like to watch."

"Yeah," Skuld chimed in, "we like to watch a mortal treat a member of the Vanir like a Valholloback girl."

"So not helping," North muttered.

"So, they're not here to help you?" I asked.

"They are never here to help me," she hissed.

Good, because the odds weren't exactly in my favor when it was just one-on-one.

"Well, that's harsh," Urðr said. "Maybe we should tell Freyja . . ."

"Freyja would enjoy the show," Skuld agreed.

"It's been ages since she's seen an *aptrgangr*," observed Verðandi.

I looked at North. "They're threatening to tattle on you?" I looked at the Norns. "Hey, ladies . . ."

They turned their attentive gazes on me to see what the heretic would say next.

". . . go Frigg yourselves!"

Skuld and Urðr looked scandalized and popped right back out, leaving Verðandi. The brunette considered the fearsome spindle in her hands, seemed to examine the thread count wrapped about its length and core, and then gave me a long look. There was the hint of a smile before she, too, disappeared.

Oh boy.

I turned back to North. "Now, where were we?"

"What . . . if . . ." she asked hesitantly, "your quest *was* finished? What if the realm of Midgard was safe and all accounts were settled? Would there be aught to prevent you from rising to your rightful reward?"

I thought about the anguished cries of a daughter from another timeline I had never known. Then I remembered those who waited for me in the Realm of the Fae. Waited, but perhaps, no longer for me; their memories of their former lives and associations bleached to whiteness by their exile among the Faerie?

Maybe their place was no longer meant to be my place, nor mine, theirs. Maybe I was best forgotten along with the hurt and chaos that seemed to find me wherever I sojourned . . .

"So, what are you asking? Would I come with you once my task was done? Once the world—or worlds—were safe and Pandora's pan-dimensional nexus portal locked, sealed, bound in chains, and tossed into an active volcano? Is that what you want to know?"

"Yes. Why would you not?"

"Maybe because I was being coerced?"

"And if there was no . . . coercion? No interference?"

I gave it a few seconds thought. "I'd be less inclined to be disinclined."

She drifted a little closer. Almost too close. "And if—instead of interfering and coercing—I was to be more helpful, even providential, in helping you fulfill your quest and find closure, would you . . . be more . . . inclined . . . to come with me after?"

"What? Go off with you to live as a hero among heroes? Feast all day on the finest victuals and quaff ale by the tankard? I don't drink ale by the way so—"

"We have a realm's worth of beverages," she interrupted.

"And then there's the sleeping arrangements," I continued. "Would it be bunkbeds in a drafty barracks where wine-soaked berserkers snore like thunder?"

"You would have your own chamber, my lord, befitting a hero who has vanquished inhuman foes as well as their mortal servitors."

I arched a brow. "And room service?"

She drifted even closer if that was even possible. "I would see to thy every need."

Despite my grin I had to swallow. "Every need?"

She leaned in and licked her lips. "Every. Need."

"You would."

"I . . ." her lips swept in close to my left ear. "And my sisters . . ."

Dear God!

"And if—in the meantime—I could send you back to Midgard's realm and you were able to complete your task?" She leaned toward me with a look of expectancy.

I fought the shrug. "I would be grateful."

"How grateful?"

Grateful dead?

I cleared my throat. "You're asking if I would come with you, then?"

"Not immediately after. You might live to be an old man."

I snorted.

"When your natural time comes round again," she offered.

"Ask me then," I answered.

She closed her eyes. "I will," she said. And drew a bright silvery dagger from the sheath on her girdle.

She drew near again and, surprisingly, put the blade to her own throat instead of mine.

"I do not know what the blood of the Vanir or the Valkyrjur can do for you, seggr, but it is the best I can offer you." And she drew the edge around the side of her neck to where a human's jugular would pulse. Light seemed to spill out from her wound. Then I saw a clearish fluid drool forth, catching the light from some internal source and reflecting and refracting it like liquid diamonds.

"Drink quickly," she murmured, pushing herself against me, "before my flesh begins to knit." Her hand came around to grasp the back of my head and she pushed my face to the crook of her neck when the slope of her shoulder began.

I did not require further instruction. I pressed my mouth to her wound and began to drink her sparkling essence.

And it did sparkle: She tasted of moonlit ice crystals and Icelandic fire. Inside my head the beat of pale wings against the snowy night seemed to throb and echo in the chambers of my heart. My pulse began to pound in a rising crescendo and I felt a gathering warmth against the coldness of The Void. My body seemed to take on weight and substance and, as it become more solid, my torn flesh began to close. I was leaking blood again but the leaking was slowing. And, as the veins and arteries were closing, new blood was starting to chase the old through the pipelines, throwing sparks of light in all of the dark corners as it spread through my flesh. I had come back from the brink of death before having drunk the blood of the Elohim but this was different. It was like sipping brightness from a full wintery moon, swallowing constellations of stars from an arctic sky, quaffing from the aurora borealis . . .

Sparkling surges of life danced and swept through my being like a blizzard. I felt my soul assuming flesh once more and the body I had known returned . . . cleansed . . . as if it had been sent out for a thorough laundering while I was absent and now it was back, swept clean, detailed, and reenergized.

The essence of immortal shieldmaiden. Potent stuff.

As I further solidified, the woman in my embrace seemed to become less substantial. And, out of the corner of my eye, The Void seemed to close in, revealing off-white walls spattered with flecks of red.

The white flesh beneath my lips was nearly closed now and I pulled back after giving the side of North's creamy neck one final lick.

"Ewwww," said an all too familiar voice behind me.

The Valkyrie seemed almost translucent, now, her inner light brightening as her outer flesh seemed to wane like a dematerializing specter.

Cold metal was pressed into my hand as she drew away. "Here. You will need this. It is blessed by the Allfather himself but you may need the ceremonies of a *Hvítakristr goði*."

Although my healing seemed complete I was still a bit dazed. "What?"

"A priest. Of the White Christ. Do not clean the blade; it is pure silver and mayhap my essence will further wound The Darkness when the hour is dire." She leaned in and kissed me briefly, a touch of the lips this time. All chaste fondness as she was taking her leave. "Live long, seggr. But look for me when Time has come round again in its final turn . . ."

And she faded from sight like a séance candle guttering down to nothingness.

I turned and saw that I was still in the back of the police van.

And, sitting together on the bench running the length of the prisoner transport were Carmella Le Fanu and my alternate daughter.

Staring at me with ridiculously wide eyes.

"Your *eye*," Stryfe whispered.

I touched my face and found my eyepatch was knocked askew. And—*ouch*—my right eye had grown back. I blinked.

I wasn't just alive; I was as good as new.

Chapter Thirteen

Somehow, somewhere, we had time-shifted while I was dead or, at the very least, unconscious.

Harkwynde, Le Fanu, and my daughter had made the transition with me.

J.D. and Volpea had not. Fatally injured, their bodies had not transitioned with us during our next phase shift into another alternate chrono-synclastic infundibulum. As to why the undead Carmella Le Fanu was still along for the ride and the dead-dead had been left behind was a question for a theoretical metaphysicist.

I certainly had no clue as to why I was still here.

Instead, Harkwynde and Le Fanu had other questions for me.

The little witch wanted to know what sorts of intel or insights I might have gained while wandering the astral realm, why the Valkyrie had deigned to bring me back, why I was gifted with a dagger to counter the forces of Darkness, and what sort of blessing/consecration/ritual I was expected to obtain for my newfound weapon.

I wanted to know why J.D. had been tasked with getting us eight leaded vials of uranium isotope.

Harkwynde didn't know other than Mama Samm D'Arbonne had made a very specific request for the U-235 and that this particular timeline was our best bet for access and the personnel able to pull it off. Beyond that, she had no clue. It was strangely comforting to know that someone else was as much in the dark as myself. Even if

179

Harkwynde had only been able to reacquire four of the original eight vials on our way out the bullet-riddled exit door into our current parallel "present."

Le Fanu wanted to know what Valkyrie blood tasted like. More importantly, she wanted to know if it gave me any superpowers.

Kirsten, on the other hand, was totally mum.

Clearly, she was still dealing with the anger/abandonment issues of parents who had died when she was young, vulnerable, and very impressionable. And wrestling with the urge to reconnect with the father who had "magically" reappeared after all of these years. It didn't help that her briefing for this particular mission included stories of my "hookups" with werewolves, vampires, elves and exotic monster sorts. Nor her own, up close and personal observations of Le Fanu's obnoxious vamping and my coming back from the dead thanks to some nasty hickey action with a scantily clad Norse demigoddess.

It all suggested a lack of reverence for her dearly departed mother and other self.

Despite the passage of years since our/their deaths across the multiple realities.

And she had been "Stryfe" so long that she chafed against her dead/beat dad calling her "Kirsten." I understood, of course, but, despite the piercings, tattoos, and purplish hair, she was still my baby girl. Calling her—or even thinking of her as—"Stryfe" was hardly an option anymore.

So, I spent the better part of the next ten hours of travel, taking turns at the wheel and retelling my sort-of offspring what had happened in my timeline.

Waking in the morgue, next to the bodies of *my* wife and daughter. My flight and fight for survival as the unique qualities of my partially transformed blood drew the attention of vampire enclaves across the country. How I was thrown into confrontations with ancient evils while building a coalition of unlikely and, often, unwanted allies.

Kirsten was less forthcoming about the events in her life. After the car crash that had killed Jennifer and me in her timeline, she had knocked about in foster care for three years before being legally adopted by Anne Harkwynde. That was when she began her apprenticeship as a *wicce* and began following the path of a "practitioner" of the Arts.

"Wait," I said. "You were adopted by Annie's mother or grandmother?"

She sighed. "Oh, Chris . . . you still don't really get it, do you?"

The van slowed to a stop. "We're here," Annie announced.

We were across the street from an old brick church.

"I assume you wanted Catholic," our chauffeur offered. "I'm not sure whether Methodists or Baptists truck in blessings for ancient weaponry."

"Good point."

"Yes," she agreed, "well, get that good point blessed so we can be on our way. This is an unscheduled stop and we really need to get going." She ducked for a better view of the sky through the windshield. "The sun will be setting in a little while and I'd like to be gone before that happens."

I looked at her. "Meaning the Forces of Darkness will be out?"

"So to speak. Meaning the vampire in the back of the truck will be awake soon and she's probably getting hungry. We don't have time to let her run around loose here . . . unless you're up for leaving her behind . . ."

I sighed and shook my head. "Can't do that. I feel responsible for her now."

Kirsten gave me one of her patented Stryfe looks and went back to pretending indifference.

"Right," I said. I opened the door and stepped down to the sidewalk. "Want to come?"

Harkwynde shook her head. "I'm going to go get gas. Be back soon." And with that, she drove off.

The church was smallish, white stone, with a single spire at the center of its face as opposed to the twin-spire, red-brick edifices that I was used to back in Louisiana.

Where were we, anyway? I had forgotten to ask since I had reawakened from my trip to the void.

I crossed the street—an old, rippled pattern of brick patched with cracked, ancient asphalt. We were either in a small town or deep in the suburbs of a distant city. Did it really matter? Pedestrians were scarce and traffic nearly nonexistent. The building, itself, seemed in good repair but looked as if it were closed. Past the sidewalk I went up a quartet of stone-flagged steps and paused before the large oaken doors.

Listened. If there was a mass underway inside, the building was well insulated.

I wasn't Catholic. And my church attendance had noticeably fallen off since I died the first time and was infected with the necrophagic virus. I looked down at the silver dagger in my hands and was suddenly glad of the dearth of witnesses: Walking into a church—or any public building nowadays with a weapon—was a good way to make a negative impression. Or get shot by a hastily summoned constabulary. I pulled my shirttails out and tried to slip the dagger through my belt so it wouldn't slip to the ground or stab me in the buttocks. A few adjustments and I was a little less threatening but now I was aware of the bullet holes in my shirt and the surrounding red stains that were crusty and raised all sorts of new questions. I did a quick sniff test and realized that I needed more than a change of clothes: I needed a serious shower with liberal amounts of soap and shampoo.

And, of course, all of my earthly goods—wardrobe, toiletries, luggage—was back on the bus or at the copshop, a timeline or two behind us. An ancient Norse dagger was all that I had to work with right now and, if getting it blessed gave me any leverage against the Forces of Darkness arrayed against us, well then, one foot in front of the other and forge ahead.

Even though I had to adopt a bizarre limp or be pricked in the butt for now. Leave it to me to battle the Forces of Darkness while emulating *Monty Python*'s Ministry of Silly Walks.

I pulled the heavy door open and slipped inside.

The sanctuary was empty at first. I slipped around the back of the main room and worked my way slowly up the side, easing past row after row of polished wooden pews. A few wicks flickered in the platoon of red votive candles arranged at the front of the sanctuary indicating that somebody was home. A stained glass dragon was drawing Saint George into shadow as the light outside began to wane. As I neared the confessional, a door opened and the priest on duty emerged with a can of wood polish and an old rag.

Thankfully he was old: I had already begun to worry that I'd find some new seminary graduate who didn't hold with old ceremonies and might lack the sacramental toolkit and engagement of the old guard. He smiled as I limped closer: a wrinkly little cherub with a halo of white, tousled hair. "May I help you, my son?"

"Father, can we go somewhere and talk?" I asked.

He gestured toward the double, freestanding closets. "How long since your last confession, my son?"

I held up a hand. "Oh, I'm not Catholic."

"What faith do you espouse?" he asked kindly.

"Uh, I don't think that's important—"

"Oh, faith is very important," he said. He looked me up and down like a tailor calculating the number of bolts of cloth for a new suit. "I sense that you are troubled and that God has brought you here for a purpose."

"Well, yes . . . about that . . . is there someplace that we can talk?"

Again, a nod toward the confessional.

"Um, no. I need to speak with you face to face. And show you something."

He turned and took in the empty chapel. Then gestured to the first pew. "We have the entire room to ourselves for now."

He sat, making room for me. I reached behind my back and produced North's dagger from under my shirttail.

He scooted back a little as I sat beside him. "You bring a weapon into God's house?" he said softly. But his voice was less friendly.

"I'm not here to harm anyone, father. I'm not here to rob the offering box. I am here to ask for a special blessing." I tried a smile that I hoped was warm and friendly.

"What sort of blessing?" he asked, his eyes not on my smile but on my bloodied shirt.

"Well . . ." I'd been dealing with my own, special, Defense Against the Dark Arts clergy back home for so long I had forgotten how out-of-this-world my request was going to sound. "I was given this dagger to protect myself from evil—" I began, holding it out to give him a better look.

He plucked it from my fingers in the blink of an eye and studied it at a remove that would have required some overreaching on my part just to get it back. I decided to give him a minute to show that I was a reasonable guy and not some crazy person. In a bloody shirt. With .45 caliber ventilation.

"Hmph. Pagan design," he pronounced, holding it up so the hilt was visible. The twinned silhouettes of endowed shield maidens, back to back, facing outward, were inscribed with old Norse runes and glyphs.

Oh yeah: I had forgotten about that "design issue."

"A mortal weapon, a weapon of violence," the old man said, "is no protection from true evil. The wickedness of the world is best combatted by faith." His words were gentle but there was an undercurrent of iron there. "And devotion."

I can be a bit slow at times but it was obvious, out of the starting gate, that this horse wasn't going to run.

"Sure, padre, you're right. I guess this was a bad idea. Silly, really. I'll just take the knife and go." I reached for the item in question but it was even farther away now. My cunning cleric had performed a little sleight of hand and now my Valkyrian switchblade was beside him on the pew. On the other side of his body.

"I have a colleague who has much more experience in battling the forces of evil," he continued, as if unconscious of his deliberate game of keep-away. "Let me call him and see if he will join us." He reached into his cassock, presumably for a cellphone with mental health services on speed dial.

"Stop!"

He froze, his moving hand still but for a slight tremor.

"Look into my eyes," I commanded.

He stared at my face as if I were the Second Coming.

"You are going to hand that dagger back to me . . ."

He reached across himself and retrieved it, turning it in his hand.

Now what? Take the dagger and leave? Use my powers of mental manipulation to make him bless the weapon? Assuming I could hold him in my thrall for that long, would a blessing at mental gunpoint have any meaning?

The door at the back of the chapel opened loudly and the priest flinched. The dagger that was moving toward my waiting hand was suddenly thrust forward.

"Holy crap, padre!" I hissed, holding up my left hand with the blade driven straight through my palm and protruding out the other side.

"Demon!" he growled back, suddenly brandishing the crucifix that he wore about his neck. "The power of Christ confounds you!"

"More like the power of the silver, pointy thing," I growled right back at him as I drew the blade from my hand. I sucked at the wound: My own superhuman healing agents along with the clotting sacks under my tongue were closing the injury and healing the damage. But it still hurt like . . . the kind of language you shouldn't use in church!

"Begone from this holy place, monster!" he shrilled as I got to my feet. "Flee back to the fires of hell that spawned you and your kind!"

"I'm going," I answered as I wobbled back down the aisle toward the exit. "Just be glad I don't have my fangs with me."

Rarely a good idea to try and have the last word: The little old man pursued me from a safe distance, hurling hymnals at my back. Hardcovers, not paperbacks, and they actually hurt. So, I blame my pettiness on a combination of annoyance and pain: I rinsed my bloodied hand in the holy water font on the way out. Two old women stood near the last pew, open-mouthed and staring as I made my way outside amid a hailstorm of songbooks and votive candles.

The sun had dropped behind the false horizon of rooflines and the overhead sky was shading to a deep azure. Soon the streetlights would be popping on. I needed to find a place to wait for my ride where Annie could find me and the authorities wouldn't—if the priest followed up with a believable phone call. *Hello, 911? I'd like to report a demon-spawn in my church. He tried to mind-suck my free will and turn me to the dark side . . .*

Maybe they'd send someone, maybe they wouldn't. Best not to take any chances. I tucked the dagger up my sleeve and began moving down the sidewalk vaguely aware that someone seemed to be pacing me from across the street.

I snuck a sideways glance. A woman. Jogger. With a funny gait.

Well, she wasn't really "jogging" or she would have passed me before I reached the next side street. But, hey, who wouldn't slow down to get a look at the guy with the bloody hand, wearing the bloody shirt, who had just been forcibly ejected from the neighborhood church?

I paused at the corner to stretch the kinks out of my back and make a surreptitious survey of my surroundings. Traffic was even more nonexistent now than when I had arrived and the only pedestrian was the redheaded jogger—or "skipper" given her unusual gait. She wore a sports bra and sweatpants, putting a toned midriff on display but keeping her legs covered, despite the summer's heat. Then I saw the running "blade" in place of an actual shoe/foot. A prosthetic leg. Which might explain her preference for the sweats. The springy, bronze colored running blade also explained her slightly altered rhythm while she paced me, as well.

Except, it didn't explain why she was pacing me.

Now that I was stopped, she stopped, too.

Stood across the street at her corner and stared at me.

I looked right at her, expecting her to look away. She didn't. She smiled. And then favored me with a wink.

Crap.

All cleaned up and properly groomed I'm not the sort of looker that causes women to spare me a second glance on the street. And since I resurrected that first time on an autopsy table in Pittsburg, Kansas, it seemed like the only members of the opposite gender who took any kind of interest in me were inhuman and generally favoring the scary zone of the monster spectrum.

And here I was: dirty, disheveled, bloody, and becoming a bit odiferous by now as my last shower was several days and timelines behind me.

Maybe that was it: I was in the wrong place, at the wrong time, and she smelled the blood on me. It was a more comforting thought than the possibility that she was one of the things that were actually hunting us. Strange town, and nonadjacent timeline—no one should know who (or what) I was here: I'll take Random Evil over Masterplan Evil any day. Or night.

Or twilight: She started toward me, a slight spring in her step as the paddled blade of her prosthesis gave and flexed with surface of the street. Her flame-colored hair seemed to flicker in the dying light like embers on the hearth. I started backing away.

"Wait," she called, halfway across the intersection, "I must speak with you!"

Double crap!

She had a noticeable accent. Not as heavy as the ones evinced by the *Graeae* or the Keres—who muddied their accents over the millennia as they pursued their prey across the earth. Still, the shared Grecian heritage was audible, none the less. Time began to slow as my limbic system flooded both brain and body with a cocktail of stimulants, hormones, and steroids, ramping up my fight-or-flight reflexes to nonhuman levels.

Unlike her mythical compatriots from Greece, she was a looker, the prosthetic appendage notwithstanding. I noted all of this as part of my micro-threat assessment. And, with every slo-mo step she now took toward me, my eyes were drawn again and again to the bronze-colored running blade that looked like a cross between a bent butter knife and the turned blade of a scythe. Weapon? Possibly. Even probably, the way alarm bells were going off in the back of my mind. *Spring-step, spring-step*, I stared at the movement of the flexing bronze metal as if hypnotized by the swing of a brass pendulum . . .

Something started to click in my mental viewfinder but she was all the way across the street now and moving into my personal space.

I backed up.

She kept coming.

This was not a viable avoidance strategy. She could probably outrun me. Leaving the church front meant I would miss my ride. And letting her maneuver me to a more isolated location seemed like an even worse idea than standing my ground. So I stopped. Gave my arm a little shake so that the dagger slid down far enough for the hilt to emerge from my sleeve and bump the inside of my wrist.

"Hi," she said, flashing a pretty smile, "my name is Emmy. What's yours?"

"Mack," I said—with a quick mental apology to Bertolt Brecht and Bobby Darrin. I tried to make my fake smile match hers.

She blinked. *Wasn't the name you were expecting, sweetheart*?

"Well . . . Mack . . . I was wondering if you could help a girl out?" Long, slender fingers fiddled with a strap on her sports bra and her bosom shifted suggestively.

"What do you need . . . Em?"

She turned her head and looked back down the still-deserted street. "Some men started following me a few blocks back and I'm afraid. Could you give me a ride back to my car?"

I followed her gaze. "I don't see anyone now." That's me: Mr. Chivalry.

"They keep ducking behind buildings. That's why I'm frightened. I think they want to have their way with me."

Well that might be believable: She was hotness half-unwrapped. And she was pumping out pheromones like Hugh Hefner's guest linens. But it wasn't protection she was looking for. And if there were any guys who had troubled her, odds were their bodies wouldn't be found until someone took a careful walk through the side alleys a few streets back.

"I'm sorry, Em; but I don't have a car. I'm on foot."

She turned her head back to stare at me but I had already caught that second, reactive blink. "Then . . . how did you get here?" she asked, a barely masked echo of incredulity in her voice.

"Took a cab," I said, working a casual smile while wondering what the hell was taking Annie so long to gas up and return.

"All by yourself?"

She looked around and I took the opportunity to do the same. Yep. All alone.

"I'm a big boy," I told her, beaming like I'd just taken my first bike ride without training wheels.

She reached out and squeezed my bicep—the one just above the forearm that trapped the Norse dagger inside my sleeve. "Yes. Yes you are . . ." She smiled and squirmed in a way that was calculated to tweak the imaginations and libidos of men since ancient Hellenic times. "Then may I ask if you would do me the honor of escorting me back to my car?"

I glanced around. Dammit, where was my ride? Set my gaze back on the church. "Well, here's the thing, Em. I had a little misunderstanding with the vicar in there and I can't really leave until I go back and apologize."

Her expression slipped a little before settling back into the slutty-damsel-in-distress look she was working so damn hard. She probably wasn't used to this much resistance from her human prey. "Can't you come back a little later? I need you now!" She leaned in and whispered: "I would be very grateful . . ." She gave her exquisite torso another little wriggle and I shivered, in turn.

Not from the bottled lust she was trying to serve but from the carrion smell that wafted across my nostrils as she murmured near my ear.

I sighed. This slow dance was all but over. Time to cue the band for something a little more lively.

"I have a question, Sporty Spice. Two, actually. If you don't mind a personal observation."

Her smile was still inviting but wary now. "Go on."

"Your prosthetic—the running blade. It doesn't look like carbon fiber. Or steel. The color—is it brass?"

Her face plainly told me now that this was the last thing she expected to be asked. "A brass alloy, actually . . ." she murmured.

"And, given the whole antiquarian evolution of mythology, I just need to know . . . are you one of the empusae? Or *The* Empusa?" I shook my arm as I spoke the last three words: The dagger slipped down another three inches and my right hand closed on the hilt to cross-draw it from my left sleeve.

Her face shifted and her white, perfect smile became a mouth full of ivory razors. She hissed and leapt on me. The dagger stopped her from a full-on embrace: I buried the silver blade in her chest up to the cross guard, right where her heart should have been.

Her teeth continued to gnash at the scant inches between her bloodred lips and my Adam's apple. Guess that getting the blade blessed by a priest of the White Christ was an important detail after all . . .

I was still alive because she had counted on the element of surprise and expected me to have the weaknesses and vulnerabilities of a straight-up human being. She would adapt now and I was about to lose those advantages to an ancient and possibly unkillable Greek demigoddess.

I fell back onto the sidewalk (ow!) and flipped her over my head, kicking her off of the knife blade and past me as hard as I could. I scrambled to my feet and glanced at the ancient weapon. Something like blood and yet not blood coated the silver in a wine-colored patina. I turned and ran back across the street, trying to buy extra moments to formulate a backup plan before she was on me again.

I should have made it to the other side, first. There was a metal "springing" sound behind me—something like a *sproing*—and I was knocked down as her weight slammed down across my upper back and shoulders. I narrowly avoided a full-on faceplant by sacrificing the skin on my left palm and right forearm to the twin surfaces of asphalt and weathered brick. Before I could worry about that, I felt her breath behind my ear. A sharp elbow to her side, behind my back, coupled with a twist and a side-roll, and her teeth closed on the slope of my shoulder instead of taking out my jugular.

I kicked her away, surrendering a mouthful of my flesh in the process.

I was up on my feet faster than any human might move but so was she. In my preternatural state, I could feel my environment slow down but my opponent was still moving at speeds comparable to my own.

I could also feel my transmundane flesh starting to knit assisted by the regenerative nanites in my system and whatever dregs of North's essence that remained. My accelerated healing factor might keep me alive a little longer in a fight to the death but it wouldn't ultimately save me if she inflicted too much damage in too short a time.

Of course: sauce for the goose . . . I slashed the knife across her chest as she came at me again. The straps of her sports bra parted and her own flesh opened but the wound began to immediately close itself as she stumbled back.

If she would hold still and let me, I might be able to eventually separate her head from her shoulders. Since she seemed disinclined to cooperate I was fighting a holding action, at best.

The thing that looked like a redheaded jogger pirouetted and took a leaping step, using the running blade in place of her right foot to spring up once more and slash at my face with her left foot.

I took a step back and parried the blow with the silver blade: The fabric of her sweatpants parted and a spray of wine-colored liquid sprayed in an arc. Through the rent in the fabric I could see that her left leg was covered in coarse, black hair.

Aside from her spring-loaded prosthesis, she could kick like a mule. Literally.

And now she was going for another spinning kick. I brought my left hand up to catch her leg, hoping to hamstring her and give me a maneuvering advantage. Instead, she pulled a half-squat, battering her donkey leg against my hip and knocking me down again. I went with the momentum and rolled. Her foot stamped down on the street where I had landed just seconds ago. A brick shattered. I kept rolling.

She leapt again, landing on the far side of my trajectory and turned into a crouch.

I stopped rolling and brought the dagger up, calculating my next move. There was none where she didn't have the advantage. She grinned, my blood still drooling from her lips.

"Delicious . . ." she crooned, licking her lips. "You are like a feast after millennia of scraps and leavings!" She seemed to glow with a soft light. "I shall take your remains back to my nest to appreciate you at my leisure . . ." She seemed to light up even more.

There was a loud bang and she was suddenly gone.

In her place was the police van still sliding to a stop.

I wobbled to my feet and limped to the vehicle, mounting the running board with a short hop. The driver's side window was down and Kirsten was at the wheel. "What was that?" she asked.

"Go!" I yelled. "Drive now! Questions later! Floor it!"

She complied. Tires spun, squealed, smoked. Just as the heavy van leapt ahead, the spring-footed creature popped back up in the headlights only to be mowed down again. There was a thumping sound as she bounced off the reinforced grill and tumbled against the undercarriage. Kirsten let up on the gas, her first probable instinct being to stop but I told her to floor it again. We picked up speed and I urged her to blow every stop sign and traffic light that she could. It didn't look that challenging: The streets were still unusually devoid of traffic.

I held onto the wing mirror mount and the open window as we shot down the road, exiting whatever town that Harkwynde had brought us to. Looking past my alternate-timeline daughter, I saw Le Fanu riding shotgun. "Where's our witch?" I asked.

"Sleeping in the back," Kirsten answered. "She's exhausted. We swapped out with the bloodsucker as soon as the sun went down. That's why we're late."

"I'm sitting right here!" the bloodsucker complained. "What was that thing?"

"Empusa," I said. "Greek demigoddess who was a monster and the mother of a bloodline of Greek vampire-types."

"I noticed her top had come off while you were . . . 'wrestling' . . ." Kirsten said in an accusatory voice.

"She looked pretty hot," Le Fanu added unhelpfully.

"The legends describe her as a beautiful woman with flame-colored hair with one leg of brass and the other the leg of a donkey. Apparently she upgraded her brass prosthetic with a running blade like they use in the Paralympics."

"Smart choice," Le Fanu said, looking at the wing mirror on her side of the cab. "She's gaining on us."

I looked back and there she was, running nearly naked now, about thirty yards behind us and gaining. The van's red taillights bathed her in a crimson glow giving her the appearance of being bathed in blood.

Maybe she was. She certainly would be if she caught up to us.

"Drive, Kirsten! As fast as you can!"

"Don't call me Kirsten, old man!"

"Then show me what you've got, *Stryfe!*"

We picked up speed and I could barely hang on. My left hand had a death grip on the mirror mount. The dagger that was sharing my right hand's grasp on the window's edge slipped from my fingers, dropping down into the cab's interior.

I looked back. She was gone.

"I think we lost her," Le Fanu called from her post at the passenger-side mirror.

There was a thud above us and the van rocked a little.

"Well, cra—" was all I was able to get out before a hand reached down from above and yanked me up to on top of the vehicle.

Kirsten slammed on the brakes and the vehicle went skidding and fishtailing across the road. I would have gone bodysurfing off the hood but the empusae pinned me to the roof of the prisoner transport with one hand on my throat and the other gripping the light bar to keep us from following the laws of mass and momentum.

"Well now," she murmured, leaning down until I could catch another whiff of her charnel-house breath. "Only one hot bite . . . and then I'll have to eat the rest of you cold, thanks to your friends." She licked her lips again. "Still, you might not be too cold if I kill the rest of them quickly . . ."

"Urk," I wheezed defiantly.

"Get away from him, you *bitch!*"

The cold hand on my throat relaxed enough for me to turn my head. Carmella Le Fanu had climbed out the passenger window of the cab and was climbing up onto the roof of the van.

The Delphic demoness arched an eyebrow in mild surprise. "Or what?" she drawled laconically. "You should have eaten him while you had the chance. He's my food now and—"

As fast as I can move compared to the human norm, Le Fanu was not only fully undead and therefore even faster, she was several centuries old which only increased her vampiric advantage. She moved before the Greek ghoul could react and counter: I was released and knocked over the side where I landed on Kirsten who had just emerged from the cab.

"You okay?" I asked, helping her up.

"Just ducky," she snarled, pushing away.

"Wake the witch," I said, turning to look for the dagger. This wasn't the time for family drama. "We need all of the help we can get."

The knife had dropped straight down inside the door to land next to the driver's seat. I eyed the shotgun in the mid-cab holster then grabbed the dagger and used the door to pull myself back up onto the top of the cab.

On the flattened roof of the transport area, the two women were wrestling for dominance. As I said, Le Fanu was several centuries old but this thing could have multiple millennia on her.

Which would make her more powerful rather than more feeble.

Even now the redhead was forcing the brunette into a kneeling position and exerting superior strength to gain greater leverage. I didn't know what I could do with an unconsecrated silver dagger since I had already stabbed her where her heart should have been. But I had to do something. I lunged at her and managed to slice her across the arm before she casually swatted me away. I caught the light bar to keep from going over the edge again and tried to get up. It took longer than it should have and I was more than a little wobbly now.

Carmella had used my distraction to turn her head and drop one shoulder, using her opponent's strength to push her off the intended trajectory and as I half crawled toward them, she opened her mouth as wide as possible and twisted her head, spiraling in to sink her fangs into the monster's thigh.

The Biter wasn't used to being bitten and she shrieked like a banshee. Well, maybe not an actual banshee: I've heard them caterwaul and it's pretty hard to match that sound and not lose your sanity in the process. But Le Fanu had sunk her fangs deep and her adversary was only starting to discover that the angle of her bite and the curvature of her elongated canines would make it difficult to pull her away without tearing out a chunk of her own leg and maybe her femoral artery along with it. Assuming she had one.

Le Fanu drank greedily, her sucking and slurping loud enough that I could hear it over the grunting and hissing as the female fiend tried to separate her from her own preternatural flesh. The look in Le Fanu's eyes was beyond what passed for normal bloodlust in the undead. There was a dark ecstasy there that seemed to border on madness as she pulled great swallows of the creature's wine-colored vintage.

And she seemed to be growing stronger—or her meal was growing weaker. Or both. I crept forward, circling around to avoid the Greek proto-vampire's grasp and sightline. As I moved closer, I could actually see the bunch and play of muscles beneath the skin as the redheaded revenant threw all of her strength into peeling her intended prey from her own inner thigh and the brunette bloodsucker hunched her shoulders and fought to stay attached.

Emmy had lost what was left of her sports bra and her sweatpants were in tatters. Le Fanu's black top was torn and both legs of her slacks were ripped from her knees to her ankles. Straining, wrestling, the proximities of lips and flesh, it was all suggestive of the pulpiest spaghetti *fumetti* or Tarantino cinema: The life-or-death struggle momentarily morphed into something primal, surreal, and erotically charged.

At which moment my daughter appeared, boosting herself up off of the back door and rolling toward the knot of squirming flesh. A taser appearing in her hand and she zapped our unwelcome passenger with it at close range.

The resulting muscle spasms caused our combatants to practically explode away from each other, both skittering across the roof and falling off of the van on opposite sides.

I dove off after our uninvited monster. If I only had a momentary advantage I needed to take it before she recovered.

But she was gone.

I jogged away from the vehicle and distracting glow of the

headlights, moving deeper into the darkness. Nothing. I slipped my gaze deeper into the infrared spectrum but nothing of human size showed up against the cooler landscape. Either she was extremely fast or her body temperature was cooler than anything warm-blooded to my view.

I turned and hurried back to the van.

Harkwynde was climbing into the driver's seat, looking a little battered from all the bouncing around and our sudden stop. "We need to move," she said. "Before it comes back." She looked at Kirsten. "Stryfe, you're in the back with Cséjthe. Carmella will ride up front with me until our next stop."

Le Fanu nodded dreamily. Kirsten had to give her a little nudge to get her moving toward the other side of the cab.

"You know what to do?" Harkwynde asked as she closed the door and started the engine.

"Piece of cake," Kirsten said, nudging me in the direction of the back door. We climbed in as Harkwynde slowly turned us back onto the road. We slammed the back door and immediately felt the acceleration as our driver worked to get us out of range before our adversary rallied.

I set the silver dagger down on the bench beside me and worked on massaging the cramps in my hand. "Where did you get a taser?" I asked my daughter as we bounced along.

"It was in the glove compartment," she said. She fiddled with a ring on her middle knuckle. "I didn't even know if it was fully charged."

"That was very brave," I told her solemnly.

"Don't patronize me," she grumbled. But she looked a little pleased at the compliment as she continued to turn the ring around and around.

Okay. Keeping monsters from killing me: hard work. Making small talk with a previously dead daughter from another timeline? A lot harder.

"So," I tried again, "do you think she has any kind of spell up her sleeve if that thing catches up with us?"

Kirsten nodded, still fiddling with a ring on the knuckle of her middle finger. "I've prepared a little spell that should help," she said, coming over to sit by me. "Look." She held up her hand and extended it so I could see the ring more closely.

There was no setting or gemstone. It wasn't even a single band but more like a bunch of fine wires, twisted and woven together into a circular snarl. She pulled her hand back and closed it into a fist. "'Night, Dad," she said. I glanced up just as she lightly punched me in the forehead.

There was a popping sound.

All was darkness.

Chapter Fourteen

"We needed to jump timelines as soon as possible," Harkwynde said as she steered around a chunk of missing roadway.

"I know," I answered, looking out the passenger window. We had left the highway behind some time back, gradually progressing through a series of increasingly narrow and less populated thoroughfares. Now we were rolling along on a private access road that was all but overtaken by the trees and underbrush crowding us on all sides.

"You needed to be asleep or unconscious for me to be able to steer the transition," she continued.

"I get it."

Kirsten and Le Fanu were in the back now as we were traveling in daylight and my daughter seemed a little fidgety about sucker-punching her old man.

"She doesn't think you do."

"Look, I'm not mad. Under the circumstances, I would have been glad to have anybody coldcock me." I frowned. "Except Le Fanu. I can't imagine the circumstances where that would ever be a good idea . . ."

"She loves you, you know."

"Kirsten?"

"Carmella."

I snorted. "Vampires can't love. Emotions like love and affection die when they're reborn as walking corpses. They're just cold-blooded predators: It's all self-interest and beneficial alliances. Betrayal is hardwired into their operating systems."

I reached over and removed the police shotgun from its upright floor mount between us. It was still unused despite the entire Empusa fracas and I checked the magazine. Loaded. Six rounds.

"So you say. But a woman knows these things," she said serenely, keeping her eyes on the road as it wove in and out of the trees. "I see the hurt in her eyes every night when you push her away . . ."

"Oh, good God! You have no idea of the history I've had with that creature—"

"Woman," she interjected.

"Whatever," I snapped, slipping the shotgun back into its mount and locking it in place. "Ever since I got myself elevated to Doman of the New York demesne, she's been trying to lure me into a sexual alliance to elevate her own status and accumulate power on the east coast."

"She risked her life for you. She threw herself against a demigoddess to save you."

"It was going to kill the rest of you after it got done with me," I answered. "Self-interest is not love."

"A woman knows another woman's heart."

"She's not a woman! She just looks like one!" I turned my head to look out through the side window again. The sun still rode high in the cloudless sky yet it had dimmed noticeably in the past hour. "That woman died when she was turned. Now she's a nosferatu . . . just wearing the face and body of its once human husk . . ."

"So . . . not a woman anymore . . ." Harkwynde let my words hang in the air for a moment. "Then I guess you aren't a man anymore, then?"

I closed my eyes and felt a wave of . . . what? Sadness? Weariness? Something alien or long dead from my previous life. "Don't twist my words. I'm not a vampire."

"Almost a vampire . . ."

"Almost only counts in horseshoes and hand grenades. I'm still alive."

"Are you?"

"What?"

"Not exactly human anymore," she said calmly.

"But not undead," I shot back.

"Maybe un-undead," she suggested with the hint of a smile.

"Where are you going with this?"

"We're almost to our destination and before you get any more distracted, you need to start sorting out your relationships with your daughter and the unusually attractive vampire who wants you physically, at the very least, and is willing to put up with your crap, and risk herself at every turn to protect you. You should have seen her when she thought you were dead. She—" Harkwynde shook her head. "Look, I'm not saying you should shag her—"

My eyebrows shot up along with my voice: "*Shag* her? Did we time-jump into the Austin Powers universe while I was unconscious?"

"I get that you're not really interested in her beyond any athletic/hormonal needs and you're the kind of honorable guy who won't exploit a situation for his own selfish ends . . ."

"Plus, I can't be shagging vampires with my kid lurking around every corner, judging me," I said dryly.

She chuckled. "There is that. But, like it or not, you've got a *woman*—" she gave me the side-eye, daring me to contradict her, "— who has an intense attachment to you and has nowhere else to go. You know you can't simply just go off and abandon her once this is all over."

I spread my hands. "What do you suggest?"

"I have nothing to suggest other than you be mindful of the situation and not treat it as if it isn't real. It is."

I sighed. "Which brings you to Kirsten," I said. "That's what you were leading into before we got sidetracked."

"She thinks you are angry about her striking you."

"I'm not!"

"Doesn't matter. She thinks you are."

"Angry? *She's* the one who's always angry! No matter what I do, no matter what I say, she's always judging me. Little girl lost mommy and daddy in a car crash that killed my wife and little girl in *my* timeline: *She's* got abandonment issues! I get it! But that wasn't me! That—me—in her timeline—is dead. Died in that timeline along with . . . Jennifer . . ." Unaccountably, I found that long-restrained emotion welling up despite my best efforts to lock it down.

Harkwynde's right hand drifted from the steering wheel to gently grasp my left. "You loved them very much, didn't you." She didn't phrase it as a question.

I nodded.

"And I killed them," I said after a moment. "And then some Thing dug them up out of the ground and used them as unholy puppets, forcing me to kill them again . . ."

"I can understand why you would never want to love someone again after such a terrible experience."

"Ya think?"

And there it was.

It wasn't just the impossibility of having some kind of relationship—having any kind of relationship since the crash and my first death . . .

It was the belief—no—the knowledge, in every single cell of my body, that everything that had come before was my *life* and that everything that followed was something else. Something different . . .

Something unnatural.

And, therefore, not defined by the laws of justice and reward, designed to permit peace and contentment . . .

Not permissible to the idea of lasting love.

I had known those things while I was still alive. Lost them when I lost my life. The fact that I still walked the earth was some kind of mistake, some accounting error on the celestial books. It wasn't a real life; nor an acceptable "afterlife." I had been distracted by the illusions of the sort of love that follows one's first love—or maybe one's best love. In life, I might have loved again. Perhaps remarried. Been some kind of happy again.

But not in this unnatural twilight existence where I had momentary bliss with a lycanthrope or a former vampire or . . .

It was well, I decided, that those I cared about were safe in the Realm of the Fae and blessed with the fading of their memories of my momentary detour through their lives.

Safe unless the portal was opened and the madness from that Dread Dimension invaded this multiverse, spreading across the timelines like an inky spill of ravenous Darkness . . .

Harkwynde's hand tightened on mine. "I need you, Christopher. I need you to be clear and undistracted. Make peace with your daughter as best you can. She does have abandonment issues, as you say. And you are more . . . formidable . . . than you know. She is only sixteen and she hasn't had the benefit of proper parenting." She chuckled. "And I had forgotten how much the hormones play havoc at this age . . ."

"Yeah, about that," I interrupted. "Just how old are you? No more beating around the bush."

"Old enough. And more."

"No," I said. "No more side-stepping. No more lyrical vagueness. If you won't say it then I will."

"Say what, Christopher?" The hand holding mine had somehow ended up back on the steering wheel.

"You're Annwn Harkwynde."

"Annwn was my grandmother. I'm Annie." She didn't even sound like she was trying anymore.

"Annwn," I insisted. "You can call yourself 'Annie' or refer to your former self in the third person but you were there the day the first atomic bomb was tested in the Jornada del Muerto desert. You were responsible in some part for the spell that changed the laws of atomic physics and saved the solar system from becoming a double-star system. I don't understand what kind of illusion or glamour you're using to pass as a teenager—"

"It's not an illusion," she interrupted, and her knuckles whitened on the wheel.

"So you really are—what—sixteen?"

She shook her head. "Chronologically? No. Biologically? Yes . . ."

We both stared at the road ahead for a few minutes.

"So . . . you're Merlin, then?"

Her mouth quirked up at its corner. "Living backwards? I suppose the analogy is apt. The blowback from our casting that day destroyed everyone in my coven and I was told that I hovered at Death's door for more than a month afterward. Several more years went by before I began to suspect that my body was no longer aging. Indeed, that it was actually the reverse."

"So, not just a disguise to keep the Wyrd Sisters off your trail."

A slight shake of her head. "And kind of pointless since I'm traveling with a human beacon for those that serve the Greater Darkness."

I wanted to ask so why the invitation for a ride-along but another thought occurred. "You've been de-aging since 1945; I don't suppose you've tried tapping the brakes in the last decade or so . . ."

"Do you really think I would wait until pimply teenage boys and creepy older men were my primary social options?" She grimaced. "No. If I live long enough, I'll end up in diapers and, eventually, a protoplasmic stem-cell factory. Beyond that?" She shrugged. "Let's change the subject. Or listen to the radio." She turned it on and found a classical music station.

Given the mood and circumstance, the musical selection should have been something like Liszt's "Totentanz" or Wagner's "Ride of the Valkyries" as we barreled along the crumbling roadway toward Fate or Destiny or Something Unfortunate from the Lemony Snicket hit-parade. Instead we were treated to sunny optimism of Mendelssohn's fourth symphony as we weaved around and between groves of trees and overgrown fields of . . . something tan and tangled. The light had noticeably dimmed, turning flora and fauna alike into sepia-toned kinetoscopes.

And then the ancient asphalt suddenly dead-ended at a serious gateway composed of tubular steel, hinged between two cinderblock security checkpoints.

I turned to the teenager at the wheel. "I thought you said we were going to James Maitland's ranch or something."

"We are. And now we've arrived." She flashed her headlights at the seemingly abandoned guard posts, though we still had hours of daylight left.

A man emerged from a tangle of brush that grew right up to the wall on the left. He approached the driver's side of the cab and Harkwynde lowered her window. He adjusted the hunting rifle slung across his right shoulder and grinned as he recognized my chauffeur.

"Lady A! Is all a'well?"

"Yes, Marcus. Have all arrived?"

"Well . . ." He scratched his head and looked toward the gate. "Nearly all. Edmond says you'll likely be the last of them that's coming."

She nodded. "And security?"

"Two perimeters. Double watches on all roads in and out. Guards-and-wards are stretched a little thin with two circles but

Edmond thought it better to round the gathering proper and cover the outer property line. The idea is we can always pull the outer circle in once The Wyrding begins and mote a more secure barrier if need arises."

"Sounds like everything is well in hand."

"Aye. Now that you're here, ma'am." He glanced up at the ashen skies. "Wildfires burning to the north and west," he added. "Nearly a hundred miles off but big enough to keep an eye out for the next couple of days." He nodded toward the gatehouse. "Open for the Lady, lads!"

Two young men, barely teenagers, emerged from behind the gatehouse and began pulling on the tubular metal gates to allow us entry. Marcus executed something between a casual salute and half-bow then turned and melted back into the woods encroaching the road.

"Not the sort of architecture I'd expect for a gated movie star's property," I observed as we rolled forward and the gate swung shut behind us.

"It's military," she said as we continued down the ancient road. "Maitland willed a portion of his land to the U.S. government for nuclear research. After the war he became obsessed with the idea of what would have happened if the Nazis had beaten us to the punch with the atom bomb."

"And so we're back to the Manhattan Project?"

"Well, this was years later. After traveling the world and amassing a peculiar collection of artifacts, objets d'art, relics, and curios, he developed an interest in the occult sciences. Bought this land here, miles from the nearest ranch or town, and built a house with a wing to house his odd, little museum."

"And here because . . ." I prompted.

"Ley lines. Chez Maitland is built on the convergence of several key earth-energy pathways—magnetic, telluric, and even lies near a convergence of the North American Blood Pentagram."

"Let's pretend I know what any of that means so we don't get pulled off topic. Maitland. U.S. Government. Land grant. Something to do with the postwar Atomic Energy Commission?"

"Circles," she answered.

"As in 'running around in'?"

"Maitland was obsessed with protective circles toward the end of his life. And the development of atomic weapons that could counter the Cold War threat. Cyclotrons had been around since the 1930s. Ditto early accelerators. Synchrotrons since the 1950s. Electron-positron colliders since the sixties. The Hadron colliders were on the horizon when he passed but none of the really large ring designs were brick and mortar accomplishments when he made out his will. And yet he deeded a loop of real estate that could accommodate a particle accelerator complex with a ring circumference of 87.1 kilometers."

"Wait," I said. "The Large Hadron Collider at CERN is something like half that circumference."

"Actually twenty-seven kilometers. The Maitland Ring would have nearly quadrupled the energy output of the CERN ring."

"But?"

She shrugged. "Ahead of its time? Budgeting overruns? All I know is the project designs were developed around 1977 and construction ran somewhere from '83 until '93 when the funding was pulled by Congress. Not hard to understand, I suppose: nearly a decade and billions sunk into the ground without anything to see for it." She gestured to the empty plains unfolding ahead. "Seventeen shafts were sunk and nearly eighty kilometers of the tunnel was completed. But all of that investment was invisible as far as the Congressional Budget Office was concerned. No above-ground construction had been started—probably prioritized by secrecy concerns. So the U.S. passed the torch to the Europeans . . ."

"And the 'God particle'—the Higgs boson—was discovered in Switzerland thanks to the Large Hadron Collider. Which Stephen Hawking says could destroy the multiverse," I finished, feeling proud that I wasn't totally clueless when it came to particle accelerator small talk.

"I thought he was concerned about extraterrestrial contact as a doomsday scenario," she smirked.

"I'm probably quoting a Stephen Hawking from another timeline. Change 'extraterrestrial' to 'pan-dimensional' and he's disturbingly prophetic."

That killed her smile.

"And, wait a minute: What about our little side trip to pick up Jerry and the U-235?"

She shook her head. "Remember, Mr. Cséjthe, when I described navigating the various time/lines like a game of three-dimensional chess? Even a good chess player can 'see' the game only so many moves ahead—the best Grandmasters can occasionally claim up to twenty. But I'm not just maneuvering us across a multilevel playing surface; the so-called board we're attempting to navigate is like a Rubik's Cube in constant rotation along multiple axes. And each tile on the board is constantly bifurcating and spawning new fractal realities so that our path, our course, our passage must consequently change as the landscape births alternate tributaries. The Jimmy Stewart of your timeline exists in multiple, adjacent timelines. His many selves have led many similar lives with a few surprising twists as the more remote fractals have unfolded different choices, opportunities, companions, accidents, tragedies across his path. . . .

"Likewise, the more distantly positioned actor, airman, officer, POW, and scarred veteran—our James Maitland—has lived multiple versions of the hand he was dealt as a World War II pilot. Some he lived a contented war hero, others he died young. In one he became a senator. In another, runner up for U.S. Poet Laureate. Among his more specific timelines, more than one attempt at constructing a superconducting supercollider. The Wyrding was originally planned for the timeline where it was actually completed, and up and running. Specifically pulling back the curtain on the Majorana fermion."

"Not the God particle?" I guessed blindly, suddenly back in dunce-cap territory.

"The Angel particle," she countered.

"Angel particle . . ." I mused. "Is this something new?"

"Not particularly," she said, emphasizing the second word as if she were crafting a pun for the kids on the short bus. "The physicist Paul Dirac predicted that every fundamental particle has an antiparticle—a twin that with an opposite charge—"

"Matter and antimatter," I said. "Should they meet: mutual annihilation, releasing a significant amount of energy. Hey, I watch *Star Trek*."

"Well," she continued, "Dirac came up with this theory in 1928. Just nine years later another physicist, Ettore Majorana, built on his hypothesis, predicting a class of particles that would have their own antiparticles—fermions. Maitland was interested in the research to actually discover the Angel particle—although it wasn't named that until the last decade or so—and granted a portion of his property to the government to research the Majorana quasiparticles.

I shook my head. "I'm confused. You're saying the construction of facilities was abandoned in this timeline. And yet you stopped off on our multiversal road trip to pick up some weaponized uranium for a facility that never went online?"

She shrugged. "Again, I don't know if the isotopes were intended for the timeline where the supercollider was finished or for a different purpose, entirely. This was D'Arbonne's contribution and we've been a bit out of touch of late. Again, imagine two Practitioners crossing a wintery river, hopping from ice floe to ice floe and calling out to each other from differing parts of the tributary while moving in differing directions. Communication is difficult under the best of circumstances."

"Slippery, too," I said, letting any *Uncle Tom's Cabin* references slide.

"You have no idea. When we first became aware of the impending breach between the multiverse and that dread dimension beyond the cusp of the Big Bang wave front, I consulted every oracle, ran the network of augurs, pulled in every divination tool at my disposal— I even wrote code and ran algorithms! When I was near done I knew only four things. That the breach would take place on Maitland's property. That it would happen within weeks, not months. That other Practitioners would be required at the nexus point with Sammathea D'Arbonne providing the missing components."

After a moment's silence I said, "That's sounds like only three things."

"Every casting, every throwing of the bones, every means of scrying, prediction, foretelling, prognostication . . . your name kept coming up."

"Why?"

Her knuckles tightened on the wheel. "My best guess? You have experience with the supernatural and the *supra*natural. And beating the odds at both. You've become unstuck in the timestreams thanks to your proximity to Cthulhu's chrono-spatial displacement in returning to his own dread dimension. But these are just guesses on my part. And I assumed the U-235 meant our target for The Wyrding would be the timeline where the Maitland Ring was completed and up and running—though apparently not.

"Maitland was right about circles: Properly activated and powered up, they can protect and even hide those things that lie within their sphere of power. Whatever his commitment to his country's development of atomic research and power, he believed that there were things on his property that needed protection above and beyond that of a fence and a locked gate. In one timeline he spent nearly five years planting rings of cedar trees around his property. True cedars, not the juniper trees they call eastern redcedars." She shook her head. "He came to believe that he held something that required extra protection and I suspect he tried to bribe the government to build him an atomic-powered circle for part of that defense."

I whistled. "And now you're saying that that's not going to be enough."

"I don't know. It very well might have. But that's not the timeline where the breach is happening. It's leaking here, where the circle was never finished. Or powered up."

"So you would seem to be wrong about needing the uranium," I observed after a moment. "Could be you're wrong about needing me, too."

She sighed. "Christopher, we're here. You might as well see things out to the end."

We came to the top of a low rise and a cacophony of tents and RVs appeared to fill the field below us.

Chapter Fifteen

Rounded by a great ring of mature English oak trees, The Wyrding looked like a cross between a gypsy farmers market, renaissance faire, and hippie commune on wheels. Antique RVs were mixed in with colorful tents and pavilions. Makeshift lanes were designated by rows of hastily thrown together stalls, tables, and booths. Where some open areas had occurred—whether by happenstance or design, the arrangement was not immediately clear—groups of attendees made music, danced, or appeared to engage in story circles.

All in all, it looked like maybe two or three hundred people were camped out on the expansive front lawn of the Maitland estate.

And there was the house, itself. The puzzle-box mansion of my hospital fever dreams.

There were three stories here, two there, and possibly a fourth hidden among the pyramidesque jumble of rooflines above the puzzle-box facade. There were towers, turrets, pediments, arches, cupolas, quoins, and a couple of balustrades. Random lancet, sash, awning, and stained glass windows dotted the hodgepodge of ashlar and rustication faced sides.

And a single, octagonal tower rose like an ancient Roman lighthouse above a sea of wild wheat and riptides of soybeans.

Unlike my dream the vaulted doorway was dark and closed, no revenant husk of my long dead wife haloed by an uncanny light from within.

Instead, a crowd quickly formed and surrounded our purloined paddy wagon like a friendly lynch mob.

"Eddy!" Annie swung down from the cab and flung herself into the arms of a distinguished older gentleman.

"Grandmother!" he cried in turn, trying to swing her around and managing a quarter-turn before his knees wobbled and he had to set her down. "We expected you days ago."

She smiled and shook her head. "The shortest distance between two points is rarely a straight line. I taught you that when you were still in short pants."

He chuckled and kissed her cheek. "Yes, you did. And we calculated for it. But I'm thinking you found trouble along the way."

"Yes. The Dark has thrown its Shadows across the skeins of the multiverse more quickly than the portents suggested. Plus, our special guest has a way of bending chaos theory like the event horizon of a black hole."

I opened my mouth to ask if I was actually being described as a black hole. And closed it as a shout went up across the campgrounds.

Smoke was billowing into the muddied sky like a vague stain that was growing darker every second.

Distant cries of "Fire!" suddenly turned to screams. Screams that grew louder as the chorus swelled and drew closer like the whistle of an approaching locomotive. I gripped the silver dagger at my hip where it was held in place by the pressure of my belt. Then dashed around to the back of the police van and pounded on the doors. "Everybody up!" I yelled. "We've got incoming!"

I glanced at the sky. It was darker now, smudged by the effluvium of distant wildfires but still not dark enough for Carmella to leave the confines of the vehicle.

Kirsten poked her head out. "What's the fuss?" she demanded sleepily.

"Don't know yet but it's coming our way." I left her and ran to the cab. The shotgun, a Mossberg 930 SPX semiautomatic, seemed reluctant to leave its holster. Meanwhile the cries were getting closer and sounds of breakage became audible.

I checked the magazine again though I had scarcely checked it an hour before: six rounds. Slugs, not shells. Three-inchers instead of the standard two-and-three-quarters. Ghost ring rear sight, an M16-style front sight. I was loaded for bear.

Too bad it wasn't a bear that was coming our way.

I hefted the shotgun and raised it to my shoulder as an ancient Airstream trailer shuddered about fifty yards away. The silver roofline crumpled like so much aluminum foil as a creature leapt atop it and paused to consider its next move.

It was vaguely humanoid but covered in a carapace of stone and reddish hues that seemed to emit an inner light of hellish aspect. Four arms sprouted from its shoulders and torso, each hand holding a spear, shield, short sword, or knife. Two heads topped its bifurcated neck, wearing ancient helmets of Corinthian or Spartan design, framing faces like crude, unfinished statuary.

"What the hell is that?" Kirsten asked as she appeared at my side.

"Just guessing?" I raised the Mossberg so I could frame one of the heads in my sights. "I figure it's one of the Makhai. Ancient Greek spirit—or daemon—of battle. Could be Homados. Or Alala. Maybe Proioxis or Palioxis . . ."

"I'm sensing a theme here," she growled.

"Get behind me," I ordered.

"Oh. There's a strategy." Apparently, sarcasm was deeply embedded in the Cséjthe DNA.

One of its heads swung in our direction and seemed to recognize that we were the non-members of this makeshift community. The second head turned and considered us, as well.

"Why is it looking at us like we're the Wiccan Wyrding Welcome Wagon?" I demanded of Annwn.

"What's a welcome wagon?" Kirsten asked.

The thing leapt off of the crushed trailer and came bounding toward us like a giant Ray Harryhausen Dynamation Kali-monster on crack-amphetamines.

"If you've got some kind of spell up your sleeve, kid, this would be a good time!"

"How about shit? S-H-I-T!" she yelled, backing up a little.

Yep: Cséjthe DNA, multiverse be damned.

I squeezed the trigger.

I have a history with firearms. Given the nature of the things that tend to hunt me, I've made it a point to have a well-stocked arsenal and spend the requisite amount of time each month decimating a small fortune's worth of paper targets. The result: I'm a fair to middling sort of marksman and I've yet to find bullets of any kind to be particularly effective against preternatural flesh.

So imagine my surprise when the first slug took the thing's head clean off.

The left one, that is.

The head (formerly) on the right turned to consider the now empty space above the shredded stump of a neck as the monstrosity stumbled to a stop.

"Hell, yeah!" Kirsten yelled behind me.

"Language, young lady," I said.

The remaining head turned back to regard us with an expression that suggested that things had just become very personal. And it began to charge at us again.

"Shit!" I said, all parental role modeling suddenly out the window. I raised the shotgun and fired again.

The multi-armed demon was a lot closer now and provided me with a bigger target—so, of course, I missed.

The third shot took off one of its arms—the one holding the dagger, I think. And then it was practically on top of us.

I turned the Mossberg to block the swing of the short sword and felt my arms go numb as the barrel bent a little, rendering the remaining slugs useless.

The spear was more awkward for it to use in close quarters but a swipe of its shield snapped my head back and I was suddenly looking up at the smoke-darkened sky, wondering just how long I'd been napping and if there would be snacks . . .

The stone-skinned giant suddenly loomed into my field of vision and a spear was thrust into the ground next to my head as a purple-tressed teen witch threw her ninety-five pound body against the monster's wounded side. She bounced off and I levered myself up, using the spear, only to fall back again as the short sword attempted a tit for my tat.

"A little help here!" I growled. Where was everybody?

I rolled to the right: The spear blocked any movement to the left. Hands? Check.

Knees? Check.

Getting back up? Nope.

The edge of the shield clipped the side of my head and sliced my ear open. And for a moment the sky was dark and full of stars.

There was an odd, fizzing sound behind the roaring in my head—not unlike the time ten-year-old me had tested the effects of drinking a soda pop with a mouth full of Pop Rocks candy. Then another sound . . . something like a roomful of people tearing apart cardboard boxes. And a shower of gravel that seemed vaguely comforting just before I passed out.

"Christopher."

I tried to orient myself but it was dark and I couldn't feel my body.

"Don' worry 'bout dat stuff. Jus' lissen."

"Sammathea?" I asked.

"You not where you s'posed to be. Or I'm not."

"Not *where* I'm supposed to be?" I asked. "Or *when*?"

"Ah . . ."

I looked around some more but it was still dark. "Am I awake?"

"No. An' if you do wake up then dis conversation is done."

I stopped looking around and tried to close my noncorporeal eyes. "So where—or when—are you?"

"We at the Four Winds Motel in Carrizozo, New Mexico. Are you close?"

"No. I'm at the Maitland Ranch somewhere near the Kansas–Oklahoma border."

"What you doin' there?"

"Sleeping, apparently. Why are you in New Mexico?" I asked.

"'Cause the augers say dis is the closest bit of civilization to where you supposed to end up. You sure you in the right place?"

"How should I know?" I groused. "Nobody ever tells me anything! Or they tell me a lot without telling me anything. Like you, with the whole Pandora's Box and 'I'll let her tell you when she finds you' preamble. Really?"

"Mister Chris, I can't jus' tell you flat out what's what 'cause you like to dodge Fate when it crosses your path."

"Yeah? Well, I've had to dodge four of them, so far. And their seeing-eye hell hounds. And a bunch of other—"

"Ahm sorry that the End of the World is turning out so inconvenient for you, baby . . ."

"A little more of a heads-up might have helped."

"You need to take dat up with the witch. What she tell you or how much not my doin.'"

"So are you coming to The Wyrding or not? I'm currently unconscious because we've got some Hellenic Hellions crashing the party and it feels like these New Age Oldsters aren't sufficiently prepped for the party-crashers."

"I don' know . . ." The uncertainty in her tone had me more worried than annoyed. "I still think you supposed to show up down here—somewhere to the northwest . . ."

"And what's to the northwest?"

"The Carrizozo Malpaís. And . . ."

"And?"

"Never you mind. You'll either end up here or not."

"There you go again!"

"Fate—" she started.

"Fate can kiss my lily-white-privileged a—" My eyes opened and this time there was a lot less darkness.

A shifting, dancing curtain of light.

There were cushions. My ear was bandaged and the scents of unguents and salves were potent yet pleasant without the harsh smell of manufactured pharmaceuticals. And, of course, there were candles. Everywhere. You can't have a pagan-themed gathering without candles. And tapers and rush lights and oil lamps . . . and was that incense? Yep. Tiny red eyes glimmered at the ends of a dozen shoots and stalks, leaning in their holders and troughs like slightly drunken stems of singed grass.

Another fragrance emerged from the salad bar of olfactory bouquets wafting through the air. Perfume?

That's when the arm across my chest moved and made its presence known.

I turned my head slowly and carefully to the left: My sore ear made contact with the pillow and I had to stop, sucking a sharp intake of air between my teeth.

A head rose from the horizon of cushions and smiled at me. "Awake, I see."

"Where—?"

"A place of healing," she answered. "You were brought here after the battle. I've been tending to your wounds."

"My ear—"

"Not all wounds may be physical," she answered. The light inside the—tent—I could see the canvas walls and vaulted ceiling now— was insufficient to make out much in the way of features. Her hair was a nimbus of darkness edged with scarlet. Her shoulder was bare. As was the breast that peeked above another cushion like a second pale moonrise. My right hand slid down my flank to confirm that I was similarly unattired.

Oh Good God! Whether this was one of those dreams or an actual waking reality, the End of the World was knocking and I needed to get up. If I'd hop-scotched into another timeline then I *really* needed to get up!

And I needed my pants.

"Faye!" a voice bellowed in the distance. "Where is he?"

I had thought myself to be already alert. Then I recognized my daughter's voice.

"Clothes?" I asked hoarsely. I congratulated myself for keeping the sudden panic out of my voice.

"But I am not finished," my cushion companion protested.

"But I am," I squeaked, trying to sit up.

Her arm across my chest was like iron and my head started to swim like Johnny Weissmuller in one of those old Tarzan movies.

"Faye!" Stryfe called again, sounding more and more like her sobriquet as she drew closer.

I fumbled among the cushions and found the flaccid drape of a coverlet. Yanked it up and over, half covering my nakedness as the tent flap was flung and my pan-dimensional spawn stormed into the tent.

"Aha!"

"Aha? Really?" answered my cuddle-buddy who, I assumed, must be "Faye."

"You moved him!" Stryfe accused.

"*We* moved him to a more restful situation."

"I specifically told *you* no sex magick!"

"Sweetie, this isn't sex magick; I'm merely cleansing his aura—"

"So—not really sex magick. Yet. Just a little conjury foreplay . . ."

"His aura is very . . . tangled. I've never seen anything like it!"

"Yeah? Well, lookie but no touchie! And lookie time is over." She grabbed a neatly stacked set of clothing off of a table and flung it at me. "Get dressed," she told me. "You're summoned to Council."

I pulled a sock off of my face. "Okay. Now that my clothes are scattered around in the dark, it's going to take a little longer. Unless someone wants to turn up the light, in which case my nakedness will be all 4K, high-def."

"I'll turn my back," Stryfe said flatly, doing just that.

The light in the tent came up as if dialed up from a dimmer switch. Sitting up was surprisingly easy, though my ear ached like thunder as I got to my feet. Faye was semi-helpful in collecting some of my clothing and producing my shoes, although her own lack of attire was somewhat distracting and potentially problematical with my daughter impatiently waiting just a few feet away. Still, she kept her back to me as I hurriedly dressed, only turning around after Faye had donned a robe and I was tying the last of my shoelaces.

Faye smiled apologetically and kissed my cheek as I stood to go. "Your aura really is quite tangled and . . ." She hesitated, seeming lost for the right words. "Come back and see me when you can. I think I can help you—"

"He's fine," Stryfe snapped. "We need to go."

Outside the sunset was augmented by a myriad of lights, strung from makeshift poles and outlining numerous tents and campsites. Some lights floated through the air like tame will-o'-the-wisps and campfires and cookfires created flickering shadow play across the walls of tents and campers. As the sun slipped below the horizon, the sinking sliver of moon echoed its reddish aspect thanks to distant smoky brush fires to the west.

"I just woke up," I told my daughter as we mounted the steps to La Casa de Maitland. "I didn't—"

"I don't care," she snapped. Then softened her tone. "Look . . . there are stories about you. Rumors. A Wyrding attracts all kinds of people. We keep the ones who follow the Left-Hand Path out of our gatherings but people are still people. There are Practitioners here who can help you and there are some who will use you to their own ends if you let them. Don't wander off and let strange women run their fingers through your . . . aura . . . until you know your way around better."

"Okay."

"Fine."

"We good?"

"Why wouldn't we be?"

I couldn't see an eyeroll but I assumed it was there.

The living room of the Maitland home was a large room made small by the multitude of chairs and sofas that had been moved into the space to accommodate the "Council." The fireplace at the far end could seat another four adults if they wanted their heads up the oversized chimney. Even more congregants were sitting on the floor in a double oval of people. A large mirror in the main hallway, beyond the arched entryway, faced the room and gave the illusion that we had assembled congresses from two adjacent timelines and had brought them together for a bicameral session.

Seated in the center were Annwn and her grandson, Edmond Harkwynde. Seated on her other side was a tall gentleman with a thick mane of silvery hair whose name I was told was Creighton. Annie seemed ridiculously young between the two even though I now knew that she was decades older than both.

"Ah," said the older gentleman as we hesitated at the doorway, "here's our guest, Mr. Cséjthe. I trust your needs have been properly tended to?"

Everyone turned and looked at me. More than a few eyebrows suggested that they knew Faye and inferred just what kind of needs had been tended to.

"Feeling better. Thanks," I answered. I eyed the hatchet tucked into the wood rack by the fireplace poker and considered whether to wait or try to fight my way out now.

Clearly my social instincts had deteriorated over the past couple of years.

"We were just discussing this latest threat," he continued. "Annwn seems to think you might be able to give us some additional insights into its meaning." His tone inferred that he was humoring one or both of us.

"Christopher," she coached, "don't just tell us what you know. Tell us what you think."

"About what?" I asked. I looked around the room. There were hardly any children and the median age seemed to be pushing fifty: some aging soccer moms and professorial hipsters, midlife-crises hippies and weekend bikers, macramé crystal new agers, tie-dye gypsies and smoky-eyeshadow and spiky-haired badass psychic wannabes. I so didn't fit in here and they knew it.

"Why is the old biddy bringing us a mundane when we need more Elders?" someone whispered.

"Good question," I answered. "Next?"

"Mr. Cséjthe," Edmond addressed me—though his tone and cadence suggested that he was lecturing the rest of the room, "my grandmother specifically sought you out and brought you here at no small risk to herself. She believes that you have a part to play in all of this. Forgive us if we are still wondering what that part is."

I nodded. "And you'll forgive me if I'm still wondering, myself." I looked around the room again and sighed. "By the pricking of my thumbs," I said dryly, "something *wiccan* this way comes."

No one cracked a smile: tough room.

"Look," I continued, "I'm not a—Practitioner—or whatever term you prefer to apply to yourselves. I don't have special powers or understand whatever spell crafts or magics or abilities you all purport to have. All that I can put on my resume is a general skillset when it comes to Evil. The malevolences that I have experience with have been both more and less than human in its physical manifestations. They have had differing agendas and manifested in differing physical avatars . . ."

I cleared my throat. "This is a little different, however. The . . . Things . . . I've encountered since Annie showed up seem to be involved in some kind of commonality that I've never . . ." *What was the word here?* ". . . felt . . . before? That is, things that seemed like major evils a few years ago feel like small potatoes now." I shrugged. *Melodrama, thy name is Christopher.*

"Oh, and the weirdest vibe off of this whole sitch: This time there's a theme."

"A theme?" Edmond echoed.

"Yeah. This time the whole Creature Feature is as Greek as moussaka from Thessaloniki."

"And what does that mean?" Creighton asked.

"Now see . . . you're all asking me to show you mine without you showing me yours. I'm having to connect the dots without all the dots being on the table. And the ones that are on the table are usually trying to kill me as soon as they pop up. But shortly before Ms. Harkwynde showed up, an acquaintance of mine suggested that someone was interested in my . . . uh . . . services, and asked me what I knew about Pandora's Box."

Some of these people were great poker players.

The rest, however, were not.

"Okay." I shifted my stance. "The Greek myth of Pandora's Box, as kids used to know—back when a grade-school education dabbled in the Classics—was the story about how evil entered the world through a cursed gift from the gods. This so-called box contained all of these ills, harms, sins, iniquities and malignancies that the gods had rounded up and imprisoned, making the world a veritable Garden of Eden. Sadly, Pandora's curiosity got the better of her and she opened the lid for a peek and nearly all of the evils within got out and the world has been a poorer place ever since."

Creighton cleared his throat. "And what does a myth about a magic box have to do with the problem before us, Mr. Cséjthe?"

"As a metaphorical tale? Nothing really. Unless the so-called 'box' is not a three-dimensional container after all but rather a portal between this dimension and The Darkness beyond the stars—a portal that was unsealed for but a few moments in our distant history but now is threatening to be reopened forever and drown us with unending Darkness."

I paused for the requisite murmuring that typically followed dramatic pronouncements like the one I had just made but Creighton just said, "Anything else, Mr. Cséjthe?"

"Yeah. So what's the plan?" I asked.

"Not to worry," the old man said. "Various binding spells are being prepared and three nights hence, at the dark of the moon, we will reinforce the seal and overlay additional incantations that should hold for another thousand years."

"Fine. Great." I cleared my throat. "And will there be a concrete coffin?"

"Excuse me?" He looked startled.

"Look, again, I don't know hocus-pocus from hokum so you may have all of the angles covered in terms of this portal thingy. But there's a three-dimensional physical container serving as the anchor point for this doorway between dimensions. Slapping a big ole preternatural padlock on the lid may keep what's on the other side from opening things from the inside-out—maybe even keep someone with your skillset from unlocking said padlock from the outside-in . . ." The ebb and flow of whispering in the corners of the room began to ebb more than flow. "But what's to keep someone on this side from taking a sledgehammer or a few sticks of dynamite to the physical package here? If you destroy the construct, does the spell craft remain intact?"

The room went absolutely quiet.

"I mean, in all of your prep and planning for what's trying to get through from the other side, did you consider the possibility of Its having friends and allies on this side? From what I've seen over the past few days . . ." *Weeks? How long was I out of it in the hospital?* ". . . there is some serious oppo out there and I doubt it's coincidental that they share a cultural and mythological commonality with the doomsday jar."

Creighton attempted to brush aside my concerns with a wave of his hand. "Yes, Mr. Cséjthe, Annwn has briefed the high council of the details that emerged during your sojourns to this place. We are adjusting our plans accordingly. So, if you're fin—"

The front door banged open and a couple of white-faced men carrying crossbows appeared in the archway from the main hall.

A silvery eyebrow arched up. "Yes, Bernard? Corbin?" Creighton asked calmly, contrasting the disturbed countenances of our two, armed buttinskis.

"The vampire . . ." One started, then faltered.

"She escaped," the other elaborated.

"Anyone hurt?" Creighton asked.

"Um . . . escaped?" I asked.

"No sir," was the answer to Creighton's question.

"Escaped from where?" I asked. "Escaped from what?"

"Search parties?" Creighton asked.

"Already organized. We'd like to do a sweep of the house."

"Hold on," I said. "She's not a hostile."

The old man nodded to the two crossbow bearers who headed back down the hall. Turning to me, he said, "She is a nosferatu."

"We wouldn't even be here without her help," I said.

"It's true, Creighton," Annie said.

"Still, she has escaped," he said, as if that settled the issue.

"Escaped from what?" I asked again. "Why did she even need to escape? Were you holding her against her will?"

"She is nosferatu," he said again, fully circular.

"Look," I said, "nobody's been hurt. Let's keep it that way. I'll go find her."

I turned and walked out of the room, half-sick at the thought that I suddenly had more faith in a nosferatu than a room full of humans tasked with saving the human race.

Chapter Sixteen

I found Carmella Le Fanu—or, rather, she found me—as soon as I left the lights of the tents and campers behind and walked into the deepening darkness of the twilight.

"Are you hunting me, Christopher?" she asked. She was ten yards away and circling to my left where a tree might provide her some cover.

"Just looking for you, Carmella."

"Is that a crossbow in your hands or are you happy to see me?"

The funny thing was, I shouldn't have been able to see her: In the dark, her body temperature was too cool to register in the enhanced infrared spectrum of my preternatural vision. Instead of a heat signature, she seemed to emit a dim phosphorescence. Not "sparkles," mind you, just a pale, bluish, pearlescent shine.

"It's not cocked." I dropped it to the ground. "It's not even loaded. I just took it along with a walkie-talkie to reassure them that I was going to handle the big, bad vampire so that they could call off their search parties and stay in camp."

She approached now, saying, "And is that what you're here to do? Handle me?"

God, she could make the word "handle" sound like a trigger word for a porn addict.

"I'm here," I said, "to make sure we don't have a bunch of clueless blood-bags running around in the dark with sharp, pointy weapons, hunting you when it's really the other way around."

She laughed without any apparent guile. "Oh, Christopher; I wouldn't harm a single hair on their heads."

"It's not their hair that I'm worried about."

"They are your allies, no?" She came up to me and placed her hand on my shoulder. "Have I not proven my worth to you in this quest of yours? I have ever been on your side and have cause, myself, to see that my world is not overrun by evils ever so much greater than the politics of the New York demesne. I want to help."

"Then what—"

"They would not let me see you. You had been hurt and they would not take me to where you were recovering. They locked me in the back of the truck and would not permit me to leave. As soon as the sun went down, I broke the lock and went looking for you. I was almost benevolent with the ones who got in my way—I tossed them aside gently, I doubt there are many bruises if even that. I saw you through the windows of the house and you seemed well enough so I sought out the deeper darkness away from the encampment and waited for you."

"And here we are," I said.

"Yes," she agreed, sliding her hand from my shoulder and down my chest. "Here we are . . ."

I reached down and pulled the two-way radio from my belt. "Cséjthe, here. I've found her. There's no problem. As long as you don't try to imprison her again. We're all on the same side, here . . ." I waited, letting that sink in. "We'll come in once I've got assurances."

There was no immediate response so I hung the walkie-talkie back on its belt clip.

"Christopher . . ." Her hand had slid down from my chest to around my side and was now behind me as she pressed up against me, her face tilted up toward mine. "It does not matter," she said softly. "I will swear a Blood-oath if you want. If they want. Or I can stay out here . . ."

"And come sunrise?" I asked.

"I have found shelter. Perhaps I am safer out here. Where I am defenseless during daylight hours."

I thought about that. How vulnerable she must feel. She was suddenly alone, without the security of family or clan. Cast adrift in a strange timeline, with no resources, her one remaining "minion" a double agent, and now she was dependent on the mercy of the humans who surrounded her at this particular moment—people that I wasn't so sure that I trusted, either.

"Will you swear a Blood-oath to me?" she murmured, her mouth suddenly close to my ear. "Will you protect me while I sleep? Keep constant watch over my body while I am helpless?"

"I will," I told her.

I could always lock her inside the police van and make sure that I had the only key.

"I have faith that you will protect me." Her lips, so close to my ear, were suddenly on my own. Surprisingly, they were warm. As was the body that suddenly filled my arms and pressed against me. Before I could push her away she broke the kiss and stepped back. "Besides, I am sure that you will want to protect them, as well." She smiled impishly with the implied threat.

"Carmella—"

"Oh, don't worry," she practically sang as she danced away, "I am fully sated. I do not think I shall need to feed for many days now."

"So . . . you are not out here to . . . hunt?" I asked carefully.

"Oh, no," she said, spinning around in a slow circle. "I am out here . . . exploring." She gestured back at the lights of the encampment. "And to avoid hurting those silly fools, of course."

"Of course," I said agreeably. Though I wasn't so sure those "silly fools" were the pushovers she seemed to assume.

"I doubt I shall ever want to feed on human blood ever again." She flung her arms out and twirled giddily like a young girl in love.

I thought I had reached a point where I was no longer stunned as how the universe could be suddenly tipped on its axis: vampires, werewolves, elves, demons, Confederate zombies, deathless Nazis, undead dragons, Greek mythology as the Destroyer of Worlds . . .

Vampires fed on humans. Those who fed on animal blood were considered pariahs and even degenerates—often considered no more than animals, themselves. Or so I was once told during my attempts to "humanize" the New York demesne.

The Le Fanus were undead royalty so this sudden change in Carmella's moral compass was confounding.

Until she opened her mouth again.

"For so long I could not understand you," she said. "Your blood mingled with the Bassarab dynasty! And, yet, you would not deign to feast on humans by blood-right!"

"Uh, still human here," I said. *Liar . . .* my conscience whispered.

"But the stories I began to hear! You drank the blood of a werewolf—forbidden by all the Laws of the Strigoi from time unknown!"

"Yeah," I snarked, "like I was the first to ever do that."

"And you drank the Loa-charged blood of the Whore of Babylon!"

"Uh, I doubt Kurt put the story in the proper contex—"

"And sipped the essence of a thousand-year-old *onryō yaojing!*" she enthused.

"Wait. Suki never said—"

"Your blood gave day-walking powers to your other vampire minion and you tasted the blood of the Wendigo!" She twirled again.

"Now wait! I never drank Wendigo blood!"

"You drank the blood of the Fey—a Faerie queen even!"

"Maybe . . . I'm not really sure what was in that bowl—"

"You were given the blood of a Seraph!"

"Stop," I said.

"You've tasted Demon blood, as well as the Spawn of Dagon and the thing we fought . . ."

"The Empusa," I said. "Now please stop."

"Her blood was potent," she said dreamily. "It has changed me. I can't begin to imagine how your feasts have changed you!"

"Whoa! Hold on! No feasts here." I waved my arms. "A sip here, a couple of draughts there—"

"And the Valkyrie! We all saw how she offered herself to you! Your potency is legendary!"

"Potency?" I said. "Legendary?" I squeaked.

"I understand now. It is not human blood that I shall ever seek again. I shall hunt monsters and curry such favors with celestials! I shall become a day-walker just like you! Perhaps I, too, will learn the mysteries of blood-walking! I shall fight at your side as your consort and warrior-wife!"

"Um . . ." I said.

"Oh, I know this is much for you to take in," she said, calming down. "You have little cause to trust me, yet. But let me show you my devotion and, in time, I know that I can please you—"

"It would please me very much to change the subject right now," I groused.

"As you wish," she said after a moment's pause. "I just want you to know that I am with you now in your endeavors. Your allies are my allies. Your other consorts shall be like sisters for me."

"I don't have—there aren't any other—okay." I looked around. "Where are we?"

"Near the property line. I've been working the perimeter. A portion of it, anyway: The property is too large to work the entire perimeter on foot before sunrise. The wall near the entrance eventually gives way to double fencing with a dirt road that follows the fence line. There are a few places where the fencing seems to have sagged with age and rust—others where the trees have grown right up to the fencing and pushed it in a bit."

I was impressed. "Did you notice any tracks or footprints on the dirt road around these areas?"

She shook her head. "The earth is pretty hard-baked and windswept so there's not much dust to be disturbed. But if one of those two-headed things . . ."

"Makhai. Greek war spirit."

". . . Yeah, one of those things would probably leave a noticeable trail. Still, I'm pretty sure that thing ported into the campgrounds through a fire. At least that's what the witness accounts seem to suggest."

"They told you that?"

"Hey," she said, "I have ears. I may be beautiful but I'm no bimbo!"

"And modest, too."

She punched my arm.

"Ow." It hurt.

"Sorry!" She grabbed my arm and began to rub the area of impact. "I forget that I'm stronger now."

"Stronger now?"

"Since I drank that Empusa blood. Like I said, I can feel myself changing."

I looked at her and again noted the soft phosphorescence of her skin under the starlight. *Yes, she was . . .*

The deepening night was beautiful.

The distant lights of the Wyrding encampment were dim to the point of near invisibility and the open sky was ablaze with stars and the luminous haze of the Milky Way. The moon, just three nights away from full opaqueness, had set earlier but we could almost see our shadows as we picked our way between the occasional tree.

It seemed a shame to turn back to camp but I was starting to flag. And, despite whatever witchy first aid I'd been rendered, the Makhai had really rung my bell. In fact, considering the abuse I'd been through over the last forty-eight hours, it was amazing that I was even up and walking around now.

"Oh, please! Not yet," she begged, at my suggestion to head back in.

"Carmella, I'm exhausted. And we've got to sort out your sleeping arrangements before the sun comes up."

"I have a place."

"Where? Outside the camp?"

"Yes. Come with me and I'll show you."

A few more minutes of walking and she led me to a circular concrete platform, rising some five feet out of the ground, some twenty yards off from the dirt road. It was maybe twenty-five feet in diameter with a ten-foot-wide concrete ramp on one side and a set of steel steps on the other. Climbing to the top there was a series of giant, inverted metal U-rings spaced around the circumference of the concrete cap. A manhole cover was set into the surface close to the steps.

"You're sleeping in a sewer?" I asked as she knelt and slid a couple of fingers into the notch where the pry bar was normally inserted.

She lifted the heavy steel cap as if it nothing more than an oversized pie tin and laid it aside. "Don't be silly," she said. "It's more like a smooth cave. Come see for yourself." She lowered her legs into the hole and dropped out of sight.

I fished a mini Maglite out of my pocket and played the beam around and into the opening. As you might expect from a man-made egress, there was a ladder leading downwards. I switched the light off and repocketed it, fished for the top rung with my right foot.

The descent was slow as I had no way of knowing which rung would be my last. The ability to see into the infrared and ultraviolet spectra is pretty much useless for descending into underground pits.

Make that underground pits with bottomless depths: some fifty-odd rungs and still counting as I continued to climb down into musty darkness. Finally, I stopped and dug the flashlight back out of my pocket while I locked my other arm around the ladder's side rail and reverse-gripped the rung at chest level. I switched it on and directed the beam downward. I was rewarded with the sight that the floor was only another thirty feet or so below. Carmella Le Fanu stepped into the spotlight of the beam and motioned for me to keep coming. Then she extended her arms into a basketlike gesture and called: "Jump! I'll catch you!"

The thing was, she was strong enough and quick enough that I could do so with no danger. No obvious danger, that is. I played the light back up the way I had come and saw that I had unknowingly passed through a couple of railed platforms where I could have exited the ladder on my way down. Not that it mattered: Carmella was waiting below.

I could have jumped the last fifteen feet. I could drop that far without injuring myself. But I was walking a fine enough line with her appetites as it was and she seemed unnecessarily insistent on my landing in her arms.

True to Carmella's description, we were standing in a man-made cave of sorts. The floor, walls and ceiling appeared to be concrete and were near circular in circumference—slightly elongated at the top and bottom, like an oval tipped onto one of its narrower ends. The open space extended in opposite directions into greater darkness like a vast tunnel.

Or giant storm-drain system.

There was no moisture, however, and the floor was clean though somewhat dusty.

"I know what this is," I said slowly. My voice echoed softly in the cavernous space. "It's the Maitland Ring."

"The what?"

"In another timeline it's a particle accelerator, nearly twice the size of the Large Hadron Collider at CERN!"

"What's a sern?" she asked.

"CERN?" I said absentmindedly as I played the flashlight beam over the distant curve of the giant tunnel. "It's the acronym for the European Organization for Nuclear Research . . ."

"You know I don't do nerdspeak," she groused, "but wouldn't that be 'EONR'?"

"What? No. CERN is taken from the French acronym, not the English." I held up my hand. "Don't ask. My French is the next best thing to nonexistent."

"So this is supposed to be some kind of nuclear reactor?"

"Not a reactor. An accelerator. But it's irrelevant: They never finished it in this timeline."

"So it's just a big hole in the ground?"

"More like a big donut-shaped hole. An underground ring. Annie said they ran out of funding before they finished the dig."

"So, an unfinished donut," she decided.

"Yeah." *How much unfinished? Something around four-and-a-half miles left undug out of a fifty-five-mile circle? More than a nibble, less than a full-sized bite out of that pastry . . .* "So, you're going to set up housekeeping down here?"

She threw her arms out and did a slow spin-turn. "Plenty of room . . . out of the sun . . . and good, soft earth for a bed."

"You'd rather sleep on dirt than a nice, comfortable bed?" The sarcasm came out a little heavier than I intended.

"It is the most natural berth for our kind. The cradle from which we all are born." The sincerity was a little less convincing than she intended.

She took my hand and pulled me along into the deeper darkness. "Let me show you."

I hardly needed the small flashlight as the space was empty and the slight curve of the floor kept our feet pointed in the right direction. "Listen," I said as we walked along, "I know that these people make you nervous. That you have no reason to trust them . . ."

"I make them nervous, too. They're all about—" her voice dropped a register and she continued in a gruff, male approximation, "—*Eevill!* We must stop The Eevill from getting through and destroying our wonderful, precious universe!"

"Well—" I started.

Her voice came back up to normal. "But, you know what? It's my wonderful, precious universe, too! And I don't want it destroyed any more than they do! But! They look at me and they see—" Her voice dropped back down into a growl. "—an Eevill Vampire! A hot. Sexy. But still *Eeeevill* Vampire!"

She looked at me meaningfully and I had to chuckle a little. "Yes. Yes, you are."

"Which?" she asked in her own voice. "Hot, sexy or evil?"

"The first two, for sure."

"But the third? The jury is still out, I see."

"Carmella, I'm not worried about your intentions. I believe you when you say that our cause is yours, as well. I think you've proved yourself as an ally and a friend." Even as the words came out of my mouth I realized that they were true. Unmoored from family and clan politics and motivations, she was finally free to be herself and not a pawn of the New York demesne. "But, as you say, they don't know you and you're a distraction right now—"

"Why do you think I left?"

"But you're more of a distraction if they don't know where you are, than if they do. Come back with me and I'll see to it that you're protected while you sleep."

"And how are you going to do that? Stand watch over my body all day long while I'm totally helpless?"

"If that's what it takes," I promised her. I owed her that at the very least, and it wasn't like I had anything else to do. I'd gotten Annie to The Wyrding, as promised. What else was there to do while I waited to see if her friends could prevent the end of the world?

Her hand gripped my upper arm. "Though I do not doubt your puissance, my intrepid warrior, their numbers and their unknown powers do give me pause. While here . . ." Her other hand tipped my free arm up so the flashlight beam revealed the end of the tunnel. The concrete-lined portion, anyway.

This is where the Maitland Ring had run out of funding and interest. The earthen wall at the terminus point had a moderate spill of loose dirt at its base but it was pretty obvious that we weren't looking at any kind of a landslide as the result of structural collapse. Instead, it appeared as though a smaller passageway had been excavated into the earth beyond. It was maybe some twelve feet high and another five feet in width. Approximately. The dig was crudely executed rather than machine drilled. I directed my light into the hole and could see nothing beyond.

"I don't know how far back it goes," Carmella said, as if reading my mind. "Maybe twenty feet back I found a comfy spot to sleep, snug as a bug in a rug. I can repose out of sight, invisible to any intruder. And I think you're the only one who knows this is down here."

"You're wrong about that," said a voice from behind us.

We both turned but already knew who it was even before I could swing the flashlight around.

"The ring will be an integral part of the ceremony," Kirsten elaborated, back in full Stryfe-mode, as she came closer. A crossbow dangled loosely from her right hand and a pistol holstered at her left hip. The flashlight in her left hand remained switched off. "The Elders already consecrated the circle up top so don't be doing anything—" Here, I got some side-eye . . . "—to deconsecrate the circle. It needs to remain sacred space until after the full binding measures are carried out."

"Can I still sleep down here during the day," Carmella asked her in a dangerously sweet voice, "if I climb the ladder to go number one or number two in the bushes topside?"

I made the smallest of gestures, hoping to wave my daughter back so that I could try a little finesse, first.

Too late: Carmella hissed softly under her breath.

I looked at her. "Be nice."

She looked at me. "Oh, please. How am I not being nice?"

I looked at her. No arched eyebrow, no mischievous smile. I directed the flashlight beam down the tunnel, past Stryfe: receding darkness.

I pointed the flashlight back toward the hole in the wall of earth. Two pinpricks of light shone back at us from within.

Eyes.

Six, maybe seven feet above the tunnel floor.

We all took several steps back.

A pale hand was emerging from one of the holes. A face surfaced into the light. Reptilian eyes and a slit of a mouth incongruously set into a humanoid face. Its skin was bluish-white and delicately scaled like a cavefish.

"I wonder what that would taste like," Carmella whispered.

"Keep wondering," I said. "Run!"

We ran. Or tried to. The third time I turned to point the flashlight and look behind us, my feet got tangled up in each other and I went down in a painful slide. Before I could get back up, I heard the twang of a crossbow string and something thudded to the ground right behind us.

I scrambled to my feet and backed up until I could see that the creature was prone, utterly still, and most likely dead, a crossbow bolt buried between her pearlescent breasts. She lay on her side, the corpse nearly fifteen feet from the top of her hairless head to the tip of her snakelike tail.

Some years before I had seen an honest-to-God *Nāga*, up close, in a demi-human nightclub in Seattle. There was a certain similarity in taxonomy: the human torso that transitioned into a great, serpent's tail from the hips on down. But the top half was less human than the bottom half was serpent-like. Its pale skin was spattered with scales that increased in number and size as they began to cluster toward the transition point, turning to variations of green and gold to match the colors of the muscular tail. The half-closed eyes were yellowish with large, split pupils that marked most venomous reptiles and her fingers were tipped with long, narrow talons rather than the flattened nails of human or simian aspect. The lipless slit of a mouth hung slack in death and displayed a pair of prominent fangs bordered by smaller, serrated teeth.

"What is that?" Carmella asked softly.

"Lamia," I said, keeping my distance. Snakes had a well-earned reputation for post-mortem biting contractions.

And, of course there were all those horror movies where someone makes the fatal mistake of leaning over the presumably dead monster.

"A lamb-what?"

"Lamia," I repeated. "Greek vampire of myth and legend. Never seen one but it fits the description. Not to mention the company we seem to keep keeping."

"You mean Grecian mythological monsters," Stryfe added unnecessarily.

I nodded. "All in consonance with the Pandoran myth."

"Looks like a hit and a myth," Carmella added in with a goofy grin.

I gave her the Dad Stare. "Ookay, again: time to leave. Let's go."

"Go ahead." Stryfe stepped past us to retrieve her crossbow bolt. "I'm right behind you."

I took a couple of steps back but I wasn't walking away until she was clear as well.

"I have to say, I'm disappointed."

I looked at Carmella. "What?"

"I mean with your reputation and all."

"My reputation?"

"Which one?" Stryfe asked as she joined us, wiping her wooden ammo on her pants leg to remove the excess ichor. "The Revenant Romeo? The Seducer of Shapeshifters? The Lothario of—"

"All right . . ." I grumped.

"I was speaking of his prowess in battle," Carmella said, "but I'm always interested in—"

"My *prowess* in battle?" I interrupted. Of the two topics, this seemed the safer course.

"You have bested every threat that the New York demesne has sent against you," she elaborated. "You have bested demons and aliens and deathless constructs!"

"And the tale grew with the telling," Stryfe snarked.

"Yet, just now," Carmella pouted, "you turned and ran away when the lamb-thing crawled out of its hole . . ."

"Hey, I left my crossbow up above so you wouldn't feel threatened. I'm unarmed. Unless you want to count the Swiss Army knife in my pocket."

"In most of the stories you are unarmed as well."

"I had nothing to improvise with here!"

"Shush!" Stryfe said.

I was confused as to which side my sort-of daughter was taking now. But as the echoes of our conversation died away they were replaced by a whispered susurrus of sound.

I turned and directed my flashlight back toward the tunnel's end. Stryfe did the same. Pinpoints of light were reflected back at us in multiple pairs, revealing that we had come across a nest as opposed to a simple burrow. The slithering sounds were now punctuated by bursts of hissing.

So much for the silence of the lamia.

"Christopher!" Carmella was hissing a bit, herself.

"What?"

"Run!"

We ran. Fortunately, the ladder wasn't that far away. Unfortunately, climbing was a lot slower than running.

And deciding who was going first.

"Ladies first," I announced, picking my daughter up by her belt and collar and tossing her upwards. She caught a rung on her way back down some ten feet above me. She glared back down at me and then began to climb with some apparent reluctance.

I turned to Carmella who said, "I'm faster than you so don't get in my way." And before I could react, she grabbed me and tossed me up the ladder. Her preternatural strength propelled me higher than Stryfe but her aim was a bit off and I hit my head on the underside of the steel platform at the thirty-foot level and fell back down. Carmella caught me just short of the concrete floor. "Quit horsing around!" she hissed and tossed me again.

I barely avoided dislodging Stryfe by catching the side rail and swinging around to the back of the ladder. She gave me another annoyed look and resumed her ascent. I looked down and found the vampress directly below me. Carmella really was faster than me and I was in her way. Now she was giving me The Look.

"What?" I asked. "You don't want to stop and watch me take on multiple monsters unarmed?"

"Oh, I get it," she growled back. "You vanquish superior foes by annoying them to death! Don't make me throw you again!"

I scrambled up the ladder after Stryfe. Who had stepped off the ladder and onto the first platform.

She was leaning over the steel railing, pointing her flashlight and her crossbow at the boiling knot of slithery vampires below us. The bad news: Two of them were climbing the ladder after us. The good news: Lacking legs, they were considerably slower at making the ascent than we were.

However, her attention was continuously fixated below and so she did not see the lamia sliding over the edge of the second platform another thirty feet above the first. It landed atop her and they both went over the railing before she knew what had hit her.

Swinging out to the side, I caught her arm as she went by; the monster and her crossbow kept going. Swinging her back onto the ladder, I looked down and saw the flicker of her lost flashlight in a knot of squirming tails and pale, grasping arms.

Carmella's hand pushed against my *gluteus maximus*. The right one. If she had pushed against both cheeks the plural form would have been *glutei maximi*. It's weird the things that flit through your mind in fight or flight situations . . .

"I said quit horsing around," she growled. "Climb!"

I climbed. Passing through the opening for the first platform, I slowed a bit to navigate the narrow passage and felt pointy teeth nip my left buttock! They didn't break the skin but . . . really?

I sped up, climbing as fast as I could while still holding a small flashlight in my right hand and periodically checking for any more surprises above us.

There were none and I pulled myself through the manhole so fast I nearly fell on top of Stryfe who was still on the ground and rolling clear. Carmella was hoisting herself up and out when she suddenly jerked and started to fall back in.

I spun around and grabbed her arm as she caught herself on the rim of the opening.

There was a momentary tug of war as I tried to pull her up and something very strong tried to pull her back down. Then Stryfe was kneeling beside me, pistol in hand. She thrust it down the manhole and emptied the full magazine into the darkness.

Carmella came free rather abruptly. Or out of the hole, at least: A male lamia was still grasping her about her legs and came up with her. A bullet had plowed a bloody furrow in his muscular tail a good eight inches below his right hip, probably causing him to lose his grip on the ladder below. Carmella twisted in his grip and sank her own fangs into the Greek vamp.

Although the human/serpent hybrid dwarfed her in weight, size, and muscle mass, he was not in the same class as the Empusa we had tangled with earlier. She was winning the suck-off and the creature began to push her away in order to escape.

Carmella was having none of it. Whatever flowed through the monster's veins, Le Fanu had a sudden acquired taste for it. Her face took on an alien countenance, an expression of divine madness resorting her features, and I recalled her words about never seeking human blood again.

It chilled me.

On the other hand, who was I to judge her pursuit on nonhuman cuisine? This was neither the time nor the place. I picked up the heavy manhole cover and bashed the creature's head in.

"Hey, I wasn't done with that!" she gasped as I rolled the lamia's body over to the opening and sent it crashing back down the ladderway into the dark depths of the tunnel.

Judging from the sounds as the corpse careened against concrete and steel, the ladder had not been completely emptied by Stryfe's gunfire. "Oh, hey," I murmured softly, after the fact, "look out below . . ." And I slammed the heavy, steel disc over the opening, tamping it down.

I looked at Stryfe. "I don't suppose you've got some kind of—"

She was ahead of me, kneeling atop the manhole cover and muttering under her breath. Her hands seemed to flicker as she placed them at various points around the metal rim. Then she stood. "That should hold things for now."

I looked off across the field. "How many other openings?"

"Enough. Possibly too many," she said. "We need to get back and deploy teams—what?"

"What?" I echoed. And then followed her gaze.

Carmella Le Fanu was already across the service road and on top of the fence that bordered the property line. She launched herself into mid-air and glided into the tree line, disappearing in a matter of seconds.

Chapter Seventeen

Carmella's escape was not well received back at Wyrding Central.

And my attempts to explain our moonlight jaunt and subsequent subterranean adventures seemed to produce more side-eye than was warranted from the so-called High Council.

My immediate discomfort was short-lived, however, as most of the camp was hastily organized and sent into action. Scouts were sent out to ascertain if there were roaming hostiles already on the grounds while work crews were assigned the task of sealing off every possible egress, hatch, doorway, capstone, chimney, and system intersection, to and from the underground ring structure. Plans were made to combine, shrink, and reinforce the inner and outer perimeters so that the tunnel fell outside of the casting and the camp proper.

In a matter of minutes the living room of Chez Maitland was emptied as everyone scurried off with a list of tasks to accomplish before the next shoe dropped in the Centipede of Fate's footwear parade. Even Stryfe, freshly rearmed and reloaded was headed for the gatehouse.

But I wasn't completely alone. Annie Harkwynde sat down next to me as her grandson and Creighton led a procession of burly male cult-types toward the east wing to "secure the portal."

"Well," she said softly, "Cséjthe saves the world again. Or should I say, The Multiverse . . ."

I turned and gave her a long look.

The youthful visage masked more than a century's worth of life and wisdom. I tried to see the crone behind the dusting of freckles across pale, unblemished skin, a face that appeared untouched by a single wrinkle—save for the dimples that bookended her subtle smile. Only her cool, grey eyes suggested the weight of years and burdens that she carried in the vault of her soul.

"I don't need propping up," I said quietly. "I know what I am and what I'm not. Tonight was another happy accident. Nothing more. Some people may believe that I'm some kind of hero or answer to prophecy or badass demon-killer, but that's because they don't really know me or they need to believe in some kind of personification of the heroic ideal. But that's not me. If anything, I'm the Forrest Gump of Armageddon's Army. My life—or afterlife—is just one, unending parade of accidents beginning with the one that killed my family and gave me this weird propensity for being in all of the wrong places at all of the not-quite-right times. I don't fight Evil as much as I just seem to stumble into Its way. I'm not a hero, I'm the thing that Evil stubs Its toe on, causing It to fall on Its ass."

"Oh, Chris," she said, her eyes taking on an uncanny luminosity, "you are so much more than that . . ."

"Yeah, I'm more," I said agreeably. "I'm God's punchline. Or punching bag. And I'm Evil's lightning rod. Which is why it's best that I move along, now. I've done what you asked; what I agreed to. I got you here. Resealing mystical portals against extra-dimensional demons is way outside of my skillset. In fact, my very presence is practically a guarantee that Something-Will-Go-Very-Wrong. The sooner—"

"No!" Something in her voice made the fine hairs on my forearms and across the back of my neck stand up like iron filings in the path of a powerful magnetic field. She reached over and grasped my hands in hers, clinging to them as if she feared I would suddenly bolt for the door.

"I need you!" There was nothing in her gaze that suggested amorous longing. The ardor in her voice was something more powerful than the desire of flesh for other flesh. "This task is not yet finished and *you*—in some way and some manner that I cannot fully ken—are essential to our success!"

I opened my mouth but she squeezed my hands and continued:

"Christopher, you see the *accident*—" she said the word as if it were in quotations, "—and all that has come after, as if it was God's personal vendetta against you. That all of the evils that The Universe has pitched at you since your first death and resurrection were manifestations of its antipathy for you, specifically. The undead, the demons, the human monsters, even the abominations of the Great Old Ones—may have seemed like singular, impossible endgames. And each, hard-won victory should have been more than any man could expect to have asked of him."

She sighed. "But have you ever considered how each of those terrible, monstrous opponents pale in comparison to the dark chaos that has brought us to this moment in time across the multiple worlds? Have you ever considered that you might be God's chosen sword and that each of your battles leading up to this event is His way of honing and sharpening His holy blade for the final War Against Darkness?"

I groaned. "Oh, please! There is never a *final* War Against Darkness. As surely as the sun rises, it sets again. Destroying evil is like playing *Whack-A-Mole* on a cosmic scale. Or even a local one. Sooner or later, you've gotta suit up—gird up your loins—whatever, and go to war against Darkness all over again.

"And, as far as God's sword? Maybe boxcutter on one or two occasions. Or penknife—Swiss Army knife on my best days. But I'm not *that* guy! I got you here and, chances are, you probably would have arrived a lot sooner and with less difficulty if I wasn't in the mix. I'm not a Witch or Practitioner or whatever is the appropriate descriptor for how you self-identify. The only thing I should be considering now is how to find our stray vampire before she gets into more trouble and then figure out what I'm going to do for a living in this new timeline." A thought occurred. "Unless, of course, another me is already here and has a fold-out couch I can bunk on while I'm getting back on my financial feet . . . hey!" I gave myself a little shake. "Do I exist here, already? I mean, is there another me that I need to avoid lest I create some kind of paradox or embarrassing identity-theft scenario?"

She shook her head and gripped my hands even tighter. "There was another you in this timeline. Married, father of four—"

"Was?"

"The Darkness that arrays its forces against us in this battle over the opening of the portal took no chances. You were taken off the board several years back in a preemptive strike. So, you see, dear Christopher, while you may not believe that your life has meaning or purpose in the grand scheme of things, vast Malevolences do."

"And my family," I asked.

"Evil does not use a scalpel," she answered. "Evil leaves nothing to chance."

I was suddenly very weary. "Then it will be coming for me, again: this me . . ."

She stood without relinquishing her grasp, pulling me to my feet as well.

"It is coming for us all," she said. "We need to rest now because we may not have the chance later."

As she led me up the staircase to a guest bedroom on the second floor, I remembered something that my father used to say when I was young: *no rest for the wicked . . . and the righteous don't need any.*

I yawned and thought: *at least I know which I am . . .*

We shared the bed.

Neither of us disrobed. We just fell onto the mattress without even bothering to turn back the covers.

I may have pushed one shoe off with the toes of my other foot but my brain was already shutting down and the only detail worth noting was Annie's soft snore ahead of my own.

Then darkness.

For a bit.

Again, I dreamt.

And, again, it began with a memory—not of pain or horror as so many times before—but of love and wonder as a tiny bundle was placed into my arms.

"Your daughter, Mr. Cséjthe."

I looked over at my wife's smiling face.

"She's so tiny, Mrs. Cséjthe," I whispered.

"Yeah? You try carrying her around for nine months."

I reached over and brushed a sweaty dark curl back from her tired face. "I'll take the next nine."

"How about we split the next nineteen?"

"Only nineteen?"

Jenny chuckled. "I can see she's going to be a real 'daddy's girl.'"

"What's wrong with that?" I murmured, tucking the hospital blanket around the tiny human in my arms. "Kirsten René Cséjthe . . . you are mine and I'm never going to let you go . . ."

My newborn daughter stretched and yawned, waving a tiny dismissive fist as if to show me how "impressed" she was with that promise.

"Ours," my wife corrected. "Now hand her over, bub. I want a little more bonding time before the next feeding."

"No fair," I grumped good-naturedly as I carefully transferred her into my wife's arms and positioned her diminutive head next to a milk-swollen breast. "You've got the goods while all I have is an empty larder."

She smiled as she rearranged my carefully tucked blanket. "Speaking of that, could you see about getting me some pudding?"

"Pudding?"

"Got to keep up my strength," she said brightly. "I need my big, bad, hunter-gatherer to hunt me down some pudding. Gather it—or them: *One* of those tiny cups is just not going to do."

"Your wish," I said gallantly, "is—"

"And bring back a real spoon," she commanded regally.

"A real spoon?"

"Well . . . it can be plastic. Just don't bring one of those flat, wooden things that look like a recycled tongue depressor."

"Yes, ma'am!" I saluted and started to rise from my chair next to the bed.

"You need to get up now and follow me," said the nurse who had been lurking in the background.

But when we exited the hospital room we were in the second-floor hallway of the Maitland mansion.

And the "nurse" turned out to be Mama Samm D'Arbonne whose only medical degree was a Cajun doctorate in Thaumaturgy. Her uniform a cream-colored pantsuit, her nurse's cap a pale turban encompassing her ropey braids.

When I had first met her, she was . . . well . . . immense. "Large" just would not do a description of her any kind of justice. Seemingly nothing more than a charlatan fortune-teller and faux psychic medium, she had turned out to be a woman of considerable power and giftedness, losing much of her sorcerous potency (and physical bulk) in a showdown with Marie Laveau and Grigori Yefimovich Rasputin. Based on what could be seen of her silhouette in the dim light filtering up the stairway, she had reacquired some of that endowment. But if her powers and abilities were truly represented by her physical volume, we were headed for Armageddon seriously low on ammo.

"What are you doing in my dre—?"

She whirled and clapped a hand over my mouth. "Shush!" she whispered. "Jus' follow me an' try to be all stealthy instead of bull in a china shop fo' a change."

The whole hand over the mouth thing felt so real that I almost forgot it was another dream message from the juju woman. Even descending the stairs felt overly real as we reached the main floor and turned toward the east wing of the house. We passed through a couple of doors and I entered a room that was back in the surreal dream territory once more.

Harkwynde had told me that Maitland had spent his later years amassing an oddball collection of curios and relics with a bent toward the macabre . . . but the considerable east wing of the mansion looked like he'd bought up all of the excess inventory from the *Ripley's Believe It or Not!* Odditoriums and Museums.

"Okay," she said. "Where is it?"

I wandered down a side aisle, looking at the various displays, some of which involved floating monstrosities in formalin-filled specimen jars.

"Where?" she asked again.

I turned. "Oh, what? I'm allowed to talk now?"

"As long as you keep it down. If someone comes tru dose doors, duck down and hide," she said.

I blinked. "New dream rules?"

"Sure. Now, hurry up."

"Aaaannnd . . . do what?"

"Find it."

"What?" I blinked. "Oh. Pandora's . . . um . . ."

"Jar," she said. "Dat's what you told me jus' before the accident. Not box. But some kind of . . ."

"Pithos," I finished. "A large, Greek urn of sorts. Often used for funerary purposes."

"Could be a funeral fo' the whole human race," she said somberly.

"Well, good news!" I told her as I worked my way back down another aisle filled with an assortment of diminutive mummies. "The coven—er, Wyrding, here, has already found it and is about to seal it up tight for another thousand years."

"Really?"

"That's what I'm told."

She gave me that Look. "Dat's what you're told? Who are you and what have you done wit' the Christopher Cséjthe I know?"

I sighed. "Look, my job was to get the girl to this Wyrding place. Mission accomplished—although I was more of a spectator than a facilitator. She's here. Her people are here. You say you need an ancient, mythical pot sealed against powerful forces? The best plan I could come up with would be to apply a liberal amount of epoxy to the lid, drop it in a well, and pour about a ton of fast-drying concrete in, after it." I returned The Look. "This is why I believe in leaving jobs like this to the professionals."

"Mister Chris, you don' even believe in magic."

"Which is why I am not inserting myself into the middle of this thing."

"Did you know they think it a box?"

I stopped my casual perusal of a scrum of shrunken heads. "What?"

"You tol' me Pandora's Box is a jug."

"Well, more like a vase, actually," I said absently. "A very big vase, though: comparable to a cask or barrel for modern storage purposes." I cocked my head. "Who thinks it's a box?"

"Meanin' its big and heavy, right. A big clay pot. Not like dose over there . . ."

I followed her gesture to the wall three aisles down. A row of five ancient, ceramic jugs were arranged in a rack over a pair of painted vases on a table top, serpentine handles adjoining their elongated necks.

"Uh, no . . ." I answered as I made my way over to the display. "These look like amphorae."

"Am-for-ay," she echoed.

"Plural. Singular would be amphora."

"An' what's the difference if it's all Greek pottery?"

"Well, not all amphorae are Greek. Some predate the Hellenic Era, going back even to the Stone Age while others can be traced to the Iron Age. There are even glass amphorae—but those would be rather rare—"

"But since we talkin' about Pandora, we be talkin' 'bout Greek pottery."

"Sure . . . as good an operating theory as any."

"An' these pithoses—pithae?"

"Pithoi, if you're looking for the plural," I said dryly.

"Are different . . . how?" she asked.

"Again, size, I guess." I shrugged. "I'm not an archeologist. Amphorae were light enough to sit on a table or have multiple jugs stored in racks." I gestured at the ready-made examples. "The larger ones might be about half the height of a human being."

"But these pithoi be a lot bigger?" she prompted.

"Yeah, more into the human-size range—some a little bigger, others a little smaller. A pithos might contain grain or oil or other goods but they were sometimes used as bathtubs and often for burial purposes. Even empty they'd be too heavy for one person to handle. Add some contents, slap the lid on and seal it for transport or shipping, and you could have 'a jug' weighing up to two tons."

"How much it weigh if you jus' gots another dimension on the inside with all kinda monsters waitin' to git out?"

"Hell. I don't know, Sammathea. And stop using that awful minstrel-show dialect. You know how I hate it."

Her smile was a crescent moon against the midnight skies of her face. "Cultural appropriation is hard work."

"Cultural appropriation? From who? Amos 'n' Andy? Leave the awful, blackface parody to the white-inferiority fringe."

"Why? Am I triggering your snowflake white ass?"

"I *know* why you do it, but I'm not your target demographic. And it demeans a woman I hold in some esteem," I growled. "Now cut it out before I retreat to a safe space."

She started to open her mouth but I raised my hand. "Buh-buh-buh-buh? Now what's this about a box?"

"Like I say . . . was saying. They think they've got Pandora's *Box*. But you had told me that it wasn't a box, it was a—"

"Pithos," I finished.

"Which I get is not the same thing," she continued. "So, help me find it."

"The pithos. Pandora's Pithos?"

"We are looking for the physical manifestation of the interdimensional portal in the shape of a pithos," she elucidated. "How hard can it be?"

"I really hate this dream . . ."

Aisle by aisle, row by row, we worked our way through the entire east wing of the mansion. Both floors. Lots o' weird stuff. No pithos.

Mama Samm was like a psychic bloodhound, tracking an invisible trail of ectoplasm through rows of séances, in search of one specific, haunted artifact.

She stopped only once and peered at a display of bottle-green pebbles. Some were dark and flintlike, imbedded with greenish, quartz-like crystals, while others had the appearance of melted emeralds, filled with tiny nebulae of dust and bubbles. They were in a clear, crystal bowl, set next to an antique Geiger counter and backed by maps purporting to show their original collection locations.

Mama Samm switched on the device and waved the "wand" over the rocks. The counter clicked and sputtered softly as the needle swung a few millimeters on the dial.

I stepped back.

Mama Samm turned the Geiger counter off and then grabbed a handful of stones out of the crystal bowl as if it were a candy dish. "Here," she said, offering me the lightly radioactive pebbles, "put these in your pockets."

"Why?" I asked, my eyes going to the title at the top of the display:

Trinitite
Sometimes referred to as Alamogordo glass or atomsite.

"Hey, this is—"

"Yes," she agreed. "Put them in your pockets."

"But—why?"

She gave me a long look. "Dream rules," she said finally. "Besides, they're not that radioactive."

"So, now you're a nuclear physicist? And what's with the whole side-trip to grab uranium isotopes?"

"Mister Chris, we have no time to waste in explanations and distractions! We've got an interdimensional portal to find and we are running out of time!"

"And timelines," I grumbled as I took the pebbles and slipped them into my pants. She took the bowl and dumped the remainder of the contents into her immense purse. She put the bowl back on the table but took the counter as she continued her search down the aisle.

"Now what?" I asked as we stood at the end of the east wing, empty-handed. So to speak.

"We search the attic and the basement," she decided.

"Basement," I blurted before I could stop myself.

"Why?"

I shrugged and discovered I had a crick in my neck. "Huge clay jar," I offered. "And heavy . . ."

"Maybe weighing thousands of pounds," she agreed. "If we run into anyone on the way, act casual."

Yeah. Sure.

We didn't run into anyone. People were either in bed and sleeping—like Annie and I were—or were out on the grounds, still dealing with the idea that The Wyrding had been infiltrated from below, compromising one of the rings that they had planned to incorporate into their sealing ceremony. Their ill humor was totally understandable but it still seemed that they could show a little gratitude to Carmella and myself for serving as canaries in their conjury coal mine.

If I thought the east wing was a cacophony of curios, the cellar was like the *Hoarders* version of the Mines of Moria. Overflowing shelves and stacks of boxes towered over our heads. Any available spaces in between were crammed to capacity with bins of baubles and crates of unknown properties. Ancient, incandescent light bulbs were trying their best, once we found the switch, but no wattage could be sufficient to reach the darker crevices in the deeper piles that towered near the ceiling like Jenga stacks of the damned. We needed spelunking gear.

"We don't have time for this," Mama Samm muttered under her breath. "Sunrise be coming soon."

"Maybe we should ask all those witchy types to pitch in and help," I suggested.

Her side-eye almost singed my eyebrows. "Mister Chris, these people are about to devote considerable resources to seal the wrong box while the Forces of Darkness on this side of the portal and the unimaginable Evils on the other side are doing their damnedest to rip the barrier wide open. At this point, I think they'd most likely be in the way." She frowned. "If they were inclined to help us at all."

"Point taken," I said, remembering Creighton's 'tude even before Carmella had moved the encampment to DEFCON 2 just a couple of hours earlier. Not that any of that was supposed to matter in a dream.

I mean, this was still a dream, right?

"So, Mister Chris . . . you sense anything?"

I looked around at the maze of boxes and the false horizon of stacks and piles beyond. "I sense that we're looking for a big pot that could weigh upwards of two tons . . . so it's not going to be anywhere on top of anything. I sense that it's probably going to be sitting on the floor . . ."

"You're a big help."

I turned to her. "I never claimed to be! You're the one who sicced the crone in teen's clothing on me and then pushed me in her direction. You want someone who knows what they're doing and has powers to detect interdimensional portals and seal same. There's nothing like that in my resume. I've never represented myself as the kind of guy who knows all about this stuff—"

"And yet you know just about the kind of stuff that nobody else would," she interrupted, jerking her head back toward the stairs and so-called experts up above and around us. "You have a knack—a history even—for thinking outside the box. Especially when said box would be a coffin for anybody else. I don't know what it is that you do or how you do it, but all of the augers indicated that you would be crucial to the success of sealing this portal before it was too late. Nothing in the original assessment or our subsequent castings for additional enlightenment—mine, hers, others—provided us with any additional details other than the strongest impressions that not only were you crucial to the solution . . ." She stopped suddenly, the unfinished thought troubling the normally implacable features of her face.

"But?" I coached.

". . . that the solution was crucial to you, as well."

"Well, duh: End-of-all-life-in-the-universe would have that effect on Yours Truly."

"Sure," she said too agreeably. "Now, let's get moving. This pithos isn't going to find itself."

We looked. Moving things seemed largely out of the question due to the apparent instability of the higher piles. And then there was the lack of floor space which would require a series of maneuvers akin to a Chinese sliding tile puzzle. And, finally, while Mama Samm had not returned to the immensity of her former form and figure, she had sufficiently returned from the brink of anorexia as to make squeezing through the narrow openings where the stacks closed in a bit of a challenge.

If we even could find this thing, I was absolutely sure that it was going to be in the very last place we looked.

Imagine my surprise when I turned a corner and literally stubbed my toe on it.

It was over five feet in height or better than one and a half meters. Other than its formidable size, it wasn't much to write home about. Most of the pithoi in illustrative photos or museum displays were more tapered with a base significantly smaller in circumference than the waist of the vessel. This thing had a silhouette like a cask or a barrel, suggesting a funerary function. The surface was covered in raised bands and faded iconography. If it had once been painted, all evidence, along with much of the patterns, had been worn away by millennia of exposure and multiple handlings.

The cover was a little more ornamented but seemed to be as one piece with the rest of the container: No seam was immediately apparent and the outer circumference of the lid was coated in a thick, resinous collar of some kind of sealant. I gingerly laid my hands against the weathered surface of the upper portion of the pot. It felt slightly cool to the touch, maybe a degree or two below room temperature. Beyond that: nothing. No aura of evil, no sensation of anything harmful—aside from some already stubbed toes. It fit the parameters of what we might expect to find in the most generic generalities.

But that was it.

I turned to Mama Samm. "Is this it?"

She huffed. "How am I supposed to know? You're the expert."

Holy Crudbunnies, I hated this dream! Give a good, old-fashioned nightmare any old . . . er . . . day. "*Not* an expert!" I hissed. "I just happen to know a little trivia point about a mythological misunderstanding and everybody seems to conflate that into me being the Sorcerer Supreme or something! So, unless you've got some sort of mojo detecting something up your hypnogogic sleeve, the only way I know to find out if this thing is the key to destroying this world and the next . . ." I paused. "And the next . . . and the next . . . and the next . . . is to pop the cork and take a look inside."

She closed her eyes and pressed her fingertips into her temples. After a moment she said, "Pick it up."

"What? Why?" I looked back at the pithos and then back at her. "What?"

"We have to go. I can't sense what's inside but I can sense what's outside. What's closing in. We have to go and we have to take it with us."

Right. "Well, go round up a dozen or so volunteers and see if we can get some blankets, rope, a block and tackle, a dolly—"

"Pick it up, Mister Chris."

I gaped at her. "You pick it up."

She huffed and planted her fists on her considerable hips. "Do I look like I am possessed of superhuman strength? You may not have fully transformed into a nasty-ass nosferatu, *cher,* but you stronger than anyone else here. And. We. Have. To. Go!" She stomped her foot. "Now!"

I bent to hug the pithos. Arguing was going to get me nowhere. And, if I couldn't lift it, further bickering would be pointless—dream rules or no.

"Lift with your legs," Mama Samm coached, "not with your back."

"Really?" I grunted, actually picking up the heavy jug with less trouble than I had anticipated—though more trouble than I might have hoped for. "Why don't you come over here and show me how it's done."

"Mister Chris, we're on a tight schedule what with the end of the multiverse and all. Don't have time for peoples getting hernias and moaning about bad backs. Time to do what has to be done and whine later. Now, suck it up and let's go." She turned and headed for the stairs.

I followed as best I could, weaving through the stacks like a drunken man, clutching an unwieldy cask of ale.

Halfway up the steps I was ready to put the thing down and rest. But there was no place to put it without risking a tumble from my grasp and a skittering cascade back down to the unyielding concrete floor below. So, I sucked it up and kept climbing, hugging the clammy clay urn as if I held the very world in my arms.

Because that was exactly what I was doing.

In multiples.

At the top of the stairs, Mama Samm helped me ease my burden back down to the floor and waited while I caught my breath. I kept expecting some kind of peevish observation about wasting time or "getting a move on" but she was uncharacteristically patient.

"Where are we taking this?" I asked as my breathing allowed single, short sentences without too much recovery time.

"Outside."

"Where outside?"

"The front porch." Her fists came back down on her mighty hips. "Now, less talking and more toting!"

No one seemed to be around. Either still sleeping or off to tamp down the manhole covers on their newfound Wagnerian Ring of the Nibble-Goblins . . .

"So, the looting has already begun," a new yet strangely familiar voice observed.

I froze and nearly lost my grip on the jug. Then I saw him, reflected in the mirror that ran the length of the staircase across from the arched entry to the main room.

With just a single occupant now the space seemed almost

cavernous compared to yesterday evening's crowded venue. Edmond sat, hunched in an overstuffed armchair like an ancient, trapdoor spider. On the floor, between his widely planted feet, sat an antique chest of lacquered, black wood with tarnished brass fittings.

I opened my mouth but he waved off any response I might have had. "Why not?" he mused absently. "The end of the world is coming. Possessions are meaningless. Ownership is illusion. We are all mummers, dancing our way toward our funeral pyre as the world prepares to burn . . ."

"Well, aren't we in a cheery mood," I wheezed, hefting the pot for a better grip.

He leaned forward a bit and seemed to peer at my face. Or, rather, the reflection of my face in the mirror as I hadn't turned toward him. "Why are you stealing knickknacks when you could be upstairs banging my grandmother?"

I started to put the pithos down so we could have a proper conversation, bare knuckles and all, but Mama Samm laid a gentling hand on my arm.

"I don't think you know who you are talking to," she said. There was an odd quality of sternness to her voice that I had never heard before.

"To whom you are speaking," I corrected under my breath. I felt curiously light- headed.

"I know who you are," he said. "Who both of you . . . what each of you . . . more importantly, *They* know." His sudden grin was both ferocious and pitying. "You should run now. It won't matter. They are coming and They will find you. No matter how fast you run. No matter where you hide. They are coming for everyone. But They will make you a priority. So, buy yourself a few more hours and run now. Maybe you can even put a couple of days between you and The Gate."

Mama Samm was tugging at my arm but I was focused on the ancient lockbox that practically radiated a sense of palpable malevolence.

"Is that what you've got there, Eddie?" I drawled with forced insouciance. "Are you the Key Master? Got Sigourney Weaver stashed in your footlocker there?"

His face changed, shading toward something reptilian. Maybe he wasn't a classic *Ghostbusters* fan. That's the trouble with the remakes:

They leave out the good parts. "Promises were made!" he hissed. "Is it my fault . . . I was chosen? That I can hear Their voices? That I was called?"

I thought of Annwn Harkwynde asleep upstairs, piteously hoping that apple did fall far from the tree.

Mama Samm squeezed my bicep hard enough to draw my attention. She cocked her head at the ancient pot in my shaky embrace.

Are you sure? she mouthed.

Sure that we had the Pandoran portal to the Dread Dimension? Well, no. Nor could I tell the difference between a product of the Ming dynasty and a Pier One Import. But I was . . . fairly . . . sure that The Gateway was a pithos and not a chest. So whatever nastiness was boxed at the old man's feet was not on the Cséjthe To-Do List at this particular moment.

I gave her the barest of nods as Harkwynde's grandson snarled more dismissals. I opened my mouth again but Sammathea D'Arbonne beat me to the punch.

"Well, good luck with that," she told him. "Come, Cséjthe, we must flee."

We didn't waste any time exiting the house and navigating the porch steps down to the great curving driveway. Still, our progress barely approached a determined stroll, never mind running or fleeing.

Off in the distance, I could hear a staccato of popping sounds as if someone were setting off strings of firecrackers.

Or several someones were rapidly firing off dozens of rounds of ammunition.

I opened my mouth again to ask about the next part of "The Plan" but a pair of headlights down the hill flashed as if on cue. An engine turned over and then the sound of grinding gears silenced all of the crickets and cicadas for ten miles in all directions. A massive truck started up the drive, making enough noise to wake the dead.

"So, we're still operating in stealth mode?" I asked, hoping that there weren't any actual "dead" around to wake up at this point.

"You never showed up when and where you were supposed to," she accused. "I'm doing the best I can to make that happen! So, try and be more helpful. I thought that Harkwynde girl and her people could help us. Clearly they are in over their heads."

"We're all in over our heads," I muttered.

"Some more than others," she agreed. "At least you aren't surrendering to The Darkness, yet."

"Yet . . ." I echoed. She couldn't hear me over the roar of the canopied, flatbed truck, grinding toward us like a locomotive on three sets of heavy-tread tires.

Yet. But I knew there would be no surrendering on my part now or in the future. It wasn't bravado or false courage or mindless ego: There simply wasn't anything to be gained in cooperating with the kind of Darkness that sets its sights on the utter corruption and annihilation of the world you inhabit—and all other worlds besides. And, anyway, I wasn't about to break The Rule for these cosmic jerkoffs if I wasn't going to break it for my own selfish desires.

Maybe twenty-four hours ago I had been ready to hand off the baton in some relativistic relay race across the multiverse. Not surrendering, of course; just assuming that there were people less clueless than me running just ahead. When you finally figure out that the people around you are worse than merely clueless—that their incompetence is more weighted by an arrogant overconfidence in sets of false assumptions that lead to extinction-level results . . . well, what is there for it but to clutch the baton—or, in this case, the pithos—to your chest and just keep running.

Or riding.

A great, old "Deuce and a Half" army truck came barreling up the long, curved drive to the front of the house. As it approached, it appeared to be a more modern version of the World War II utility trucks—though more of a throwback to the 1950s than the 1990s. The tented canopy over the extended bed was peeled halfway back exposing three metal support hoops and pedestal-mounted anti-aircraft gun. It arrived with a loud grinding of gears and the engine immediately died as if the driver was a novice at handling a large, manual transmission gearbox.

"Well, I don't drive stick!" a vaguely familiar voice complained. "In fact, I don't drive period! As Doman, I have drivers. Who drive me. The last time I drove myself, was maybe fifty years ago and it was an automatic. I don't drive and I certainly don't drive stick. Gods and Monsters, the damned thing has three axels! Ten big-ass tires! This isn't a truck, it's a Macy's Day Parade float!"

"Okay, shove over," another familiar voice answered, "this driving lesson is done." I set the pithos down to rest my arms.

The cab's passenger door opened and a ghostly figure swung down to the ground. He appeared to be solid enough, nothing of transparency about his pinstriped shirt with the rolled-up sleeves nor the unbuttoned suit vest revealing the loosely knotted, silk necktie. The cuffs of his trousers covered his socks, resting atop his very expensive-looking wingtips. The face beneath his rakishly tipped, grey fedora was moonlight pale.

"Dennis?" I said. Then turned to Mama Samm. "Don't tell me; he's not my Dennis Smirl."

"*Your* Dennis Smirl?" the Enforcer for the Chicago demesne growled. "You're reading way too much into my leaving my post and driving across the country with your juju woman to save the world!"

"Actually he is the Dennis Smirl from your timeline," she said quietly. And then raised her voice to address him: "And you are reading way too much into our working relationship to call me *his* juju woman!"

"Yeah, yeah," Stefan Pagelovitch said as he came around the truck into the creamy wash of the headlights. Although he was more practically dressed for a nocturnal excursion into enemy territory—black shirt, black slacks, ebony Gucci trainers—he was just as expensively and elegantly attired as Smirl was in his tailored Loro Piana, albeit a little less rumpled. "But if Cséjthe wasn't involved in this, I doubt if she would have convinced any of us to come along," he added.

As I looked at the Doman of the Seattle demesne, two things occurred to me. First, both Pagelovitch and Smirl had gone missing around the same time my accountant had disappeared . . . and Stefan had said *any of us* as opposed to *either of us*.

The vampire looked toward the back of the truck. "Where is—is she sleeping in my coffin again?"

As irrational as it seemed, the thought of Lupé leapt to the forefront of my attention. Or Deirdre. I ran to the rear of the cargo area and hoisted myself over the tailgate. And stopped. A gun barrel was pointed at my face.

More disquieting, the bore of said barrel looked big enough to swallow a quarter—maybe a half-dollar.

Worse, yet: the face staring at me from the other side of the anti-aircraft sight was at least two thousand years old, familiar, and decidedly unfriendly.

Chapter Eighteen

"Well," I asked after a long, uncomfortable pause, "who let the dog out? Who, who, who, who—?"

The dark man with the baroque mullet sighed and leaned on the grips of the pedestal- mounted machine gun, tilting the impressive muzzle skyward. He wore a dark, military-style tee and camo-patterned fatigue pants over combat boots. It seemed as natural on him now as the boiled-leather armor and caligae he had worn two millennia before.

"'Twas not funny the first time you shared the pictures that move on your talking device. It hath gained no additional humor as you speak the words once again," he growled.

"But you are—or, at least, were the Hound of Ulster," I said.

"A cognomen," he argued. "Before I was the Hound of Ulster, I was Culann's Hound. But my true, given name at birth is Sétanta."

"Aye," a feminine voice countered. "But two millennia have passed and you are—by all the scribes of history—Cúchulainn." As he sat back in the unexpected La-Z-Boy recliner on the truck bed, Fand appeared, out of the shadows, her pale, elven beauty almost a light in the darkness of the night and the shadowy depths of the cargo area. She virtually draped herself over her mythic lover from behind the overstuffed chair. "How now, Cséjthe?"

I dipped in a mock curtsy. "Your Majesty. You're far from home." I tried to peer into the darkness behind her. "Anyone else on vacay from The Realm?"

"My sister deemed it dangerous to come lest she fall once more under your . . ." the Faerie queen made a distasteful face, ". . . influence."

I wasn't asking about Liban—though I wouldn't have objected to seeing that particular Fae again. "I was wondering about my people . . ."

"They are no longer 'your' people, Cséjthe," she scolded gently. "They are inhabitants of The Realm. And, as such, their past lives are set aside. Along with such memories—"

"Yeah, yeah; I know," I said bitterly. "Out of sight, out of mind."

"Out of heart," she added.

"Speaking of heart," I said, changing the subject before disappointment could close its black fingers about mine, "I see that you and the boytoy are still together. I thought Manny and the druids put a stop to that."

Her face softened. "We are long-lived but none of us are eternal. After Manannán mac Lir passed into the Eternal, his spell was weakened. And the draught of the *Draoidh* loosed its hold on me after the first millennia . . ."

I glanced at Sétanta who still seemed largely indifferent to his elven lover's caresses. "But not the mostly mortal mullet, I'm guessing . . ."

She gave him a thoughtful look. "There are costs to bringing a mortal back from the brink of death . . . as you should so well know. Should you live for tens of hundreds of years—"

I shook my head. "Let's not go down that road."

"We have other roads to travel for now," Mama Samm's voice said at my back.

I turned and then moved to drop the tailgate as Smirl and Pagelovitch approached, bearing the pithos.

"This is the prize?" Fand asked as I knelt to take the big jug into my embrace.

"Yeah. Prize," I grunted, trying to lift the giant clay pot into the back of the truck. "Hopefully the Door prize and not a Booby prize."

"Sétanta," Fand ordered, "help him secure the portal. Handle it carefully!" she barked as he ham-handedly tried to wrest it from the three of us.

I followed him into the depths of the cargo area where he stashed it in a pile of blankets and moving pads stacked next to the ornate casket that I presumed was Pagelovitch's. A scattering of mattresses, sleeping bags, a couple of yard-sale armchairs, folding card table, and several beanbag chairs seemed to be the extent of the furnishings for this road trip. Not exactly the intuitive travel comfort for transporting Faerie royalty, a master vampire, a Celtic legend, or a Chicago top brass enforcer with shapeshifting abilities that were apparently just the tip of the arcane catalogue. I would have rented a Winnebago, Class A Lux edition.

But then there wouldn't have been a place to put the pedestal-mounted anti-aircraft gun that Sétanta had returned to caressing: a .50 caliber Browning with boxes and belts of ridiculously oversized ammo. Off to the side were more boxes, opened to reveal enough armament to give the anti-NRA lobby nightmares for years to come.

A flamethrower rig appeared to be carelessly stashed next to a box of grenades.

"Well, damn," I said softly, "someone forgot to bring the tactical nukes."

"Cséjthe?" Smirl asked, holding up a set of keys. "You know how to drive stick?"

I nodded.

That's when the screaming started.

It started off with a bang.

A jet of flame shot into the sky, maybe a mile away. Keening wails drifted our way from the brief blowtorch effect and the flame died back down to a scattering of red and yellow embers.

A second column of flame pierced the night, punctuated by more screams and more gunfire. This time it was closer, maybe a half a mile away or closer. The spray of embers near its base moved erratically, as if they were living entities caught in the throes of madness.

"Your turn!" Smirl tossed the keys to me and then climbed up into the back, followed by Pagelovitch who muttered, "Thank gods!" Passing me, the pale man handed me a couple of earplugs. "You'll need these," he said, "not that they'll do much good."

"Wait," I said. "Annie's upstairs!"

Mama Samm grabbed my face. "Cséjthe! Focus! We have a world to save! Else everyone and everything be lost!"

I stepped back, pulling my chin from her grasp. "We don't even know if we have the right jar!"

Something passed overhead, low enough that I could feel the vortex and wash of impossibly large wings. The stars overhead vanished and took an impossible amount of time to reappear, suggesting a sizable silhouette of dread and malevolence. I dropped the earplugs into my shirt pocket and slapped the keys into Mama Samm's palm. "Five minutes. I'll still drive if you want to wait but I suggest you have the engine running and everything strapped down before I get back."

I turned and ran back to the porch, hitting every other step on my way to the front door.

I spared a glance through the archway as I hit the stairs to the second floor and noticed that Eddie had acquired a hand axe from the wood rack next to the fireplace and was giving the locked chest considerable thought. I heard another voice, maybe two, but I was mounting the landing now and taking the turn toward the second floor. Let the dead bury the dead: I was going to get Annie, find Kirsten, and blow this popsicle stand.

She was still on the bed, right where I'd left her. Along with my left shoe. Which might explain some of the difficulty I'd had walking for the past hour or so. I gave her a little shake to wake her as I sat on the bed to reacquire my footwear. "C'mon, sleepyhead. Rise and shine. Everything's just moved to 6.9 on the Mordor Scale . . ."

She stirred a little but obstinately refused to rise, much less shine.

Someone was shouting downstairs.

Okay. I leaned over her and slid my arms under her back and legs. She came up off the bed as if she hardly weighed anything at all. Nothing like the Jug of the Damned, anyway. I turned and headed for the door. As light as she was in my arms, it was still awkward trying to get us both through the opening and into the hallway. By the time I was at the top of the stairs I could hear a number of voices drifting up from the first floor.

"Stop!"

"What are you doing?"

"Are you mad?"

I recognized Creighton's voice in the mix. And Edmond's—though I wasn't sure who was saying what. Other voices were indistinct, though generally expressing dismay.

As I reached the bottom of the stairs I could see that there were six or seven people in the room, facing off against Annie's grandson who was keeping them at bay with the hatchet now. For an elderly dude he had a pretty good swing. The ornate, lacquered chest had been upended and was next to his right foot. The brass fittings were freshly scarred and scraped, the dark wood was pockmarked with splintered gouges where the axe head had bitten deep.

"Edmond?" Annie was awake, her eyes wide and stricken. "What are you—?" The question died in her throat as his gaze swung to hers. The room seemed to pivot with the movement and I fought the urge to shift my weight to accommodate an imaginary tilt to the floor.

He hissed. The outer corners of his eyes drew back and the planes of his face shifted into something vaguely reptilian.

Someone behind him tried to make a move. Without looking away he swung the hatchet in a three-quarter arc, twisting sinuously like a boneless contortionist and opening his would-be assailant from shoulder to breastbone. There was blood. There was screaming. There was a great deal of both and Eddy hadn't lost his hold on his hand axe or his grandmother's gaze.

The room seemed to fill with an uncertain, wobbly light.

I was suddenly aware that he was only four of five running steps away from us and my arms were relatively useless as they were currently occupied. I glanced toward the front door off to my right. The Thing using Edmond Harkwynde's mortal remains as Its own personal Airbnb, saw my eyes and the tensing of my body, and hurled the axe right at us.

The world shattered.

Then I realized that we had both forgotten that we were watching each other's reflection in the great mirror opposite the main room's archway.

The hatchet was buried in the wall beneath the stairs. A third of the mirror was in pieces on the floor beneath it, the remainder riven with cracks and fault lines that crept toward its outer frame even as I stood there.

Annie started to struggle in my arms and I looked at Edmond's distorted reflection in the broken glass to see what he would do next. He bent and retrieved another throwing weapon as the room grew brighter still: He lifted the ornate chest and raised it over his head, taking a step and then another toward the archway. My cover would be gone in another three steps.

And then the room shattered again.

Or, rather, the great picture window shattered as a large truck crashed into the front of the house. Shards of glass, chunks of masonry, and people went flying across the room. Edmond looked surprised and vaguely disappointed as the chest tumbled from his grasp and he flew sideways with a long, jagged, crystalline dagger protruding from his ear.

Surprisingly, I managed to stay on my feet though I lost my grip on Annie. She landed in a crouch with one hand on the floor and the other raised in a seemingly protective gesture.

A voice that was not Edmond's said, "Oh my G—" and then all was still.

Except for a vague hissing sound.

Edmond?

Annie rose and took a step toward the archway.

I grabbed her upper arm and tugged her back. "Wait . . ."

Aside from swirling clouds of dust and fine debris, the remainder of the mirror revealed no movement in the next room. No one stood up to cast a reflection. No one moaned. No one groaned or cursed. I couldn't see where anyone had fallen. I couldn't see if the Thing that looked like Edmond was, even now, crawling or creeping or scuttling like a spider around the furniture to make an unexpected leap at us at any given moment.

I sidled toward the front door, pulling a vaguely resistant tweenager with me.

And then I saw it.

Several its.

The pile of antique silvered glass beneath the hand axe that angled out of the remains of the mirror offered a dozen or so tilted eyes back into the room.

Reflected in one was an arm and hand, positioned awkwardly in mid-fall. The flesh grey as if long dead.

A leg and foot were revealed by another piece of the great mirror, as still as stone.

And then there was an angled view of the antique chest, its lid and one hinge twisted into a gaping maw and the head of a snake corkscrewing toward it, as if seeking sanctuary. A second serpent joined it. Neither seemed to be making any progress.

The faint hissing sound became louder and less distinct now. The sound issuing from a chorus of tiny throats . . .

And now the view of a *mythic* decapitation in another of the fallen shards of mirror.

But this seemingly mortal wound was not fresh. The separation of head from shoulders was ancient. This death had been meted out millennia ago. Only the scalp was still alive, bristling with dozens if not a hundred and more snaky tresses.

They hissed at my reflection.

"Σκατά!" I hissed back. I grasped Annie's chin in an iron grip and turned her face away from the archway as I used my other hand on her arm to move her along. "Don't look back," I told her. "We have to go and go now!"

As we stumbled out the front door I could see the cab of a gasoline truck buried nose-deep into the crushed wall fronting the house. Stonework from the outer facade had collapsed across the windshield and hood, shielding the driver from the immediate danger of a line-of-sight view. If there was a driver. No silhouette was visible through the driver side window.

Annie made a move toward the tanker but I pulled her back again. "Not that truck," I told her. I pointed at the Deuce and a Half: "That one."

Mama Samm D'Arbonne had the passenger door open to the cab, her dark skin nearly indistinguishable from the night while the white turban that confined her hair seemed to float like a disembodied ghost at the roofline. Dennis Smirl's pale face was visible behind the steering wheel, awash in greenish light from the dashboard instrumentation.

"Cséjthe!" she bellowed. The sounds of screaming and gunfire were closer and louder, now. As were a couple more columns of flame and maybe twenty or thirty smaller fires that seemed to stagger about on two limbs or four. It was still too far away to tell if any of them were human.

And I wasn't keen on knowing . . .

"I'm not leaving without my daughter," I bellowed back, expecting an argument.

She merely pointed at the rear of the fuel tanker.

There was enough ambient light from the house, from the vehicles, from the distant flares, to see a length of heavy canvas hose trailing behind the truck like a prehensile tail. The grass in its wake was wet and the smell of gasoline lent a sickly-sweet perfume to the night air.

Yeah, that wasn't good.

I waved her back into the Deuce. "Follow the drive around and down to the gate. You can wait for me there. Or not. But I'm not leaving without Kirsten." I gave Annie a little nudge. "Go on, climb into the back. I can travel faster on my own . . ."

"No, you can't," she said. "And I can call her."

"Okay," I said. Arguing wasted precious time. "Go ahead. Do what you can do. But we gotta move now." I waved off Mama Samm again. "Wait at the gate. Or not. Ten more minutes and I don't think it will really matter."

Mama Samm shook her head but stepped up onto the running board. "We can't do this without you, Christopher. You'd be surprised what matters."

"Sure," I muttered.

She nodded and gave Smirl the sign to drive.

The old military truck lurched forward with a roar and laboriously made a looping turn to mostly follow the circle drive back down toward the main gate.

I looked over at the nearest pyre, a smudge of yellow and orange flame lighting the way to a succession of distant candles in the predawn darkness. The last time I had seen my daughter she had been heading toward the front gate. A series of explosions, pyrotechnics, and a whole lotta screamin' goin' on would have surely drawn her away to the east to engage the threat.

Even if I hadn't seen her in action, she was a Cséjthe. It was in her genes.

Without even a word to Annie I pivoted on my heel and took three steps toward the flickering lights and got clotheslined by a shaved gorilla.

A twelve-foot tall, shaved gorilla with four arms!

Or, rather, two upper arms that bifurcated at the elbows into four forearms!

Which was just so wrong without even taking the implied pun into account.

The creature's leathern skin was hairless and colored a midnight, purple-black which camouflaged it in the darkness until it was right on top of me.

And now it *was* right on top of me!

A hand closed around my throat. I felt more than saw that it wasn't anything like a mammalian hand with four fingers and an opposable thumb, but rather something akin to a great raptor's foot with three, heavily muscled digits, each tipped with a long, curved talon, tapering to a venomous-looking tip. A huge, toothy maw split its head open, leaning down to take a big bite out of me . . .

. . . but its impossibly wide mouth bisected its curiously flattened head from front to back rather than the typical side-to-side taxonomy: My gorilla analogy was officially out the window and well in the rearview mirror. Its skull fell open like it was split in two and a giant, serpentine tongue reared out of its neck like an octopus tentacle. It licked across ridiculously long and sharpened teeth that literally glowed in the dark like phosphorescent icicles.

". . . Run . . ." I gasped, hoping that Annie was smart enough to understand the concept of "lost causes."

The gargantuan beast sprouted another arm, this one smaller, pale white, and ending in a human, five-fingered hand.

The hand reached across the monster's negligible throat and got a grip on the opposite shoulder.

A second head appeared. Human. Or close enough: Carmella.

Her mouth was full of teeth, too. And wider than I remembered. It was like her fangs had gone from the adolescent phase to full-blown adulthood and had lots of babies! Which looked well on their way to becoming adolescents themselves!

She grinned at me and I shivered.

"Hello, Christopher," she cooed. "Miss me?"

Then she leaned in and took a tremendous bite out of the beast's neck.

The wound erupted in a geyser of inky fluid, more ichor than actual blood, but the vampress tucked back in and began slurping at a veritable river of pulsing goo.

I heroically fought off my gag reflex: Who was I to look a gift vampire in the mouth? Carmella had the monster's full attention now. I scooted backwards like a crab as it released me and reared up, all four er—forearms—flailing like a quixotical windmill. Dodging my reflexive punch, Annie jumped behind me and helped me back up to my feet.

In the meantime, Carmella Le Fanu nearly went flying as the monster found its own, so-called, feet and began to whirl about, spraying us all with greasy fluids like a demonic lawn sprinkler. She managed to hook one hand on the edge of those terrible jaws as she swung about in a near full circle. Without thinking—because it's the one thing I'm so good at—I tucked my head, bent at the waist, and tried to ram the creature to knock it off balance.

I was moderately successful. I did ram the thing head-on—I could hardly miss given its size and proximity. I hit it hard, at the juncture of its lower limbs, and bounced off without achieving any discernable result—it remained upright—other than the disturbing impression that there may have been genitalia involved. As I staggered back, I saw the vampire's other hand catch the opposing jaw on the thing's bifurcated head. The gleaming maw, already stretched implausibly wide, opened even further until the glowing chompers were pushed one hundred eighty degrees apart . . .

Then one-ninety . . .

Two hundred . . .

There was a hoarse, high-pitched keening, fracturing into shrieking noises. Then a wet, tearing sound as the jaws were forced apart past the breaking point. The monster collapsed in a shuddering heap and lay still. Or relatively still, given the mandatory twitching—the byproduct of misfiring neurons as they sputtered into collective oblivion.

Carmella Le Fanu dismounted the heap like an Olympic gymnast and strode toward us, a ghastly figure drenched in blood, gore, and things that didn't bear close examination.

Other than that, she looked disgustingly healthy.

"You came back," was all that I could think to say.

She stopped and looked at me like I had said something disrespectful.

"What?" She looked past me, presumably at Harkwynde, and frowned. Then back at me and frowned a little less. "Did you think I had abandoned you?"

"Well . . . I . . ."

"Christopher!" I winced. My mother had used that tone with me when I had, upon rare occasion, disappointed her. "We had just uncovered a nest of—what did you call them? Sheepala . . ."

"Lamia," I corrected.

"Right. And what did you expect me to do?" she asked. Rhetorically, I was betting. "Turn myself over to the bitches?"

"Witches," I corrected.

"Practitioners," Annie elucidated.

"Bumblefucks," Carmella decided. "They discover an underground ring running beneath their ceremonial grounds and don't even run a decent security check? I'm supposed to rely on these paragons of wisdom to see that I'm not the threat, here?"

It hardly seemed the moment to point out that she was the scariest thing I'd seen here over the past twenty-four hours so I let it slide.

"I don't think these people could pour blood out of a boot if the instructions were written on the heel! So, somebody had to do something!"

"Which you did . . ." I guessed.

"Yes! I went out and hijacked a fuel truck!" she said, pointing at the obvious reference just a few yards away. "Drove it back here, through the front gate, led a parade of crossbow-wielding geniuses to the far access hatch and—thanks to your cranky little girl—managed to start a Johnny Cash classic before all of the rats got out of the bag!"

"Johnny Ca—?" I started and then stopped.

She put her hands on her slimy hips and stared at me. "Go on, work it out," she taunted.

There was a muffled explosion and a manhole cover was launched to the west of us on a column of flame.

"Ring of Fire," I mumbled lamely.

"That's right, my Doman!" she said snarkily. "Why, thank you, Carmella! That was brilliant, Carmella! You were so smart, so innovative, not to mention brave to come back and save the torches-and-pitchforks mob who were shooting at you—" Her eyebrow ascended sharply. "—and your daughter, as you were risking life and limb to save their—and your—sorry asses instead of—as you apparently thought—running away to selfishly only think of myself!"

"I'm sorry," I said.

"I'm sorry, Carmella!" she steamrollered over me. "Forgive me, Carmella! You're the best, Carmella!"

"You really are," I said.

"That's right!" she said. Then stopped and blinked at me. "Really? You think I'm the best?"

Well, at least for the moment. But I didn't say that. I just nodded. "And extra points for the *Deus ex Exxon* solution."

"Oh . . . Christopher!" She moved in for a sloppy, gore-slicked embrace and I stood there and took it like a man. I did manage to get my fingers up and between our lips before we ended up swapping fluids that did not bear even the most oblique consideration.

"We can't stay here," I told her. I pointed at the hose trailing the crashed fuel tanker. Off in the distance a serpentine thread of fire was wending its way toward us at an alarming rate.

Carmella nodded and practically lifted me to set me aside. Instead of running away from the repository of so much volatile gasoline, however, she ran to the truck, mounting the step up to the cab and ripped the driver's side door out of the frame. Flinging it aside, she reached in and lifted the diminutive driver out, tossing her over her shoulder. "Run!" she yelled to us as she jumped down. Taking her own advice, she blew past us and Annie and I followed in her wake as the flames finally caught up to the tanker's hose.

Fortunately, both Carmella and I could move inhumanly fast— her with my daughter in a fireman's carry and me with Annie practically airborne as I pulled her along by her upper arm. It must have taken the burning fuel a few extra seconds to breach the valve at the other end of the hose: By the time the shockwave of the blast flung us another twenty yards through the air, we were beyond the primary effect of the fireball. Ditto most of the shrapnel although I did have to pull a nine-inch metal splinter from my left buttock. The wound was less troublesome than the implied metaphor.

I staggered over to Kirsten who was crumpled on the ground. "She's alright," the vampress assured me. "She just can't drive a stick for shit."

I glanced up at the Deuce idling down the hill near the gatehouse. "A lot of that going around," I murmured.

Kirsten coughed and began to rouse.

"Easy, young lady," I said, putting a restraining hand on her shoulder as she started to sit up. "Let's make sure nothing's broken before you start moving around."

"It's not," Annie decided as she knelt beside me. She gave me a look and tilted her head up, adding: "We've got bigger worries than broken bones, anyways."

"Like those Greek monsters you've got all stirred up," Carmella agreed.

"Um," I mumbled, "that last thing? Not Greek. Not any mythology I'm familiar with . . ."

Annie said something that sounded like "glug."

Kirsten shoved my hand away. "'M a'right!" her head wobbled a bit before she managed to find a point of reference. "L'right," she reaffirmed. "Help up," she demanded.

Just like that, Kirsten was gone and Stryfe was back again.

"Honey," Annie told her, "we gotta go. Right now. You can either let your daddy carry you or the nasty-ass thing that used to be a vampire."

"Hey," the nasty-ass thing that used to be a vampire said.

"Well," I said, "I don't know what all sorts of bloodlike fluids you've been drinking, but you're clearly metamorphosing into something else entirely." I let the specific anatomical reference slide.

"I'm transforming like you, Christopher," she said. "You have shown me the Secret of Becoming!"

Becoming what?

I decided that this was hardly the time to point out that we had been ordering off of different menus. Being offered the "blood" of the Elohim and a Valkyrie was hardly the same as treating a monster slaughterfest as an all-you-can-eat buffet.

Smirl leaned on the horn and I hoisted Kirsten into my arms. Surprisingly, she let me: I guess the difference in external viscera content made my embrace a little less objectional.

As we sprinted toward the Deuce, Smirl swung down from the cab and gestured to the seat behind the wheel. "You said you can handle a manual transmission, right?" he asked, lifting Kirsten from my arms.

"Yeah?"

"Then get us down the road. Her Highness will take care of the rest."

A horde of things that made the four-armed, split-headed,

shaved-gorilla creature look like an escapee from a petting zoo were headed down the hill toward us. Like I said, arguing just wastes precious time: I climbed up into the cab and slammed the door behind me. Fand was sitting in the passenger seat. She gave me the once over, taking in the Rorschach application of viscera on my clothes. Then, like true elven royalty, she sniffed and turned her attention to the vista beyond the windshield as if we were already on our way.

"Roll up your window," she said.

"Why?" I asked, fumbling the key into the ignition. "Does the AC work?" I was kidding: Despite this being a post–WWII design, there was nothing in the cockpit design that suggested any kind of comfort technology.

"The *Curuni* said that we should—to quote—roll up the windows and lock the doors before starting out."

Curuni? "Yeah? Well, the Curuni is not the boss of me."

"Cséjthe!" Sammathea bellowed from behind me.

Fand gestured. "You tell her."

Oh.

I hand-cranked the glass up despite the summer's heat and pressed down on the post that locked my door.

"Is there a problem up there?" D'Arbonne's voice sounded uncharacteristically brittle and that worried me more than the hideous mob in my rearview mirror. "Why are we not moving?"

I turned the key in the ignition and the engine jumped to attention with a roar. Literally. I fumbled in my pocket for the ear plugs. My teeth were literally vibrating. Smirl was right: The ear plugs made the noise bearable, but just barely. I ran a visual assessment of the dashboard. There was more instrumentation than on anything I'd ever driven: It took me a few precious moments to figure out what was important for right now and what I could figure out down the road.

The Browning in the back of the truck opened up, suggesting that the mutant menagerie from the Dread Dimension was closing in fast.

The stick shift rose out of the floor like an iron walking stick in the throes of a grand mal seizure. There were five speeds, not counting Neutral, Reverse, or the "Transfer Case" with faded instructions indicating the "Low Down" and "High Up" settings with the required speeds for each gear in each setting.

I only thought I knew how to "drive stick" it seemed.

I wrestled the gearshift through a series of grinding noises and the truck lurched forward. The stutter of the .50 caliber behind the cab was now punctuated by the unsteady boom-shaka-lakas of frantic grenade tosses that suggested time was up for my student driver exam. I danced a counterpoint jig on the clutch pedal as the truck grunted into first and then gradually into second gear as we rambled toward the gateway to the outer road.

"You need to go faster," Fand admonished.

"Maybe you should get out and push," I suggested, trying to coax, then insist that the stick move into third gear.

I felt a slight leftward dip in the cab as if something heavy jumped onto the driver's side running board. Then something went splat against my door and I turned to see a large, greasy, four-fingered hand pressed against the glass. There was a lipless mouth where the palm should have been, ringed with rows of curved, needlelike teeth.

You would think a mutant army of demon spawn from the Dread Dimension would bring their own wheels for the Great Invasion instead of resorting to hitchhiking . . .

The hand or paw or whatever kind of appendage that was licking at the glass reared back and smashed through the window to lay a sloppy grip on my shoulder, just as I managed to move the gearshift into some semblance of fourth gear. I moved my right hand from the stick to the steering wheel and my left hand from the wheel to the crank on the driver's side door: I turned the crank like a man possessed.

Or soon to be . . .

What was left of the window retracted back down into the doorframe and the jagged opening forced the appendage down, too, finally severing the hideous hand in a spray of blackish ichor that seemed to miss the Faerie queen to my immediate right while completely drenching me.

Still, the thing on the running board persisted, hissing and squalling until I opened the door a couple of times while sideswiping a concrete post as we exited the gateway to the Maitland estate.

"Check your side mirror," I told Fand. "I doubt if any of those things can catch us on foot, now, but . . ."

And that was when I saw the swoop of a bat-like creature on the periphery of our headlights further up the road.

Saying "bat-like" in this instance was like saying "cat-like" to describe a sabretooth tiger sprouting luminous, barbed spines and extra limbs ending in serrated pincers.

"Well, that's not good," I muttered. If stating the obvious was a superpower, I'd have a closet full of capes.

Something heavy landed behind the cab and I could feel the rear suspension dip low over the second and third axles. The tires screeched and hissed as the undercarriage kissed spinning rubber.

The Browning opened up and shredded canvas from the rear tenting went sailing past my window.

Fand touched my shoulder and I could hear her voice as if we were conversing in a quiet room. "You must convey us away from this place and, as soon as we reach an area of open roadway, clear of hand or hoof or paw, I shall open The Way."

Open the way?

Then I remembered her sister, Liban, "opening The Way" for my houseboat to travel from northern Louisiana to New Orleans by something akin to translocation.

Oboy.

"Any reason you can't be doing that right now?" I asked as a series of thumps increasingly dented the cab roof over our heads.

"I require open space with direct line of sight for at least one kilometer," she said. Glancing up at our descending ceiling, she added, "A tranquil environment is more conducive to proving an accurate portage . . ."

"You may have to settle for kicking the door open and making a blind leap."

"I will not chance taking a creature such as this into my Realm," she insisted, removing her hand from my shoulder.

And that's when The Hound of Ulster did a belly-flop on the hood of the Deuce.

The bumpy surface of the broken and ancient asphalt was bouncing him down the inclined surface of the engine cover but his hands shot out, grabbing a windshield wiper apiece in each of his ham-sized fists.

I fought off the fleeting impulse to look for the wiper controls on the dashboard.

"You must stop the truck!" Her Highness hollered, no longer in whisper mode.

That was not happening, not with the hordes of hell barely behind us. I leaned over the wheel and thrust my arm out the side window, waving at his right hand. It was just beyond my grasp.

"Take the wheel!" I told her.

"I—cannot drive stick!" she cried.

"Just try to keep us on the road and away from the trees!" I opened my door and scooted toward the edge of my seat. My foot lost pressure on the gas pedal and I had to contort my body so that my right leg could keep us from losing acceleration while I could dangle my mangled left buttock off the cushion. Hyperextending my left arm between the semi-open door and the frame, I grabbed Sétanta's right wrist. And started to pull . . .

And that's when we sideswiped a tree.

I lost my grip—nearly lost my arm as the door was slammed back against the frame—and saw that Fand was maintaining a strong steady grip, both hands white-knuckled and firmly on the dashboard. The steering wheel was completely in play and rolling to and fro like an unsecured barrel on the deck of a storm-tossed ship. I leaned back in and made sure we were pointed back toward the open space between the woods on either side.

"Help him!" she shrieked.

"Help me so I can help him!" I yelled back at her. "Take the damn wheel!"

But Cúchulainn was already helping himself. His right hand dropped to his belt from which he plucked a dagger with an eight-inch blade. He raised up and plunged said blade into the hood, just in front of the windshield. The dagger pieced the sheet metal like it was hot butter.

Using the hilt as an anchor, he leveraged himself back up, reaching above the windscreen to find purchase higher up.

Unfortunately that meant I could see more of him than I could of the terrain. "Come on, come on! Move, ya big lug!"

The tip of a glowing, spiny tail slithered about the top of the windshield, leaving smoking, brown spiderweb traceries in the glass. He caught hold with a great bellow, his eyes flashing amber and orange, his hair standing up on his head with coruscations of static electricity: Suddenly he was flipped up and over the cab, leaving an unobscured view of the roadway.

Which was missing. Replaced by an army of trees charging right at us!

I wrenched the wheel, taking a fifty-fifty guess at which direction would put us back on the road again.

For once, luck appeared to be on my side.

Which probably meant that when the stakes were really high I would be running a luck deficit again.

The thumping and thrashing sounds were becoming more extreme and, once again, something went hurtling over the cab, missing the hood entirely and landing beyond the wash of our headlights.

Fand touched my shoulder so she could speak without yelling once more. "I believe that was your vampire girlfriend."

"I don't have a vampire girlfriend," I muttered.

The headlights suddenly revealed a battered and even bloodier Carmella Le Fanu getting to her feet. She went down again with a thump and disturbing bounce to the vehicle's shocks and suspension before I could even twitch toward the brakes.

And then she was back up again, springing to her feet in my side mirror. A runner in red, washed by the crimson glow of the taillights as she sprinted to catch back up as I steered all over the road in a moment of indecision.

We weren't going fast enough. To slow down or stop would mean death for all of us. And death for all of us meant the portal would fall into the enemy's hands. Or claws or tentacles. The Greek would inherit the earths. Darkness and eldritch madness would spread through the multiverse.

And all because Cséjthe couldn't get an old Army transport truck into fifth gear.

And then, just like an answer to prayer (someone else's, I was all out), the road straightened out and the trees fell back, giving way to open fields bordered with scrub and underbrush. I looked at Fand who had rolled down her window and stuck her head out to see how her once mortal lover was faring with Fuck the Magic Dragon up top.

I grabbed her arm and shook it. "We need an exit strategy, Highness! Like right now!"

She turned around and blinked. "The road . . ." she said. "I cannot see if it lays straight-wise . . ."

Our headlights were old and weak and an unfocused yellow wash barely reached thirty feet ahead. The stars and the sliver of moon were all but lost in the pall of smoke that covered the sky like a dirty shroud. Either the Maitland estate was burning big time or the wildfires had made considerable gains on our location.

Or maybe the world, itself, was starting to burn, consuming itself like a vast funeral pyre in preparation for the final oblivion that was nearly upon us now.

Where were we going? What was the plan? Just to keep the portal out of the Enemy's clutches for a few more days? Hours? Moments . . . ?

Nothing more than a useless defiance until the inevitable end?

If there was a chance, a plan, anything beyond simply running from the Darkness . . . anything that we could run toward . . . God hadn't clued Cséjthe in on the plan.

Annwn Harkwynde's plan had proven to be a bust.

And Mama Samm D'Arbonne hadn't . . .

What?

Said something about not being where I was supposed to be. And when . . .

Something about a motel in New Mexico.

Pazuzu?

I shook my head as if that would help me concentrate.

Carrizozo!

I bared my teeth. "Someone call up Death and cancel that appointment in Samarra. We're rescheduling for the Four Winds Motel in Carrizozo!" I shook Fand's arm again. "Open the way, now, Princess! Up the road or the middle of the field! I figure we've got enough mass to run over a wire fence and ground should be dry enough to keep us from bogging down for a couple of miles, at least . . ." I gave her one last shake and dropped her arm to take a death grip on the steering wheel. "Open it! Now!"

And she did.

Chapter Nineteen

Maybe it was the difference of traveling through openness and not tunneling through water. Or Fand's powers were different from her sister's.

A silvery coin appeared off to my left, in the middle of a field: a lighted doorway in the night.

I took the truck off-road as gently as I could—which was not very but the incline was less severe than it might have been and I couldn't drop speed if we wanted the best chance of breaching the fence.

A chorus of "Cséjthes" erupted from the back along with a few other "names" best not repeated here.

A spiny, not-so-glowy, bat-dragon hybrid went tumbling across the hood and off to the left, so I cut right, steering us over a fencepost and cutting our speed in half as we bounced onto the field and began cross-plowing furrows of milo or emerging soybeans. Tangled clusters of wire bunched up between our tires and the undercarriage, grabbing at the transmission with a momentary fingerhold, then peeling off as we dragged a hundred feet of fencing behind us like fishing nets on a trawler.

Our speed halved again as the soil was loose and soft from the plow and tiller.

The coin-sized opening in the field had grown from a shiny dime to a glimmering silver dollar but our speed was more akin to a neighborhood jogger than an Olympic runner now. The terrain required a return to third gear, which the transmission gratefully accommodated with an almost palpable sense of relief. The motor evened out and it felt like we would make it without any further difficulties.

If only "slow and steady wins the race" was a maxim that would hold true in this case.

But apparently not.

Even as we rumbled forward, I could see additional lights in the sky, soaring and swooping behind us in my side mirror. And everyone in the back of the truck was bailing out. Even Mama Samm managed a stately jog up to the cab and swung up to the running board on my side. "This isn't going to work," she observed. "We'll travel faster on foot. We've got to reach the Realm of the Fae before . . ." She gestured to the things behind us.

"Even carrying the pithos?"

As the words left my mouth I saw Stefan Pagelovitch run ahead of us, holding the massive jug as if it were crafted of papier-mâché. Carmella Le Fanu was dogging his footsteps, offering to help.

"Cséjthe, you are no longer the strongest or the fastest among us. It is no longer your burden alone."

Her words should have brought a sense of relief. Instead, it felt like I was being cut from the team. "Well," I said, "at least I can drive stick."

She fixed me with that old familiar look. "Barely. Now, git down off'n that thing! We gots to run!"

She was right: Everyone else had already run on ahead. Even Fand had abandoned the cab, supporting a limping Sétanta as they moved toward the opening before us.

We both jumped down and began to run. D'Arbonne, while still more svelte than her pre–Hurricane Eibon days, was still arguably human while everyone else—save maybe Annie—was not. I scooped her up, tossed her over my shoulder, and began to really tear across the open ground.

"Mister Chris," she groused to my backside, "I really do not appreciate you being so familiar with my person but I'm inclined to give you a pass under the circumstances . . ." Her attempt at maintaining a tone of dignity was somewhat undermined by the rhythmic interruptions of bouncing up and down on my shoulder. ". . . but I must ask that you do not use this occasion to stare at my . . . derrière . . . while you carry me!"

There were several optional responses that immediately occurred to me—and she probably deserved any or all of them. Instead, I merely said, "Yes, ma'am." And kept running.

Fand and Cúchulainn limped across the threshold behind me. I'd lost track of Annie in the turmoil but a teenage girl could apparently outrun a Queen of the Fae and an ancient incarnated Celtic god in a three-legged race. Smirl and Kirsten had salvaged firearms from the back of the truck and had discouraged the aerial pursuit until everyone else was inside and then stepped across the threshold, as well. The Hound of Ulster dropped wearily to his knees as Fand turned and "Closed" The Way.

The field and the night skies faded from view.

We were now encompassed by a silvery fog, luminescent, yet providing very little distinction in regard to landmarks, terrain, or even distance.

"How long?" Annwn asked the Faerie queen. "How long before they can breach this place?"

"I do not know," Fand answered. "We must not remain here ere long. 'Tis best to move on for both this task's end and to deny those who might find us more easily where we linger."

"Which way?" Pagelovitch asked. The weight of the pithos would not trouble a master vampire but its size and shape made it awkward to manage for more than a short time or distance.

Fand looked at Mama Samm. The black woman walked up to her and placed something in her hand. "This will guide you," she said.

Fand closed her hand. After a moment her eyes widened and her breath hissed through her teeth. Then she looked over at her wounded warrior. "Can you travel, my love?"

He grimaced, struggling to his feet. "Not well. Not fast. But I can move. Give me leave to summon others and mount a rearguard defense."

The struggle was evident in her face. There were very few things that could enter the Realm of the Fae unbidden but the Things that were hot on our heels had already proven themselves adept at breaching interdimensional barriers. If this was, literally, The End of The World, she could not bear to be parted from him. But our best chance at stopping said End of The World—if we had any chance at all—required that we escape as fast as we could. Sétanta understood this. Fand understood this. And that we couldn't navigate in her Realm without her.

"The sooner you depart, the sooner you can return," he told her, making shooing motions with his big, meaty hands.

She moved between them and threw her arms around his size 15 neck. Their parting kiss was both heartbreaking and NSFW. We all looked away—well, except for Carmella who watched avidly, then shot me a meaningful look and licked her lips.

I might never want sex again.

Finally, he said, "I grow impatient for your return, my queen."

For all my ragging on him since our first unfortunate encounter, in that moment I'd rarely respected anyone more.

Pagelovitch and Smirl stayed with Sétanta. The best egress into The Realm right now was the place where Fand had opened and reclosed The Way. Any pan-dimensional creature in pursuit would be drawn to that recent change in the fabric of Reality. And it would remain more permeable for the foreseeable future, so someone had to cover our retreat and defend that access point to Fand's Realm while she was away serving as our preternatural pathfinder. Kirsten even handed over the two pistols she had liberated from the back of the truck, albeit a little reluctantly, handing them over to the vampire and the Celt. Smirl seemed adequately armed for one "dragon." God help them if anything more got through before the Queen of the Seelie returned.

My parting from the Seattle Doman and the Chicago Enforcer was briefer and less complicated. I would come back as soon as my part in this was done and we would share an epic pub crawl where stories would be told, songs would be sung, and we'd all have a good laugh . . .

Yeah . . . it was a serviceable illusion.

As we moved out they were quickly swallowed up in the silvery fog in our wake.

Fand wasn't very talkative at first but I eventually learned that we were traveling *through* The Realm rather than "through" The Realm. We were utilizing some sort of nexus space . . . like some sort of Einsteinian Faerie wormhole.

This explained the lack of sumptuous Fairyland landscapes and magical architecture.

Which was fine as we didn't have time to sightsee anyway and getting from Point A to Point P while skipping Points B through O was far more convenient.

Einstein also said that "time is relative."

You don't have to understand $E = mc^2$, the Special versus the General theories, or temporal distortion effects approaching the speed of light. Anytime your relatives come to visit, time seems to slow down. Especially after the third day.

I don't know how long we slogged across the foggy, grayscale landscape—a couple of hours, four, five, nineteen . . . probably not the latter as I doubt I could walk that long on my best days and I was still limping and leaking where I'd pulled the sliver of shrapnel from my hapless heinie.

Le Fanu and I all took turns hauling Pandora's Jug to keep from tiring and dropping the damned thing. Especially since it was a Damned Thing and dropping it might be the metaphysical equivalent of dropping a hydrogen bomb.

But it gave me time to think again. Something I hadn't had any real time to do since . . . when? Since the long drive up to the Maitland estate while the teenybopper suggested I do couples counseling with the power-mad vampress with stalker issues while grappling with alternate-timeline Kirsten's daddy dearest complex.

Since then, The End of the Multiverse was starting to take on a certain appeal . . .

Eventually, I checked in with Harkwynde. Who was looking even younger than she did when she first showed up on the I-20 off-ramp . . . how many days ago, now? Time and timelines, I had lost track of so much now. But, most importantly, I'd lost track of what the plan was supposed to be at this point. Seal the portal? Destroy the portal? Hide the portal? Boobytrap the portal?

I was starting to get a little giddy.

A short conversation with Annie didn't help. Her plan to use The Wyrding to gather enough "Practitioners" to reinforce the thaumaturgic wards and seals on The Portal had gone up in flames, figuratively and literally. Worse, she was still shaken by Edmond's subversion, suddenly revealed as a catspaw for The Darkness Beyond. She was spending most of her time consulting with Kirsten and Mama Samm in a hushed, three-way dialog. The look on their faces did not invite a fourth buttinski. And I was more than a little distracted by Carmella Le Fanu.

The vampress had once been a beautiful woman. She had retained that beauty over the centuries as a nosferatu, only displaying her "scary face" when the bloodlust was heavily upon her. But there was something more alien beneath the surface features of her face, now. Her body, while not misshapen, was subtly . . . off. Her unholy repasts were making her physical husk into something different, something even less human. And I wasn't sure what was left of her inside that husk, as well.

And how long before her addiction to power-feeding turned her growing appetite back to my own, high-octane biofuel?

As for Fand, she remained tightlipped about any elven prophecy or insight into the endgame for our journey. Nor was she prepared to open a side-trip into her Realm to offer food, rest, alternate transportations, or even a washbasin and some clean towels. I couldn't really blame her for her inhospitality: If the Bestiary from Beyond did breach the nexus she didn't want to make it any easier for them to invade The Realm proper. There would be time for showers and clean clothes once our job was done.

And if we failed it wouldn't matter anyway.

After carrying the pithos for another indeterminate time I finally stopped, lowered it to the ground, and waited.

Everyone else finally noticed and stopped, as well.

Mama Samm walked over and pointed at Carmella and then at the pithos.

Surprisingly, Le Fanu picked it up without a word.

"You got something to say to me," she told me, "you can walk while you talk. We can't be stopping now. Not after how far we've come and how close we are." She started walking ahead and everyone else followed suit.

"You were waiting for me in New Mexico," I told her as I limped up next to her. It wasn't hard to match her stride; she was starting to flag a little, herself.

"Seems like I'm always waiting on you to catch up, Cséjthe," she said with barely a hint of a snark at all.

"Well, I lost my super-secret decoder ring," I said. "It would help if people would let me in on the plan at the very beginning instead of keeping me in the dark until the very end."

"And then some," she said.

"And then some," I agreed.

She sighed. "Christopher, there was never 'A Plan.'"

"There wasn't?" Well, that would explain a lot.

"Like everything in life, there were *Plans*. I assume you know the old canard, 'the battleplan ceases to exist as soon as the first shot is fired'?"

"The actual quote is—"

She shook her head. "Don't start with your Liberal Arts degree literary quotage! I'm trying to explain to you what I know, what I think, what I don't know, and what I can only hope and pray for."

I shut up. I was too tired for verbal repartee and happy to let her be less cryptic if that's where the moment was taking us.

"We come to know things. Patterns emerge. Augurs are revealed. Prophecies converge." She took a breath. "When I say 'we' I mean people like Annwn Harkwynde, the Fae, and others who Fate and Circumstance and The Gifts are given to . . . people and Powers who live and exist on the fringe between that which is commonly understood and that which is glimpsed through study and practice and giftedness . . ."

I held up a hand. "Okay, I get it. I had my peeks behind the curtains even though I'm not a Power or Practitioner or gifted—"

"But you are," she argued. "Just in different ways that you do not understand or even admit to yourself. But it is the reason why, time and again, that you are drawn into the conflicts of The Darkness and The Light. You are the Fisher King who is eternally wounded and eternally renewed to do battle—"

"Getting a giant splinter in my ass does not make me the Fisher King," I interrupted. "For God's sake, I can't even stand to put a worm on a hook! And as for tying flies . . ."

So much for deciding to not snark.

"The point which I am trying to make, Christopher, is that we come to our understandings in much the same way that you do: by study and by trial and error, by gradual unfolding of events and, all the while, trying to make sense of the random and cryptic clues that the Great Unknown deigns to reveal in Its own ways and times.

"But," she continued, "you have emerged in those times and clues and augurs and prophecies, time and again for this precarious moment in time."

"Really? Like my name, Christopher L. Cséjthe, keeps popping up in ancient scrolls and stuff?"

"Almost never by name."

Almost never?

"But the signs are there. The evidence mounts. And your preparation . . . we have enough scholars and Practitioners. What we don't have enough of are the ones who can wage holy war with your unique perspective and tactical improvisation. Who can survive what no mortal might endure and keep a heart that is true in the Darkness that presents as endless and relentless."

I cleared my throat. "I'm looking for a strategy, not a Hallmark card sentiment."

She was silent for a moment. Several long moments actually.

"You had an appointment in New Mexico," she said finally. "You missed it."

"A prophecy?" I asked.

"An augur. I pray we are not too late."

"Well," I said. After my own, long, several moments' pause. "As much as I'd love to check out the suites at the Four Winds Motel in Carrizozo, we can't just pop out of thin air in any population center, no matter how sparse or how small. And, given the pattern of The Darkness's minions showing up like they know where we're going to be before we do, I'm betting that there's a better than even chance that Something—or a whole bunch of Somethings—have already researched your reservations, staked out your rooms, and are lying in wait even as we speak."

"We are not going to Carrizozo," she countered calmly. "I said you were supposed to come to New Mexico. Carrizozo was merely the most convenient place to wait for you."

"So we're not going to the motel. Nor the town. So, where?"

She sighed. If I had a dollar for every time she sighed since our first meeting in a fortune teller's shop in Monroe, Louisiana, I could . . . well the math was considerable.

"Not just where, Christopher, but when."

"Yeah, I get it: I'm late. So where?"

She sighed again. Like I was the one not getting it.

"The Jornada del Muerto desert. Or about forty miles north, northeast of there to be more precise."

The Journey of the Dead? Yeah, that sounded about right. And not just because it sounded remote from any population centers. And then I remembered Annie's story about her coven, in the desert, July 1945. My head began to swim with a serious onset of déjà vu-doo.

I opened my mouth to ask my next question but Fand beat me to the punch. "We draw nigh," she said.

"Cséjthe," Mama Samm ordered, "empty your pockets. Divide the stones between her highness, me, Annwn and yourself."

Stones? I plunged my hands into my pockets and pulled out pebbles of melted greenish glass.

Trinitite.

"Oh, shit."

We emerged into the predawn twilight next to a twelve-foot obelisk of dark, jagged stone mortared together with concrete. A mountain range stretched in the distance but the ground was relatively flat and unbroken save for patches of scrubby desert plants and a gravel parking lot nearby.

Carmella Le Fanu gingerly set the pithos down under Mama Samm's supervision while I walked over to the stone spindle, rising out of a cement base like the mummified finger of a long dead giant.

There were two brass plaques affixed to the side I was on. The first read:

TRINITY SITE
WHERE
THE WORLD'S FIRST
NUCLEAR DEVICE
WAS EXPLODED ON
JULY 16, 1945

I glanced at the wording below but the light was bad and my mind wasn't processing printed text any more.

"Um, guys? We're on government property . . ."

I could palpably feel Mama Samm nodding behind me. "Yes, Cséjthe."

"More specifically," I said, backing up, "this is White Sands Missile Range. We're on a military base."

"Test range," Mama Samm corrected.

"But I thought this part was open to the public," Annie said.

"Only a couple of times a year," I said. "So, if we've got somewhere else to be, we'd better get moving. Or if we're doing it here, we'd better get doing. Sooner or later they'll send soldiers with guns to arrest us."

And that's who we'd rather find us, I thought, repressing a shudder.

"We are where we are supposed to be," Mama Samm said with a calmness that made me sound a little hysterical by contrast.

I looked around. "And?"

"We just aren't *when* we're supposed to be."

"All right, already. I'm late. You've made that abundantly clear—"

"Of course," Annie said, smiling for the first time since we'd arrived at the Maitland Manse. "Give it a moment to sink in."

"Will this take long?" Fand asked. "I must needs return . . ." She stared into the distance thoughtfully.

"Nearly four score years from beginning to end," Annie said quietly. She reached into her pockets and produced the four vials she had salvaged from J.D.'s lead-lined suitcase. She handed one to me, one to Kirsten, and the third to Sammathea. Carmella looked bewildered and vaguely hurt.

"I will see you on your way," the Fae said quietly, "but I cannot journey with you."

"That should be enough and more." Mama Samm D'Arbonne motioned us in toward the pithos. "Kirsten, to my left . . ."

"Stryfe," my daughter corrected.

It was my turn to sigh.

"Annwn," D'Arbonne continued, "to her left, now." As they formed a half circle about the great urn, she turned to me and said, "Christopher, one last journey. Before the sun shines brightest you can lay down your sword and shield . . ."

"And study war no more?" I murmured.

She nodded and her smile was dazzling. She held out her right hand and I took it in my left.

I almost said, "Promise?" But there was a weight to her words that would not permit disrespect in any form or utterance.

"What about me?" Carmella whined. She looked at me. "You're not ditching me now!"

"This is a one-way trip, Strigoi," my daughter told her with a hint of iron in her voice.

Le Fanu ignored her, looking at me. "Whither thou goest—"

"Oh my God, just *stop* already!" my little girl muttered.

Mama Samm motioned to her. "Stand next to the pithos, inside the circle." She released my hand, momentarily, to let her through.

Off in the distance a line of dark smoke appeared. Man-made or other, I could not tell but it was headed our way.

"And now we close the circle," Annie intoned. "Join hands." She took my right hand in her left and squeezed it gently.

"Time, Ms. Harkwynde?" D'Arbonne asked.

Without releasing her grip, the young woman consulted her watch. "Six-twenty-four." She glanced at the crimson limning of the horizon to the east. "A.M.," she added unnecessarily.

"Central time," I guessed. "So . . . five-twenty-four, Mountain time?"

"Something approaches," Fand said. "I must depart! Now!"

"If you will but help us on our way," D'Arbonne agreed.

Fand stepped in and placed her dainty hands on my back and Annie's.

"Give my love to . . ." I whispered. But she was gone.

Along with the obelisk.

In a burst of darkness.

The dry desert air was suddenly logy with humidity and the lightening skies overrun with clouds where none had existed a moment before. Looking around and up I saw a black square overhead, like a trapdoor falling up into the Black Pit of Tartarus. The smell of ozone hung in the air.

And then the smell of gunpowder as a small rocket shot up from the ground and burst like a half-hearted, Fourth of July, afterthought. In the flickering sprig of falling flares I saw the support legs of the framework tower that surrounded us. Steel trusses rose from concrete footings on four sides of us, rising maybe thirty meters into the sky where they anchored the four corners of the black square above. A scattering of soggy, military bunk mattresses surrounded us like a haphazard nest.

"What happened?" Le Fanu clung to the pithos like a drowning woman to a life raft. "Is this another timeline?"

I started to step back to get a better sense of what I was looking at but Mama Samm squeezed my left hand with a ferocity matched only by the death grip Annwn had on my right.

"Do. Not. Break. The. Circle!" she hissed.

"Not another timeline, vampire," Kirsten told her, "just another time."

Somewhere, off in the distance, a voice was counting down over a speaker.

"This is what you meant," I said, looking at D'Arbonne and then Harkwynde. "When you said it wasn't just a matter of *where* I was supposed to be but, also, *when*?" I looked up again. The cloud cover was dispersing and the sun was about to break the horizon. I could make out the planking a hundred feet above us: the oaken floor of a corrugated iron shack, open on the western side. A bundle of cables climbed one of the tower's legs to the bomb inside . . .

Gadget, I corrected myself. *Not bomb but gadget.*

The bombs would follow within a month. Fat Man and Little Boy. Hiroshima and Nagasaki.

But today it was just a test device, a gadget.

The Gadget. Anyone who truly understood what was locked inside its plutonium core would not want to think of it in terms of a "bomb." Not yet.

And, if wishing were so, maybe never . . .

I looked back at Annie. "I told Creighton and the others that they ought to bury the portal in a concrete coffin. Their heads were all wrapped around the metaphysical aspects of the portal and hadn't even considered its physical vulnerabilities."

I looked at Mama Samm. "But you had. You already had a plan. Part A was bury The Portal in the heart of a star instead of cement. Part B was keeping everyone in the dark. As usual."

"One person can keep a secret," she answered. "Two cannot."

"Edmond," I said.

"You knew?" Now Annie's voice was thick with the sense of betrayal.

Mama Samm shook her head. "Not specifically. Not him, necessarily. But there were too many people involved in too many meetings and planning sessions . . ."

"A whole spectrum of vulnerabilities and weaknesses to be probed and exploited by The Enemy," I agreed.

"And plans evolve," my daughter added quietly. "We've had to adjust . . . adapt."

"Bringing us to this moment in time," I observed. "So . . . I'm wondering. The translocating across adjacent timelines was impressive enough that I never thought to ask if you could go backward or forward in any given timeline . . ."

"Time travel? You think we could've fixed things with time travel?" Kirsten scoffed, back in full Stryfe mode. "You start trying to reset a row of fallen dominos and you just end up knocking over dominos that were originally supposed to stand. It—"

"There are limitations to how much and how often we could do something like this," Mama Samm interrupted. "Even with Fand and Stryfe and Annwn and I powering this potential paradox. Alignments are required . . ."

"One such alignment is that I am already here," Harkwynde said. "Even now I am powering another spell with my old coven some twenty miles to the northwest."

"Soooo, paradox?" I asked.

"No. We will not meet nor will this manifestation remain long enough to leave any mark. Disturb one butterfly—or a thousand: At ground zero it will make no difference in a matter of moments."

"And there are components that link us to this place and this moment in time," D'Arbonne continued. "The isotope and the green glass nuggets of fused sand that we've shared among us."

"Trinitite," I murmured.

She nodded. "Annwn and I have prepared the groundwork for such a spell, very carefully and very thoroughly in advance. It was conceived for different purposes, different contingencies . . ."

"When?" Le Fanu wanted to know.

"Before Stryfe was embedded in your demesne, vampire. Annwn Harkwynde began her tutelage but I have contributed to her curriculum along the way. Still, we could not anchor our destination without one, final component of the spell." She gave me a meaningful look.

"You, Christopher."

I sighed. "Makes sense. Going to blow things up? Invite Cséjthe to the party. End of the World event? Wouldn't be a thing if I wasn't sitting in the front row. Pain, death and suffering? Well, pain and suffering, for sure but, based on years of experience now: I can't really die."

"Can't you?" Mama Samm said softly.

I thought about that. It was one thing to come back from catastrophic blood loss and mortal trauma.

Subatomic disassembly? All the king's horses . . .

"Christopher," she said tenderly, giving my hand a gentle squeeze. "You've been in so much pain for so long. I know you're tired, baby. And I know that you don't think you can ever have anything like what you've lost. That God or the universe doesn't care about all you've sacrificed, all you've done . . .

"Well, this is your answer," she said softly, in voice like my mother's. "The closing of the circle. We are the Hand of God. A fist of Light."

"Oh, I get it," Carmella grumbled, "you people are the fingers. I'm just the thumb."

"Christopher," Sammathea continued, "listen to me: The hand that closes, can open again. As can the heart."

I bowed my head. "I don't mind," I said. "I'm okay with this. It's a good ending."

"Daddy . . ." my daughter hiccupped. "Every ending is just a new beginning."

I looked back up. Considered telling her that that was about the cruelest thing that anyone could say to me now that my release was finally in sight. But I just smiled and told her that I loved her and was proud and that I was sorry that I would never get to know my little girl all grown up.

"Just. Don't. Break. The. Circle," Kirsten answered, with a seriousness that was almost comical.

Yeah, like there's going to be a refrigerator around a nuclear test site when you really need one.

And that's when the Thing slid over the edge of the platform above us.

I got a glimpse of amorphous mass of ooze and eyes and tentacles and dozens of hissing, snapping, ravenous mouths filled with teeth and fangs and even hook-like beaks. It fell on us like deadly fruitcake of foul putrescence and cancerous evil ruining my perfect Rick Jones moment.

Carmella performed one, last service: Reacting with inhuman speed, she leapt up to meet it in midair.

Only to stop . . .

Freeze-frame style . . .

The vampire-mutate and the abomination hovering just a few feet above our upturned faces . . .

And then the world became every color of light that you could imagine.

And some you couldn't.

Colors more felt than seen . . .

Gold, purple, violet, gray, blue . . . a warm brilliant yellow-white as we stood in the instant, at the very heart of the birth of an earthbound star.

The portal was instantly deconstructed.

Anything on the other side of that arcane doorway was consumed in an unimaginable blowtorch of stellar proportions. Anything, in the deepest, darkest corners of that Stygian pocket dimension, that might survive the terrible light and heat that streamed through that dissolving passageway, was forever cut off. The door was forever closed to our corner of the multiverse.

Everything at the heart of that man-made sun on the barren plains of the Alamogordo Bombing Range, also called the Journey of the Dead or Jornada del Muerto, was instantly vaporized.

Including a small circle of fragile humans, holding hands at the very end, so that uncounted worlds might live.

Chapter Twenty

Waking up in heaven was like waking up in an old hospital bed with a lumpy mattress.

The sunlight was softened by fabric blinds but still bright enough to turn the backs of my eyelids a warm, chocolate brown, stirring me to wakefulness.

I rolled over and discovered that I actually was in some sort of a hospital bed. And that turning over took a great deal of effort.

As to the latter: I had lost muscle mass. Not exactly skin and bones but definitely below my longstanding debates with the bathroom scales. And moving felt like my joints had not been lubricated in a very long while.

As to the former? There was an IV in the back of my hand and a catheter in . . . well, where catheters typically go. I was wearing pajamas—the kind of sleeping apparel I had abandoned before starting high school and had never seen a need to return to.

Under the pajamas: an adult diaper.

The room and its furnishings did not exactly carry a NASA long-term space mission vibe so I was thinking the astronaut theory was less likely than the long-term convalescent theory.

And why not? Standing at the core of an atomic chain reaction was sure to have some long-term deleterious effects on the human body . . .

Like total vaporization?

I shook my head and went to work on extracting the IV. The back of my hand was a bouquet of black, purple, and blue blossoms and hurt like hell.

The catheter was almost easier: I'd had previous experience in taking out my own catheter.

It wasn't any more pleasant this time around than the last.

Sitting up felt like the equivalent of the Marines raising the flag on Iwo Jima. Which isn't really a fair comparison as there had been six of them and there was only one of me. The vertigo made my head swim like Michael Phelps chasing a gold medal.

It felt like I'd been horizontal for a long time. A very long time.

But well-tended from the looks of things. My face was freshly shaved, my pajamas clean and faintly smelling of fabric softener. The adult diaper must have been changed recently: no unpleasant surprises there.

The room around me was unfamiliar but clean and tidy. Apparently a small bedroom, repurposed as a home office, re-repurposed as a sickroom: hospital-style bed with IV poles, biowaste bin, stethoscope and blood-pressure cuff on the nightstand. A small desk across the room held a laptop and a stack of books. Picture frames on the walls displayed the covers of books bearing my name—or, rather, the pseudonym I had once used when trying my hand at some sci-fi parody back in my college days. Something related to virtual reality and computer games. These covers suggested stories with a bent toward horror. The faces were . . . familiar . . .

A door slammed somewhere below me.

I looked down at my bare feet. The floor was so much farther below: It didn't look like I could step out of bed without falling another ten feet or more. Why was I so high up? My head began to swim again.

I had been holding hands with a . . . witch? Practitioner. And another. She was . . . she knew . . . things . . . had powers. . . .

I was looking into the eyes of my daughter when the world ended.

My dead daughter.

Who was alive because there were times . . . lines . . . parallel to ours. . . .

I clutched at the head of the bed to keep from falling over: I was so dizzy!

It was hard to think. . . .

To remember. . . .

"Moooom!" a strangely familiar voice whined from downstairs. "Will's not helping with the groceries!"

"I'll get the sacks in the trunk," another voice—a voice from the distant past answered. "You go check on your father. William? No TV until everything's brought in and put away."

I had not heard that voice in years. It was a voice I could never hear again.

Jenny.

The sound of footsteps. Stair steps.

The bedroom door creaked open like an ingress in a haunted house.

A ghost entered and stared at me, fear and hope and sadness and a hint of dawning joy on her young features.

The piercings were gone. Her hair was long, symmetrical, unshaved, undyed. Her face bore a trace of life's disappointment but none of the hardness of her orphaned doppelganger.

"D-daddy?"

My mouth was dry, my throat as unaccustomed to use as my limbs. I managed to croak: "K . . . ir . . . sten . . ."

She started to cry and the years fell away from her visage. "Mommy! Oh, mom—*mommeee!*"

Something crashed downstairs, followed by the thunder of footsteps approaching from below.

Another ghost swept into the room, sweeping my daughter into the protective circle of her arms. And then her eyes met mine.

Overflowed.

"*Chris?*"

I was home.

A young boy ran into the room. "What happened?" he demanded. Then looked at me.

"Dad?"

Well, mostly home.

It took time.

Time to rebuild wasted muscles.

Tolerate solid food.

Time to sort out this particular timeline.

Another car wreck at the intersection of 103 and US 69 outside Weir, Kansas. My wife and daughter and newly minted toddler son turned out to be relatively okay.

I, however, did not.

The diagnosis had shifted over the years: "Persistent vegetative state" was eventually changed to "unresponsive wakefulness syndrome" then various versions of what was called a "minimally conscious state." Likewise, I was shipped from hospital to hospice to convalescent center to "rest home" and finally to just home. I didn't require that much upkeep—fed and watered like an amenable plant—and once the insurance ran out, there simply was no other choice. Fortunately, I was breathing on my own without the necessity of a ventilator or any other assistive devices. I was generally compliant in being moved, bathed, dressed, or fed soft foods and a liquid diet. I had just never achieved full consciousness over the years since the accident.

Until three weeks ago.

When I awoke from the light.

Now I was sneaking around in the dark.

I was strong enough to leave my bed and make my way to the door—as long as I took my time and frequently used the wall to steady myself.

A miraculous recovery, the doctors said. As if I hadn't been bedfast these past several years. It was as if I had retained muscle tone from an alternate existence where I spent a lot of time running, leaping, fighting, wrestling, lugging giant clay jars, fleeing for my life. . . .

The stairs were more of a challenge but navigable by draping most of my upper body over the bannister as a counterweight to my trembling legs.

Halfway down I encountered a softball I'd been throwing in the back yard with Will earlier in the day: him running all about, a ball of frenetic energy, me comfortably ensconced in a lawn chair. The trick now was to get around the ball without sending it on a noisy trajectory down the rest of the steps.

I managed. Maybe slipping through all of those tombs and lairs and crypts and graveyards had honed my getting-a-midnight-snack stealth-skills.

Three more book covers in frames were hung on the descending wall opposite the railing. My face on the book jackets was somewhat familiar and yet vaguely different. That Christopher L. Cséjthe had led a slightly different life. As had Jenny, who's face showed the years of struggling alone while I napped. Still beautiful after all this time, maybe even more so as she had aged like a fine vintage in just a few years that should have been the equivalent of decades in any other life.

At the bottom of the stairs I paused to catch my breath and get my bearings in the darkened house.

It wasn't any house I'd lived in. Not in my original timeline.

Unless that was a hallucination. A dream that had seemed more unreal with each passing day. If I was to capture its details on my laptop before they faded, I'd have to bump up my daily wordcount by another thousand, at least.

I shook my head.

I had a son, now.

A daughter who didn't hate me.

And a wife I thought I had lost forever and several lifetimes ago.

True horror isn't monsters or demons or dread dimensions. True horror is life without love. A life alone.

Maybe, I was beginning to think; just maybe, God didn't hate me after all. . . .

I swiped at my eyes. There were bills to pay and I needed to figure out this interrupted writing career. . . .

But good times were fleeting, love was precious, and I was never going to take my family for granted, ever again.

Even if my "son" Will was unborn in at least two other timelines.

This was here.

This was *now*.

Even if my current existence was encapsulated in a micro time-bubble, on the edge of an Einstein-Rosen bridge, at the heart of a nuclear furnace over seventy years in the past. For this micro-instant, caught between two heartbeats of Eternity, I was home and I was going to suck the marrow from every bone that the universe saw fit to toss me.

And speaking of marrow . . .

I made my way to the refrigerator using furniture, tables, and chairs as an impromptu lifeline.

Standing in the wash of the dim, interior light, I did a quick inventory: rabbit food, rabbit food, rabbit food, hamster snack, squirrel snack . . . voilà!

Blood pudding.

Overcooked, just the way Jenny knew that I liked it: Protein was essential to my full recovery so I knew there would be more tomorrow.

I finished it off quickly but neatly as I had a non-hospital and decidedly conjugal bed to return to upstairs. I carried my empties to the sink and quietly rinsed the dish and utensils, cupping my hand under the tap to wash down the remains of the sausage with a couple of swallows of water.

And that's when I heard the tapping . . .

As if someone gently rapping, rapping at my own back door.

"'Tis some visitor," I muttered, "tapping at my chamber door— only this and nothing more . . ."

Unimpressed, the tapping continued, growing a bit louder. Along with the sounds of a little scuffling.

I shook my head and hurried to the back door, off of the kitchen, hoping to avoid rousting the entire family from their beds.

The door opened into the back yard and a warm autumn night. Moonlight silvered the grass and the increasingly denuded tree branches that impotently clutched at a descending leaf here and there.

Also outlined in the lunar limning: a pair of young women seemingly intent on auditioning for some sort of space-theme night on a cable pay-per-view wrestling program. Both wore clear, bubble-style helmets and space suits that were only slightly less transparent but applied some sort of compression technology. The scientific term that immediately came to mind was: shrink-wrapped. Both of them looked as if they had just stepped off the covers of the 1930s sci-fi pulps my grandfather had stored in his attic with one notable exception.

Apparently, George Lucas was right: There is no underwear in space.

I cleared my throat and they immediately stopped trying to pull each other's hair—a pointless task due to the goldfish bowl headgear enclosing both coifs.

The one on my left stepped toward me. "You are the Deathless One?" she asked with an air of expectation.

"Uhhhh," I said, taking in her lovely, green features.

"The Walker Between Worlds?" queried the one on the right.

"Ummmm," I answered, noticing that she was just as lovely, albeit with crimson skin in contrast to the first's emerald hue.

"The Orion Syndicate has need of your talents!" the green girl announced, following up with a thrown elbow at her rival.

"Barsoom is under attack!" countered the fuchsia femme, with a little pushback to the competition.

"Well, that doesn't sound good," I empathized.

"We need the Daybinder!" insisted my first visitor, leaning so far forward that I was pretty sure the green went all the way down.

"We must have the Bloodwalker!" cooed the other, making sure I knew that there was a whole lotta red going on in her spacesuit.

"Gee, that's too bad," I sympathized.

They looked at me uncertainly. Gave each other the same look, with an extra dollop of suspicion. Looked back at me.

"Are you not he?" they both asked in near synchronicity.

I smiled innocently. "No."

"No?"

"You are not the one the Terrans call Christopher Cséjthe?"

I shook my head. "No. Nope. *Non*. *Nein*. *Nyet*. Negatory. Nay. You ladies must have the wrong address."

"Well . . ."

They looked about uncertainly. Back at me.

I smiled innocently but it was probably the pajamas that helped sell it. Both of them took a step back.

"Good luck with that," I said pleasantly.

I stepped back, closed the door and relocked and latched it.

Waited quietly for a few minutes but heard nothing more than the gradual return of the susurrus of wind-stirred leaves and cricketsong.

And then I carefully made my way back upstairs where I crawled back into bed with my love, my long-lost wife, to sleep another deep and blessedly dreamless sleep.